DISASTERS, RELIEF AND THE MEDIA

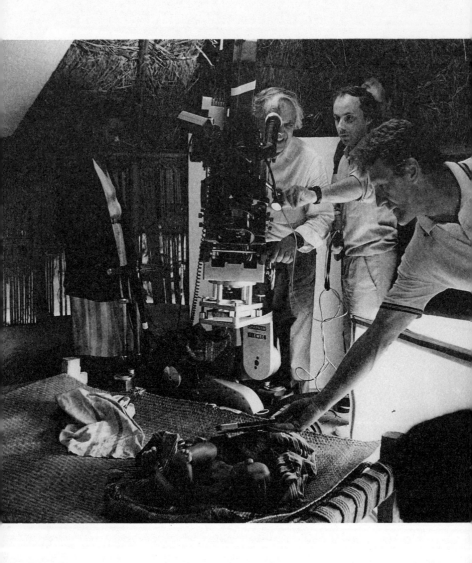

Jonathan Benthall

disasters, relief and the media

I.B.Tauris & Co Ltd
Publishers
London · New York

Published in 1993 by
I.B.Tauris & Co Ltd
45 Bloomsbury Square
London WC1A 2HY

175 Fifth Avenue
New York
NY 10010

In the United States of America
and Canada distributed by
St Martin's Press
175 Fifth Avenue
New York
NY 10010

A CIP record for this book is available from the British Library.

A full CIP record for this book is available from the Library of Congress

ISBN 1–85043–642–8 (hardback)
ISBN 1–85043–737–8 (paperback)

Title spread. Making a commercial for Sport Aid, Shepperton Studios,
London, 1986. (© *Caroline Penn / Format.*)

Typeset by Photoprint, Torquay, Devon
Printed and bound in Great Britain by
WBC Ltd, Bridgend, Mid Glamorgan

To Zamira

Contents

Acknowledgments

I am extremely grateful to John de Salis for his generous and untiring advice, information and encouragement.

Others who have been specially helpful include Paddy Coulter (International Broadcasting Trust), Lady Limerick (British Red Cross Society) and Anne Winter (Unicef, Geneva).

Having served for many years on a number of advisory committees for Save the Children (UK), I have a special admiration for it, though I have tried to be objective in writing this book. Michael Aaranson, Mark Bowden, Rodney Bream, Michael Edwards, Nicholas Hinton, Peter Poore, Hazel Richards, John Seaman, Andrew Timpson and Sharon Welch have given valuable help.

Others who have given information or help include:
Martin Griffiths (ActionAid, formerly Save the Children UK), Pascale Sotias (Aide Médicale Internationale), Kathy Rampsberger (American Red Cross), George Alagiah, Mark Damazer, Marmaduke Hussey, John MacCormick and Michael Stevenson (BBC), Michael Whitlam and Michael Meyer (British Red Cross), Julian Filochowski (CAFOD), Julian Hopkins (CARE), Martha Teichner (CBS News), Derrick Knight, Kate Phillips, Chris Roles and Revd Michael Taylor (Christian Aid), Kevin Cahill, Will Day and Jane Tewson (Comic Relief), David Turton (*Disasters* journal), Dee O'Connell and Sir John Johnston (Disasters Emergency Committee), Zia Alvi (Doctors Overseas Charity), Michel Bonnot and Bernard Kouchner (French Government), Mallory Wober (Independent Television Commission), Glyn Mathias

(ITN), Michel Convers, Michèle Mercier, Paul-Henri Morard, Rémi Russbach and Karen Saddler (ICRC), Robert Rossborough (Licross-Volags, Geneva), Rosemary Gosling, Ioan Lewis, Peter Loïzos and Sonia Livingstone (London School of Economics), Patrick Aeberhard (Médecins du Monde), Antoine Crouant and Xavier Emmanuelli (Médecins sans Frontières), Tim Allen and Henriette Lidchi (Open University), Alfred von Boeselager (Order of Malta), Andrew Bearpark (Overseas Development Administration), Audrey Bronsteen, Peter Davies, Justin Forsyth, Margaret Hardiman, John Magrath, Elizabeth Stamp, Guy Stringer and Robert Wells (Oxfam), Barbara Harrell-Bond (Refugee Studies Programme, Oxford University), John Knight, Chris Pinney and Roslyn Poignant (Royal Anthropological Institute), Shepard Harder (ISCA, Geneva), A. H. M. Kirk-Greene (St Antony's College, Oxford), Alan Macgregor (*The Times* correspondent, Geneva), Prince Sadruddin Aga Khan (United Nations), F. Mayrhofer-Grunbuhel (UNDRO), Jeff Crisp (UNHCR), Thérèse Gastaut and H. A. Hamad-Elneil (WHO), Susan Barber, C. Malcolm Carruthers, Charles Clayton, Jeff Thindwa and Alan Whaites (World Vision); Hugo D'Aybaury, Rt Revd Simon Barrington-Ward, Michael Behr, Léon Davico, John Kelly, John O'Neill, Elizabeth Pitt, John Ryle and Harold Sumption.

A paper by Sue Wright on media representation in the Gulf War, in an RAI public seminar in April 1991 on 'Cultural aspects of the Middle East conflict', was of help during the early stages of planning this book.

I was due to meet Frédéric Maurice of the ICRC to discuss the theme of the book, on which he contributed some stimulating and valuable ideas in writing, but tragically he died of wounds as a result of a mortar attack on a Red Cross convoy outside Sarajevo on 19 May 1992.

Loulou Brown made fruitful comments on a draft of the book, and Anna Enayat of I. B. Tauris has been supportive as commissioning editor. Mike Kirkwood copy-edited the manuscript with care and skill. My employer, the Royal Anthropological Institute, allowed me to combine research for this book with my normal work.

None of the above bears responsibility for any mistakes.

Lastly I acknowledge my debt to Zamira, my wife, and to my sons Dominic and William.

A NOTE ON SOURCES

All translations from the French, unless otherwise indicated, are by the author. I have tried to give published sources for as much as possible of the information presented here. Some material, however, has been gleaned from personal interviews or conversations. Anyone using the book for scholarly purposes should bear in mind that newspaper sources are particularly prone to error.

Abbreviations

AMI	Aide Médicale Internationale
ASC	Corps Suisse pour l'Aide en Cas de Catastrophes (see SDR)
BBC	British Broadcasting Corporation
BRC	British Refugee Council
CAFOD	Catholic Fund for Overseas Development
CICR	Comité International de la Croix Rouge (see ICRC)
CNN	Cable News Network
DEC	Disasters Emergency Committee
EC	European Community
FAO	Food and Agriculture Organization
FCO	Foreign and Commonwealth Office
GDP	gross domestic product
GNP	gross national product
IBA	Independent Broadcasting Authority (1974–1990: now ITC)
IBT	International Broadcasting Trust
ICRC	International Committee of the Red Cross
IEFR	International Emergency Food Reserve (WFP)
IGO	International Governmental Organization
ISCA	International Save the Children Alliance
ITC	Independent Television Commission (since 1991: formerly IBA)
ITN	Independent Television News
ITV	Independent Television
IWA	International Workers' Aid
MDM	Médecins du Monde
MSF	Médecins sans Frontières

NGO	non-governmental organization
ODA	Overseas Development Administration
ODI	Overseas Development Institute
OECD	Organization for Economic Cooperation and Development
OEOA	Office for Emergency Operations in Africa (UN)
PLO	Palestine Liberation Organization
PVO (US usage)	private voluntary organization
SCF	Save the Children Fund
SDR	Swiss Disaster Relief Unit (see ASC)
SSR	Soviet Socialist Republic
UN	United Nations
UNA	United Nations Association
UNDP	United Nations Development Programme
UNDRO	Office of the United Nations Disaster Relief Coordinator
UNHCR	United Nations High Commissioner for Refugees
Unicef	United Nations Children's Fund
USAID	United States Agency for International Development
volag	voluntary agency
VSO	Voluntary Service Overseas
WFP	World Food Programme
WHO	World Health Organization
WV	World Vision
WVI	World Vision International

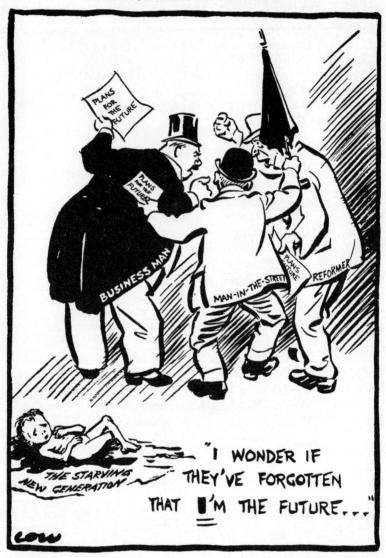

Cartoon by David Low, specially drawn for *The Record of the Save the Children Fund*, 1st August 1921. Reproduced by permission of Save the Children Fund.

Introduction

'I think that the boat people disaster is, ironically, good news for Somalia.' These are the words, to *The Times*, of a 'senior aid official who has worked in Somalia for seven years'. The official was speaking of the slaughter of about 70 Somali refugees and the rape of scores of women trapped on a ship carrying them from their devastated capital, Mogadishu, to Yemen. Refused permission to dock at a Yemeni port, they had wandered the Gulf of Aden for 16 days with dwindling food and water before being hijacked by an armed gang.

The aid official considered this 'good news' because 'It will get it into the media and perhaps the world might try to stop the worst holocaust since the second world war.' In the same report, the *Times* Africa correspondent noted that five million people were estimated to be near death from starvation in Somalia.[1] 'At least 200 people, mostly children, are dying every day in Mogadishu where bandits recently looted a planeload of food for children and last week attempted to steal the entire contents of a ship which was bringing in 5,000 tonnes of grain for famine victims.'

One might be forgiven for thinking 'the media' to be an implacable Moloch which demands blood sacrifices – and maybe this is how our aid official, grimly reckoning the costs and benefits, has come to perceive its power.

A day after his words were reported, world headlines were grabbed by the French President's daring surprise visit to Sarajevo on 28 June. It could be argued that the UN was at the time moving to secure the airport for a humanitarian airlift, or that President Mitterrand's visit was a piece of theatre which did not actually change the relationships responsible for a hideous civil war. Nevertheless, Mitterrand's courageous use of his own person as proof of solidarity with a grossly abused city had the instant effect of forcing Sarajevo onto prime-time news, and relief planes sent by Western governments did get through intermittently after his visit. Bosnia was on the front pages for months afterwards.

But the other story of the massacre of Somali refugees did not become a major headline. No star reporter, no photographers, no television crew were on the spot – no 'disaster tourists'.[2] The *Times* correspondent, Sam Kiley, filed his report from Nairobi, some 1,000 miles from the Yemen coast. Somalia did become a major news story later in the summer of 1992 after outcries by the Red Cross, Save the Children and other agencies. Historians may identify the turning-point as the end of July when the new Egyptian Secretary-General of the UN, Boutros Boutros-Ghali, accused the UN of being too much interested in the rich people's war in Yugoslavia and too little in Somalia, provoking indignation from a number of Western diplomats. A Swiss newspaper chose the headline, 'Boutros-Ghali l'Africain'.[3] Many observers of the Third World today hold that, following the end of the Cold War during which the major powers competed for geopolitical influence, much of it – in particular, most of Africa – is almost falling off the political and economic map as drawn by the West.

We have certainly witnessed over the last 25 years or so the emergence of what may be called a media regime, to which the humanitarian agencies and politicians are increasingly having to adapt, and we need to understand it better. This understanding will not itself solve the problems of relieving disasters and making the world a fairer place, but it is a precondition for finding solutions.

'Journalists are parasites on human suffering.' So observed a senior medical doctor in the course of a tense committee meeting on overseas relief aid, following the spate of major overseas disasters in early 1991. Perhaps the doctor was thinking of the famous Billy Wilder film *Ace in the Hole* (1951), in which a reporter, down on his luck, delays the rescue of a man trapped in a cave in New Mexico in order to create a 'media circus'. I felt when I heard these words that if such an intelligent and influential person could hold this simplified view of complicated issues, there was room for a book that would try to elucidate them clearly and thoroughly.

CENTRAL AIMS OF THIS BOOK

My central topic is the relationship between the relief agencies and the media. I shall explore how major disasters, both natural and man-made, are represented by the media in Britain and other Western countries, and the dilemmas which face the agencies when fund-raising priorities, developmental strategies and educational values do not harmonize. These agencies have to cohabit with a media regime which can often appear arbitrary and ruthless at the same time as it stirs compassion and action. The theme has even more importance than may meet the eye – but I will set out the reasoning for this contention in the Conclusion rather than the Introduction, leaving the reader to evaluate it.

In order to keep the book within manageable limits I have chosen to focus on the relief of emergencies in non-Western countries, especially as it is channelled through the 'voluntary agencies' or Non-Governmental Organizations (volags or NGOs). Yet many of the agencies that respond to emergencies most effectively are actually more committed to 'development', or helping to build up prosperity from a base of poverty. The 'development' debate is an intellectual minefield generally outside the scope of this book but bound to crop up at some points. While maintaining the focus on disasters and emergency relief as they figure in the media, this book also turns to the history and organization of some of the most important aid agencies, and in doing so cannot avoid wider topics – including not only development but also human rights, environmental degradation, wars, and the concept of humanitarian protection.

The harrowing details of actual human suffering matter in this book, but it is also interested in how they are refracted by modern marketing techniques, broadcasting politics, the cultural styles of national humanitarian movements, the visual imagery and narrative formulae through which disasters and relief are represented, and the peculiar power and enchantment of television. The book is intended to explore issues and ideas, and makes no claim to be a reference book. I have not attempted, therefore, to give equitable coverage to each country and each agency in proportion to their size and importance.

The United Kingdom as base-line

Britain is almost certainly the first country in which the issues addressed in this book have come to the fore and received serious attention. There are two historical reasons for this.

First, though the leading role in humanitarian aid in modern times has been taken by the Swiss, the independent NGO scene in Britain is particularly well-developed and diverse – despite the country's declining influence in many other fields. This is partly because Britain is larger than other countries with a strong tradition of humanitarian aid such as Switzerland, the Netherlands, Sweden and Norway. Britain is also a former imperial power with close residual links to many developing countries. But also, as the cultural critic Richard Hoggart has argued, the multiplicity of voluntary associations in Britain is a feature of national life which positively distinguishes the British people.

Second, several other countries have a national press which is as diverse and sophisticated as the British, and a few have newspapers (such as the French *Le Monde*) which excel against any competition for serious coverage of world affairs; but it is doubtful whether any can rival the quality of British television and radio at their best. This is the heritage of a system of benign 'regulation' by broadcasting authorities which goes back to the foundation of the British Broadcasting Corporation (BBC) in the 1920s, and which has hitherto avoided the excesses of both state control and commercial opportunism. The overall standard of television documentaries, in particular, is high, and so is that of professional and public debate about the role of the media.[4]

Hence it is not accidental that Britain has led the way in, for instance, the debate about 'development education' (informing the home public about the underlying problems which make charitable giving necessary) and in disaster studies;[5]

or that its system for coordinating appeals for major disasters, the Disasters Emergency Committee (DEC), is widely admired in other countries.

The USA is well-known for the generosity of its private citizens to charity, but American voluntary agencies have to resort to publicity of a brashness that would never succeed in Britain, and they have little to teach British agencies about development education. Japan, with all its wealth, has produced no NGOs of international significance; nor has Italy, though it is said to have recently overtaken Britain in GNP. The wealthier Islamic states have not yet developed a strong tradition of independent voluntary agencies.

The close interaction between the British media and the agencies has lent weight to the voluntary sector. As one agency director put it to me, the media in Britain act as a watchdog over the voluntary sector, and they also give it much assistance.

Structure of the book

In Chapter 1, I examine the international response to disasters today, concentrating on the build-up of disasters in the first half of 1991, and giving detailed attention to the functioning of the Disasters Emergency Committee, which in many ways encapsulates a distinctively British style of humanitarian action.

Chapter 2 considers the tensions or ambivalences within the voluntary agencies which flow from their divided loyalties: towards beneficiaries and towards the home constituencies.

Both these chapters draw extensively on the British scene. But I have taken steps to guard against the risks of both a near-sighted adherence to topical issues of the hour, and of national parochialism. In Chapter 3, I step back to review first the Nigerian civil war of the late 1960s, and, second, the Armenian earthquake of 1988. This historical chapter tells the stories of two major disasters and the problems of relieving them, with special reference to the influence of the media: the first of the disasters was man-made, the second 'natural' (though aggravated by human improvidence).

Chapter 4 adopts a 'lateral' approach, considering a number of cultural styles in the international world of voluntary agencies which differ from what we might otherwise take for granted as a British, DEC-centred norm. I hope not only to give solid information about some important non-British traditions, but also to stimulate comparative questioning of values and shared assumptions, including, of course, those of the British. These non-British traditions are those of the 'French doctors', the International Committee of the Red Cross, and World Vision – for all of which, relations with the media are most important concerns. I also give a brief glance at two 'null cases' of major agencies that do not yet have to worry about the media, for different reasons.

Chapter 5 considers a range of issues relating to the visual imagery and narrative conventions of disasters and relief, with special attention to the power of television. Readers whose primary interest is in the media rather than in the relief agencies might turn to Chapter 5 first.

In the Conclusion, I argue that the humanitarian NGOs occupy a pivotal position as the world faces major crises, both short-term and long-term.

THE MORAL BASIS OF HUMANITARIAN AID

Largely as a result of successful communication through the media – across a world shrunk by telecommunications, aviation, radio and television – the humanitarian voluntary agencies attract wide support in Western industrial countries. But this consensus is not universal and it is worth examining what kinds of people do *not* give it.

To start with, charitable giving of any kind presupposes a minimum level of disposable income. It would appear that when poorer people in Western countries give to charity, they usually select local or domestic causes. All giving to Third World causes used to be a largely middle-class activity, but this has to some extent changed with the advent of the telethon and televised rock concerts.

There is still a vestigial resistance among some intellectuals of the Left against the very idea of charity. Socialists and Marxists used often to argue that private charity was irrelevant, or by addressing symptoms rather than causes may even slow down the coming revolution which will correct every injustice. This argument is seldom heard any more in its pure form. The fair and important point remains that the presence of private charity can be used by governments to exonerate them from allocating public funds; but the more responsible agencies are alert to the risks of being made use of in this way.

A more serious obstacle is the assumption of many people that their own privileged group has an exclusive, god-given right to security and prosperity. This kind of sectarian, class-based or ethnicist perception of the world is common. However, the concept of human rights – derived from an older Judaeo-Christian principle of equality before God, but extended to secular society – has gained ground over the centuries, and has been buttressed by contributions from moral philosophy and non-Western religions. It is now the moral basis of the humanitarian agencies of the United Nations – however much they may stand in practical need of reform and reinvigoration – and of the mainstream Christian churches; also of many other organizations, from the Order of Malta and the Red Cross to more specialized agencies such as Amnesty International and the Minority Rights Group.

Inertia and quietism can lead all of us to take refuge in the apparent certainties of the bonds of family and neighbour-hood, religion and ethnic grouping – and none of these loyalties should be disparaged, for they are the elements in each individual's cultural identity. Some journalists of the Right argue that these are a sufficient and ample context for morality in the 1990s. The political tradition they belong to is that of Enoch Powell, and it will be surprising if it does not gain more adherents amid the present political and economic turbulence.

However, John Donne wrote that 'No man is an island' nearly four centuries ago – enunciating a central strand in the philosophy of Christianity, the love of one's neighbour as oneself, exemplified in the parable of the Good Samaritan. Scientists concerned with the global environment have been endorsing the same message on common-sense, practical grounds for some thirty years at least, adding to Donne's epigram the observation that no island is an island, either.

Opponents of overseas relief and development agencies sometimes adduce in their support Dickens's brilliantly portrayed Mrs Jellyby in his novel *Bleak House*. Mrs Jellyby's passionate devotion to the welfare of the natives of Borrioboola-ga in Africa was matched by her neglect of her own close family. But we must remember that Dickens, though championing the victims of poverty and oppression in his own country, was even by the standards of his day an out-and-out racial supremacist who derided those philanthropic institutions which are the precursors of today's overseas agencies.[6] It is true, however, that the satire was partly deserved and has relevance for the humanitarian movement today, for successful careers in the humanitarian world can be built, like other careers, at the expense of someone's own family or household.[7]

There are indeed many needs for humanitarian charities to address within the industrialized countries. Save the Children in both Britain and the USA spend about one third of their budgets on community development and health projects within their own domestic territories. In the USA, one of the richest countries, about one in five children is born below the official poverty line, and the proportion is expected to increase to one in four by the end of the century.[8] A similar estimate of one in four children has been suggested for the UK, though the exact definition of poverty in countries that are generally affluent is a matter of political controversy.

A kind of journalistic calculus governs our concern for the victims of disaster, a calculus in which the main variables are first, numbers of victims, and second, proximity – geographical but also ethnic and economic (for a disaster in an industrialized country seems to attract more coverage, per head of victims, than one in a less developed country). The media work out their equations routinely. However, such is the power of the first-hand narrative and – even more so today – of the visual image that the calculus is now and then unpredictably upset, so that concern is suddenly, but usually briefly, generated for a set of distant victims.

Avoiding parasitism

It is of course true that journalists are sometimes parasitic on human suffering. But the same is true of humanitarian workers, of doctors, and indeed of anyone who writes a book such as this one.

Everyone should keep in mind two principles: first, that it is for the sake of victims and survivors of disasters themselves that sophisticated systems of communication and assistance should be designed; and second, that in the efforts to relieve suffering, a huge contribution is made by people who never receive public recognition or appear in the media.

Both principles are occasionally lost sight of, even in the most admirable humanitarian agencies, and frequently by journalists and writers.[9]

1  The International Response to Disasters in the 1990s

Trevor McDonald, Britain's much loved veteran Black newscaster, is speaking gravely of the need to save millions of people from dying in Africa. Donations soon pour in through the mail, through banks and post offices, through telephoned payments by credit card.

The Disasters Emergency Committee is in action. Though it has almost no paid staff and is completely non-operational, the DEC provides a structure for cooperation between the relief agencies and the broadcasting authorities in Britain. The DEC is only a small part of the structure of relief aid in Britain, yet it occupies a nodal position in that structure, so that a detailed description of its working can give a useful insight into the national system as a whole.

But first we need to survey – from the widest global perspective and always mindful of the ambient power of the media – what disasters are, and how the present system of humanitarian response operates. We will also summarize the dismaying pile-up of major disasters that faced the agencies during the first half of 1991.

WHEN IS A DISASTER?

The Bible records numerous plagues, floods, famines and destructions of cities. In 79 BC, the city of Pompeii in southern Italy was buried in volcanic ash. The most damaging earthquakes have killed hundreds of thousands of people at a time and destroyed whole cities. Millions of people have died at various times as a result of flooding of one river in

China, the Hoang Ho; 21 million from the worldwide influenza epidemic of 1918–9; 1.5 million from the Irish famines of the 1840s. These estimates take no account of the sufferings and privations of survivors, or of the economic impact. The impact of extreme physical events is invariably more devastating when it occurs among poor, vulnerable populations.

Large numbers of people live in areas prone to the risk of natural disasters such as flood plains or geological fault zones. 'Natural' disasters in ordinary usage are those which do not result primarily from human actions, yet their effects can be greatly mitigated with proper foresight and preparedness. Many disasters which appear to be 'natural' are in fact symptoms of the incompetence or irrationality with which we manage resources. This applies particularly to food shortages: some of the most seriously famine-hit parts of Africa are only a few hundred miles from the massive oil wealth of Saudi Arabia, and the developed countries frequently allow 'mountains' of food to rot as a matter of economic policy because of our agricultural over-production.

Man-made disasters of the past have been equally widespread. There is no need here to recount the effects of wars and pogroms in human history, the destruction of productive environments by over-exploitation, and more recently the tragedy of large-scale industrial accidents. One political doctrine, Stalinism, has led to disaster conditions over large areas of the former Eastern bloc.

Fortunately a large proportion of the world's populations live out their lives in relative freedom from disaster. But we cannot be sure that it will not strike us, however secure we may feel, and we can no longer ignore disasters which are far away, if only because television and photo-journalism bring them ever closer to us. Yet it will be argued in this book that the coverage of disasters by the press and the media is so selective and arbitrary that, in an important sense, they 'create' a disaster when they decide to recognize it. To be more precise, they give institutional endorsement or attestation to bad events which otherwise have a reality restricted to a local circle of victims. Such endorsement is a prerequisite for the marshalling of external relief and reconstructive effort.

The endorsement is not decided by some mysterious Moloch but by quite small numbers of professional editors and reporters, whose decisions on whether or not to apply the 'hallmark' of recognition can have far-reaching chains of consequences, both positive and negative.

The vast majority of natural disasters such as floods and earthquakes are not reported at all in the international media. Some cases of warfare and civil strife might be happening on the dark side of the moon for all we read or hear about them. The media in each country understandably record their own disasters, and in Western countries a priority is accorded to disasters afflicting citizens of the wealthier countries. The media tend to be specially concerned by high death counts, as opposed to the longer-term effects of disasters on economic and social life; yet even high death counts do not guarantee that a particular disaster gets onto the front pages and the television screens.

Disasters may be roughly classified as follows:[1]

1 The *sudden elemental*, prompted by climatic and geological forces (though often aggravated by man-made errors). As in the case of earthquakes, these are often to a great extent unpredictable. Some elemental events can be tracked in advance by a few weeks (for instance, river floods) or a few days (for instance, tropical hurricanes).
2 The *foreseeable*, such as most famines and epidemics.
3 The *deliberate*, resulting from wars and civil strife.
4 The *accidental*, resulting from some kind of technological mishap.

Some disasters include elements of all four types.

It is now generally recognized that even the 'sudden elemental' disasters nearly always include a human element. Many occur in vulnerable populated areas, that is, places where human beings have created conditions of vulnerability. Buildings are the principal cause of death from earthquakes. According to the USA's Overseas Development Council, agricultural modernization and demographic pressure push six out of ten poor people to live on land which is specially vulnerable to disasters.[2] At least one whole sovereign state, the Republic of the Maldives, is at serious risk from a rise in the sea level, and much of Bangladesh is endemically prone to tidal waves and flooding. This is one category of disaster which may actually be increasing in incidence and gravity, because of land degradation and population pressures.

A more useful distinction, cutting across that between natural and man-made disasters, can be drawn between sudden and chronic. The sudden disasters are generally easier to cope with. When on a large scale they frequently attract considerable media interest which stimulates compassion and an urgent response. Chronic disasters pose more complex problems. Among chronic disasters we must include environmental emergencies such as deforestation and the pollution of air and water, and epidemic or endemic diseases such as cholera and AIDS, which are so closely linked in the Third World with poverty. The relief of such chronic disasters merges conceptually with long-term development aid.

The most severe disasters can have demographic effects which damage a nation's potential for reconstruction: examples of these are the civil war in Cambodia and the current HIV pandemic in parts of Africa. In such cases, a heavy death toll from the productive age groups leaves an imbalance of children and the elderly.

THE ORGANIZATION OF RELIEF AND RECONSTRUCTION

Over many decades and from small beginnings, institutions have grown up to respond to disasters. We may regard them as forming a functioning system, though not a system which has been purposefully designed.

At various points in this book, we will look back in passing at the history of some of the more important humanitarian agencies. Here we will review the system as it functions today, beginning at the global level with the UN-based International Governmental Organizations (IGOs) and working down through government and inter-government programmes to the independent agencies (Non-governmental Organizations or NGOs) in different Western countries. After this overview, we will examine in some detail the major relief NGOs in Britain as they interact with the media, on mutually agreed occasions of major overseas disaster, through the Disasters Emergency Committee.

Though the emphasis in this whole book is on international and 'Western' agencies, it is important to stress that – in the opinion of all the more experienced international and national agencies – the priority must be to reinforce *local* response mechanisms after a disaster. There are indeed some emergencies, such a major earthquake, where the immediate arrival of trained and well-coordinated rescuers and doctors can save many lives. However, an experienced relief organizer has written:

> We must have the courage of our convictions and admit that the most appropriate reaction is sometimes to do nothing during the first few days. One must constantly remember that before organizing help one must have a clear idea of the problems which may arise, and also evaluate the situation correctly before acting. It is not enough 'to do something'.[3]

After urgent measures to save lives have been taken as far as possible, the task is then to persuade donors and relief agencies to commit resources first to rehabilitation and reconstruction, then to preparing against repetition of the same disaster. The media-prominence of a great flood or earthquake can be productively used by the agencies. Furthermore, sudden disasters and their aftermaths tend to follow fairly well-understood common patterns. For instance, even a severe flood which has caused many deaths from drowning tends to leave only a few injured people to be cared for, which is not the case with earthquakes.

Obviously, the dangers of war and civil strife can make it difficult or impossible to bring any effective external relief to victims. Special problems, too, are raised when disaster is coupled with refugee movements, in which case the concept of a local response mechanism to disaster has to be supple-

mented by a model of relations between host communities and
strangers.

The United Nations agencies

Since the charter of the United Nations Organization was
signed in 1945, a bewildering number of agencies have
proliferated. The following list includes only those concerned
with disaster relief.

- The Rome-based Food and Agriculture Organization
  (FAO) is concerned both with early warning on countries
  prone to food shortages or pest infestation, and with
  providing post-disaster food aid and supplies such as seeds,
  tools, animal vaccines, fertilizers and fishing equipment
  needed for rehabilitation.
- The World Food Programme (WFP), a smaller organization also based in Rome and partially accountable to the
  FAO, devotes a large part of its resources to feeding disaster
  victims, and is now generally seen as the leading UN
  agency for food aid coordination and logistics management.
  Its emergency response capacity is known as the International Emergency Food Reserve (IEFR).
- UNDRO (the Office of the UN Disaster Relief Coordinator) has the task of mobilizing and coordinating the
  various organizations of the UN in response to a request
  from a stricken State, liaising with NGOs, assisting with
  assessment of the State's needs, and communicating these
  needs to donors; and generally acting as a clearing-house
  for assistance, study, prevention, control and prediction of
  natural disasters. UNDRO is not restricted to natural as
  opposed to man-made disasters, but will take a leading
  role in the International Decade for Natural Disaster
  Reduction. This is coordinated by the Scientific and
  Technical Committee of the UN General Assembly,[4] and is
  largely oriented towards a technological approach, for
  instance improving earthquake prediction.
- The Office of the UN High Commissioner for Refugees
  (UNHCR) provides all types of assistance to refugees, and
  has a subsidiary role (as yet no more than marginal) of
  trying to prevent refugee movements.

- Unicef (United Nations Children's Fund), having the function of providing assistance for mothers and children, assumes the leading role in a number of non-food sectors including the provision of shelter, drinking water and cooking utensils, immunization programmes, treatment of diarrhoeal diseases, grassroots training, and priority inputs to help reestablish basic primary school capabilities.
- The World Health Organization (WHO) has a new but active Emergency Planning and Response department, and has special expertise in providing technical advice on medical and health issues.
- The World Bank, the biggest of all the UN agencies, provides emergency lending for post-disaster reconstruction, and regular lending for emergency preparedness and early warning systems.
- The Development Programme (UNDP) has Resident Representatives in developing countries who are also representatives of UNDRO and the World Food Programme. They have a central role in coordinating relief in disaster-prone countries.

This list of the major UN organizations relevant to disasters is by no means complete. In terms of size and importance in their contributions to disaster relief, the three largest are Unicef, WFP and UNHCR, followed by WHO and UNDP.

Weaknesses in the UN system and proposals for reform

Understandably, the problem of coordinating all these organizations in their efforts, especially at times of stress, is highly complicated. It is generally agreed that there is room for improvement, indeed for a thoroughgoing reorganization of the UN's humanitarian programmes from the top down.

One line of criticism, exemplified by the journalist Graham Hancock's *Lords of Poverty*, targets the UN system as a whole with its massive overhead expenses including tax-free salaries, perks and travel on a well-worn conference circuit.[5] Criticism is also levelled at the lack of genuine accountability in the UN system, which leads to featherbedded management and people in the wrong jobs or receiving promotion for the wrong reasons; and at rivalry between the various agencies (since the major agencies were set up some four decades ago, the UN has tended to respond to new problems by creating new agencies).

However, the leaner parts of the UN can function quite well at times. In the field of disaster relief, the Office for Emergency Operations in Africa (OEOA) was set up in 1984 as an *ad hoc* operation under the Secretary-General and was not unsuccessful during a short but critical period. 'Special representatives' of the Secretary-General heading *ad hoc* operations directed from New York – such as Sadruddin Aga Khan, who in July 1991 headed a mission to Iraq on humanitarian needs following the Gulf war – are often given enough leeway to produce clearly written reports with incisive recommendations, even if these are not always followed up.

The UN is also under the scrutiny of member states and NGOs. In 1990, four Nordic countries published a study, *Responding to Emergencies: the Role of the UN in Emergencies and ad hoc Operations*, which is among other things a sharp indictment of the work of UNDRO since its foundation in 1971 after the earthquake in Skopje, Yugoslavia. In August 1991, the International Save the Children Alliance criticized the international system as a whole for 'a lack of political will, forward planning and institutional learning'. These critiques echo a particularly hard-hitting study prepared by Sadruddin Aga Khan in 1987 for the United Nations Association of the USA, in which he wrote that

UNDRO has the dubious distinction of being the object of continuous critical evaluation throughout a 16-year history. . . . Although the inference of these reports is that UNDRO is unable to fulfill its mandate, they have had little impact on changing UNDRO's operations other than to cause UNDRO executives to expend considerable energy in lobbying member governments and other agencies to safeguard its position. However, as UNDRO has no governing council, one may legitimately ask how else UNDRO can act to promote its interests.[6]

Latterly, UNDRO appears to be scaling down its operations.

Unicef, which depends more than other UN agencies on private funding, is and has been for many years one of the more dynamic parts of the UN. WHO, though burdened with an ineffective regional structure, carries out indispensable work in epidemiology and other fields. Most informed observers believe there would be hope for the UN if a real effort were made to bring the weak elements up to the level of the stronger ones, and to enable the many able and devoted people working in its agencies to realize their full potential.

Some journalists and politicians have called for a humanitarian Rapid Deployment Force:

> If there really is to be a 'new world order', let it begin with a humanitarian Rapid Deployment Force that saves people rather than killing them – a multinational standby capacity with ready emergency supplies of food and water, clothing and medicine, and the transportation and manpower of armies, navies and air forces to respond to God's disasters and man's inhumanity to man.
>
> And let that Rapid Deployment Force be backed by the military power of the big countries, so that it is not restrained by national boundaries and world or regional politics. The model should be postwar Iraq, where the United States did move, reluctantly at first, to feed and protect some Kurds and Shiites under attack from their own government.[7]

It is argued in favour of a Rapid Deployment Force that the armies of Western nations have increasingly little to do now that the cold war is over, and that only they can airlift large quantities of helicopters, for example, or set up satellite communications. Operation Provide Comfort, conceived to set up the safety zone for the Kurds in 1991, cost the US many hundreds of millions of dollars. Such sums can be found relatively easily in the slack that is generally allowed for in military budgets, whereas they are far beyond the resources of NGOs. But the force would have to be closely supervised by a humanitarian rather than a military overseer, with careful attention to long-term consequences. Soldiers are generally trained to achieve short-term objectives, and military inter-vention invariably brings unplanned havoc in its train.

The UN has resources to respond to disasters but their efficient coordination has so far proved beyond it. The Nordic UN study, despairing of UNDRO which should be fulfilling the coordinating role, recommended a Standing Inter-Agency Group for Emergencies, sitting both in Geneva and in New York and consisting of representatives of each UN agency actively involved in emergencies. The International Save the Children Alliance made similar proposals, emphasizing the need for better coordination both within and outside the UN.[8] Others call for a more radical restructuring of the agencies, with one or two being eliminated altogether in the interests of efficiency and overcoming inertia. With the hope of stronger management than the UN has had in past years, following the appointment of a new Secretary-General in Boutros Boutros-Ghali, it may be that these problems will be tackled more effectively.

In response to an Anglo-German proposal, the UN appointed in February 1992 a coordinator to take charge of humanitarian relief. He is Jan Eliasson, formerly Sweden's ambassador to the UN. He heads the new Department of Humanitarian Affairs, and will have a revolving fund of $50 million at his disposal as well as direct access to the Secretary-General. UNDRO may soon disappear as an independent office. The coordinator's office is in New York, along with the Security Council, the political organs of the UN, Unicef and UNDP – but too distant, perhaps, from most of the UN humanitarian agencies, which are in Geneva (indeed, the new department has an office there too). Some regret that a high-profile public figure was not appointed, able to 'knock heads together'. Others more optimistically hope that the outsider Eliasson will be able to coordinate the UN's fiefdoms more easily than an insider. The Swiss government, keen to maintain Geneva's position as the centre of the humanitarian movement, immediately paid $2 million into Eliasson's revolving fund, much more than its normal quota.[9] So far, the NGO community (to whom so much was left in Somalia and Kurdistan) is not over-impressed with the UN's humanitarian record during 1992. It is noted that, as one among numerous

Under-Secretaries-General, Eliasson does not have enough seniority to coordinate the powerful agency heads effectively.

By contrast, the UN High Commissioner for Refugees newly appointed in 1991, Mrs Sagato Ogata, is considered to be doing a good job in an agency hitherto somewhat demoralized and lacking direction, and now grossly over-stretched by the demands made on it, especially in ex-Yugoslavia.

The administrative problems of the UN are not dissimilar from those experienced by many large multinational commercial firms. These adopt the remedy of strict accountability, with a board of directors holding the ultimate responsibility to shareholders. An alternative model might be the accountability of State civil servants to ministers and hence to the elected parliament of a Westminster-style democracy. Though the UN was originally intended to function as a disinterested international civil service, it has always been prone to political interference by powerful individual member States and blocs of less powerful States. The Secretary-General is usually a second-tier official entrusted with overwhelming problems in which the UN's political, peacekeeping and humanitarian roles become blurred. Sadly, there may be mere talk of change.

The humanitarian agencies have been arguing about coordination for at least twenty years. The 1971 documentary film *Diplomacy*, in Roger Graef's television series *The Space between Words*, follows the negotiations between various national diplomats in Geneva, among each other and with representatives of the humanitarian agencies (including the League of Red Cross Societies), about the role of a new UN office for coordination of relief for natural disasters. The negotiations depend on the interpretation to be given to the word 'direct': will the new official give substantive operational orders, or merely 'direct' in the way a policeman directs traffic? The negotiations end with a diplomatic fudge.

Government and multi-governmental action

Most Western governments have introduced procedures for responding to disasters. This is known as 'bilateral' aid since it involves only the donor and the recipient nations – as opposed to 'multilateral' aid, when donor nations' funds are channelled through a supranational entity. The largest national agency is the United States Agency for International Development (USAID). One of its most prominent activities in the disaster field is in early warning systems to forestall famines in Africa.

The Swiss Disaster Relief Unit (SDR) is one of the most effective national organizations, based on the principle of a militia or reserve army. It was founded as an instrument of Swiss foreign policy and has provided operational humanitarian aid abroad since 1974, funded by the federal government. It is a corps of about 1,200 professionally and personally well-qualified men and women who, with the agreement of their employers, have committed themselves to undertake humanitarian work abroad for a limited period of time. The volunteers all speak foreign languages, have experience of disaster missions and are between 23 and 55 years of age. They are coordinated by the Federal Council's Delegate for Disaster Relief Abroad, supported by a small staff in Bern. Their missions abroad, of which there have been over 200 to date, are always led by volunteers. They are planned to last for one year at the most, then to be handed over. Each individual's commitment is limited to between two and four months.[10]

Britain channels its relief aid through the Overseas Development Administration (ODA), which is part of the Foreign and Commonwealth Office. The ODA Disaster Unit's main role is that of a funding agency, working closely with the UN, the Red Cross movement, the European Commission and the voluntary sector. ODA states clearly that the extent and direction of the Government's emergency relief aid is determined 'primarily by humanitarian and logistical considerations' but it 'may also be affected by political considerations, although lack of diplomatic relations does not stop the sending of humanitarian aid.' Information comes to the Disaster Unit from British embassies, voluntary agencies and UNDRO.

The Disaster Unit officials are empowered to grant funds on their own initiative without bureaucratic impediments; in fact, this is one of the least bureaucratic of government departments. They rely to a great extent on the experience and track record of three agencies – Save the Children Fund (SCF), Oxfam and the British Red Cross – with ActionAid almost achieving this category of recognition. Other agencies are eligible to apply for funds to the Disaster Unit but their applications receive closer individual scrutiny.[11]

The Disaster Unit can now mount its own response to emergencies overseas (the Disaster Relief Initiative, announced in August 1991), obtaining rapid assessment of need and sending skilled teams of people to help on the ground. The first occasion on which this happened was in northern Iraq in April – May 1991. A register of volunteers is now maintained so that teams of firemen, medics, engineers and others can be assembled at short notice. In the past the Armed Services have been used for disaster relief: for instance, in contributing to famine relief efforts in Ethiopia and Sudan in 1984 and 1985, and after the Nepal earthquake in 1988.

The Commission of the European Communities recently overhauled its organization and set up a European Office for Emergency Humanitarian Aid as from 1 March 1992. Its regular total aid resources amount to about £570 million per year, to cover Eastern Europe and the former USSR as well as the Third World. The Commission appears to have resented its 'low visibility' as a mere channel for humanitarian aid through UN agencies and NGOs, acting 'more as a banker than a partner'.[12] It will continue to work with traditional humanitarian organizations, but will gradually adopt a more direct role, 'enhancing the Community's presence on the ground'. The new Office's work will be reviewed regularly and evaluated thoroughly after seven years.

It is clear that a concern with presentation of the EC's image through the media was an important factor in this organizational change; the Commission also wanted more control over the outcome of political decisions on relief aid that the EC might make in future. Some officers of major British and French NGOs are disturbed that both national government and the EC are becoming too motivated by the desire to secure a political 'profile'. There is concern lest the NGOs should be pushed into a position of becoming no more than contractors for governments.

Relief and development NGOs

The core of international humanitarian aid outside the control of governments – though enshrined in law and treaties – is the Red Cross and Red Crescent Movement. This will be the subject of a special section in Chapter 4. Here it will suffice to distinguish the International Committee of the Red Cross (ICRC), concerned mainly with the results of human conflict, from the Federation (until recently known as the League) of Red Cross and Red Crescent Societies, which also has its headquarters in Geneva but is a much more diffuse organization with a broader mission which includes special responsibility for natural disasters.

A great variety of humanitarian NGOs have developed in Western countries. Some of these are federated across national boundaries, for instance the federation of Catholic agencies called Caritas Internationalis, of which the British member is CAFOD, the Catholic Fund for Overseas Development.

As already mentioned, many of the agencies concerned with 'relief' are in fact more interested in development as part of their fundamental philosophy: this would certainly apply to Oxfam, Save the Children, Christian Aid, CAFOD and Unicef. Much work sponsored by these organizations, mainly based in communities of a few hundred or a few thousand though also at a national level, is pursued as a regular part of their programmes, attracting little publicity but earning the approval of informed private citizens and academic institutions, and also the support of donor governments. As a general rule, such projects aim to generate self-reliance through training and through strengthening weak points in a system of economic support and/or health care.

Potential pitfalls beset all long-term development projects. These can occur particularly when a government seeks to impose some ambitious scheme on an unwilling population – by large-scale resettlement of pastoralists, by building a dam, or in countless other ways. One of the commonest pitfalls is that grant-aided import of food or other commodities can depress prices, thereby ruining local markets and small producers' livelihoods. Anthropologists have traditionally been a thorn in the side of development planners, pointing out the unintended consequences which so often arise from well-meaning schemes.

Development is a controversial field and sometimes the controversy spills into politics. We will consider this question in Chapter 2. Within the development agencies, internal debate frequently addresses the desirable balance between development and relief. Within Oxfam, for instance, there are field officers whose preoccupation with urgent relief needs in Africa and elsewhere makes them rather sceptical about the development-oriented priorities of Oxfam House in north Oxford. Oxfam copes with the problem by having a separate department for emergencies, on which it has recently spent as much as 45 per cent of its annual budget. Save the Children Fund (UK) prefers to integrate emergency relief into its normal regional structure. Both agencies see direct emergency relief as a smaller part than it used to be of their total mission.

Nicholas Hinton, SCF's director-general, whom I interviewed, comments that the European Community and the UN are better at shifting millions of tons of food than the NGOs; SCF has done particularly well by putting pressure on the United Nations and Oxfam in their relationship with the EC. Hinton believes that the distinction between short-term and long-term aid is overdrawn. SCF can often get access to a country where there is a disaster, and is then able to do long-term work there. SCF's role in a disaster, according to him, tends to be an intensification of what they normally do. This view no doubt reflects SCF's overall strategy in managing its budget, and would not necessarily be endorsed by other agencies. When there is a disaster, SCF's expenses in a particular region shoot up; when the emergency is over they do not drop to the previous level, but reach another plateau. SCF's total income – which reached nearly £100 million during the exceptional year of 1991 – follows a similar pattern of irregular growth from year to year.

One experienced coordinator of refugee and relief services, now working in Geneva, believes (like the Oxfam field officers mentioned above) that with so much urgent need for relief in the world, there is an element of humbug in talk about 'development'. This practical 'field view' is shared by many others, but for a variety of different reasons: by those market economists who hold that development aid can actually be destructive in encouraging dependency and corruption, and by some anthropologists and others who question the whole ideology of modernization.

Yet most observers who have seen 'grassroots' projects at their best coming to fruition take the view that the development agencies deserve support, despite the mistakes which they at times inevitably make. The experienced NGOs – imbued with a healthy spirit of self-criticism and openness with each other about mistakes – are most able to offer planning and management without the bureaucratic top-heaviness of some UN agencies. They are likely to come under increasing pressure to be more open with outsiders as well as insiders about projects which are flops. Some commentators have called for the idiom of good service and value for money – with the intended beneficiaries in the role of the consumer – to be adopted by the agencies, who have become too used to interacting with governments and being assessed by fellow professionals.[13]

To complement the larger agencies, there is always room for the innovative specialist agency. Examples of these in Britain are Survival International, which is devoted to the interests of indigenous peoples; or Action for Disability and Development, which has carved out a special role to help disabled people to help themselves, especially in Africa, and to challenge their persistent marginalization – even by some NGOs devoted to working with the 'poorest of the poor'.[14]

Other agencies such as Médecins sans Frontières (discussed in detail in Chapter 4) are primarily concerned with emergency relief. The British Red Cross is an example of an agency moving in the opposite direction from Oxfam or SCF – from its traditional response to disasters to a complementary commitment to long-term community development. It is not intended that this will become a major part of its budget, but experience in community development should make the emergency relief work more sensitive. The British Red Cross has a few overseas delegates of its own but mostly operates either through the ICRC or the Federation, or bilaterally with sister societies.

A small office in Geneva, the Standing Committee for

Humanitarian Response (formerly the Licross/Volags Steering Committee for Disasters), coordinates the efforts of the Federation, a number of Christian agency federations, the International Save the Children Alliance (ISCA) and Oxfam. The Standing Committee also cooperates with the Humanitarian Liaison Working Group of Ambassadors, an association of OECD (Organization for Economic Cooperation and Development) donor governments. The Standing Committee is concerned neither with fund-raising nor with day-to-day operations but with the allocation of tasks to the agencies, by geographical areas and sometimes by special expertise.

The cost-effectiveness of most of the NGOs is a crucial point in their favour. Organizations like Oxfam and Save the Children demonstrate that highly effective staff can be attracted and retained without huge salaries being paid. Even their senior directors earn quite modest sums of money by the standards of commerce or even the Civil Service. Job satisfaction compensates to a great extent for the low pay (which is, of course, not low pay at all by the standards of most poor countries). Some charities go to the opposite extreme of cutting down ruthlessly on the costs of professional staff, with a view to making sure that 'every penny goes to the beneficiaries'. However, such a policy is not generally practicable in the field of overseas relief and development where professionalism as well as dedication is essential, and where money and supplies can easily be lost or diverted without proper supervision. There is a current trend in charity circles to stress the importance of good administration rather than the need to cut overheads to the barest minimum.[15] Some agencies make a point of relying on the 'voluntary', or unpaid, services of doctors, firemen and others. Others deliberately choose to be 'non-operational', raising funds to send to local partners overseas while remaining accountable to their donors for the auditing of these programmes.

DISASTERS AS MEDIA CONSTRUCTS

Before we review the sequence of major disasters covered by the media during 1991, consider those which do *not* get into the media. To start with, Communist countries pre-*perestroika* did not encourage publicity for their disasters, natural or man-made. The mere fact that journalists now have access to areas where there have been floods or earthquakes, or industrial accidents like Chernobyl, has greatly broadened the geographical range of news about disasters.

In the late 1950s a nuclear waste accident in the eastern Soviet Union resulted in many small communities being removed from Soviet maps (the area is now known as the Eastern Urals Radioactive Trace). The Tangshan earthquake in eastern China in 1976, which struck an industrial city of a million people at night without warning, is said to have claimed 240,000 lives and obliterated some 7,000 families; though it was reported in the world media, the Chinese government of the day relied entirely on its own resources for relief and reconstruction.[16]

Planned violations of human rights such as the Chinese destruction of the Tibetan monasteries, and the slaughter of hundreds of thousands of Tibetans by Chinese security forces, caused minimal protest in the Western world, largely because journalists had no access to Tibet and were therefore unable to report the atrocities. In East Timor people have lost their lives at the hands of the Indonesian government over many years while attracting hardly any journalistic interest until recently, even though the UN Security Council resolutions in 1975 and 1976 called on the Indonesian government to withdraw. A few human rights organizations, helped by dedicated journalists and campaigners, have sustained some degree of public concern in the West for Tibet and East Timor, but not enough to convince Western governments to put any substantial pressures on China or Indonesia respectively.

It can be said, therefore, that disasters do not exist – except for their unfortunate victims and those who suffer in their aftermaths – unless publicized by the media. In this sense the media actually *construct* disasters. The disasters which are assured of ample coverage are the more unusual ones, such as the extraordinary explosion of Lake Nyos in Cameroon in August 1986, which released a cloud of carbon dioxide that killed 1,746 people as well as nearly all other living things that it touched.[17] A well-publicized disaster or civil war in one part of the world takes the media heat off other countries, enabling leaders to choose their moment to do things which they do not want to be widely known.

The major NGOs have long-term commitments in their chosen operational countries which they adhere to despite lack of media interest. This is easiest for those with substantial free reserves. The ICRC to its credit has had a presence in East Timor, for instance, since 1978. Though much of the work is to focus concern for individual detainees, they also carry out a water and sanitation programme in selected villages, and one assumes that the presence of two staff members in the capital, Dili, has had some restraining effect on the behaviour of the occupying power. (The danger, of which the ICRC is well aware, is that its presence can be exploited by repressive governments to give them an appearance of respectability.)

Governments and national relief agencies come under intense pressure to respond to those emergencies which are in the public eye. A great responsibility therefore rests on those who control and filter the news. The news system appears to aspire to having one disaster at a time to wrack the public's conscience. This has been described by a French television journalist as the 'funnel effect' (*phénomène de l'entonnoir*): 'There is only room for one overwhelming emotion a day or week. . . . There'll always be forgotten countries.'[18] This may be a function of the way the human brain works; more likely, it is a professional assumption of journalists.

Paul-Henri Morard of the ICRC says[19] that after many years of experience he cannot understand the reasons for which the media will pick up one disaster story rather than another, and then just as suddenly drop it. For instance, in July 1991 when I interviewed him he was trying to get the media interested in filming 350,000 exhausted Ethiopian soldiers walking down from the Aswan Dam to Addis Ababa, since their plight had hardly been reported and there was thus no interest from governments in supporting ICRC efforts to assist them. This was as visually dramatic and emotionally poignant an event as the retreat of Napoleon's army from Russia. Yet no one was interested in filming it: the television companies' money had been spent covering the Gulf war, and their attention was currently all on Yugoslavia. Sometimes, he says, a well-known person or a TV crew will light on a trouble-spot somewhere and there will be a snowball effect. (Another experienced journalist has adduced the parable of the Gadarene swine.) Morard thinks it is pointless to try to change the direction of the media unless you have a huge network of influence, and probably not even then.

MULTIPLE DISASTERS IN 1991

A convergence of media-prominent emergencies put the international relief system under immense strain in the first half of 1991. In 1988 there had been a similar convergence, when in Britain the Disasters Emergency Committee mounted three appeals within two months for the Sudan emergency, Bangladesh floods and a hurricane in the Caribbean. But in 1988, famine in Africa did not threaten so many millions, nor did any of the 1988 emergencies come anywhere near equalling the political drama of the Persian Gulf crisis. This unprecedented strain on the system provoked criticism in the press. Why were Bangladesh's flood shelters so inadequate? Why was emergency food aid shipped to north-east Africa so late? A summary of the most prominent disasters of 1991 and their consequences will bring out many of the issues explored by this book. This is not, however, an exhaustive list of the disasters of 1991, which also included (to name but two) a flood in Malawi and the eruption of Pinatubo, a volcano in the Philippines which had been dormant for six centuries.

African famine
During the first few months of 1991, the relief agencies were preoccupied with the famine in Ethiopia, Sudan, Somalia, Mozambique, Malawi, Angola and Liberia.[20] The early warning systems set up over the last decade were reasonably effective and by October and November 1990 the agencies were reporting danger signals: failed harvests for the second year running, families gathering wild foods or moving to

towns, low water supplies, alarming death rates among cattle and goats. Urgent international action was required.

However, it was not until December 1990 that the British Government and the EC signed food aid contracts, leaving little time for grain to be transported before the rainy season in May (the big contracts did not come until April–May). By January, reports from Eritrea in Ethiopia, where civil war still raged, were worsening. Thousands of Somalian refugees, fleeing another civil war, arrived in an Ethiopian border camp. By May, it was confirmed that in Sudan and Ethiopia the food situation was worse than in 1984/5. SCF (UK) estimated that 26 million people were in need of immediate food aid.[21]

An Ethiopia Famine Appeal had already been launched on British television and radio in December 1989 through the DEC, raising £10.2 million to purchase food, trucks and medical supplies for people in the north of Ethiopia, with a view to enabling them to stay on their land rather than sell their cattle, tools and seeds and migrate in search of food.[22] A major British contribution was the Joint Trucking Operation, established jointly by Oxfam and SCF since the mid-1980s, which now provided a fleet of 38 trucks for relief supplies on a corridor route through both government- and rebel-held areas.

On 8 January 1991, the DEC launched a further Crisis in Africa appeal, the seventh for African food relief in the last twenty years. It was intended to help prevent deaths all over the continent caused by a drought exacerbated by civil strife – by means of delivering food so that people could stay in their own houses. Thus it was hoped that horrific camps, of the kind seen on television in 1984–5, would be unnecessary. The funds were also used to provide seeds and tools to optimize the chances of a good harvest in 1991, and for water provision, medical care and transport facilities. In spring 1991, SCF launched its successful 'Skip lunch, save a life' campaign. A number of other British agencies cooperated in a project called Wings over Africa, wherein a group of journalists was taken on a tour of Africa in a plane lent by British Airways. A further DEC appeal, Action for Africa, was launched in April

1991. All in all, at least £30 million was raised specifically for Africa by British agencies in the first half of 1991.

At the same time as it strove to relieve immediate starvation in Africa, SCF's overseas staff were meeting in conference to discuss how such crises could in future be headed off at an earlier stage, through enabling people to maintain their livelihoods and thus preventing economic collapse. The very concept of 'famine' was called into question, as defined by the political objectives of donors, including their institutional need to move food aid; focusing on 'famine' buttresses the position of some donors that nothing can be done until people are actually starving, and the more positive concept of 'food security' was suggested.[23] SCF now urges that food aid should be provided before people become destitute and are forced to abandon their homes, thereby running further risks to their safety and health and leaving their farmland untended. SCF supports such policies as channelling aid into community programmes through 'food for work' and 'cash for work' schemes; stabilizing market prices so that staple foods remain affordable; and financing rural credit, grain bank and income generation projects.[24]

Oxfam launched a campaign in early 1991 called 'Don't Forget Africa', and took a leading role in putting pressure on governments and the European Community to increase food aid. Ironically, with world food prices at low levels it was costing the EC more in export subsidies to dispose of surplus cereals on the world markets than it would to transport them to most of the famine-hit areas.[25] In March, Oxfam took the unusual step of chartering its own ship to deliver 5,000 tonnes of grain for 350,000 people – partly to draw attention to the failure of the major Western food donors to deliver the 750,000 extra tonnes needed. Stimulated by angry Oxfam press releases about the EC ministers' 'dithering', a *Guardian* leader said that public attention to disasters, stimulated by tele-vision, is too short: 'as it recedes from the latest horror, the non-governmental aid agencies are left in the position of social workers desperately trying to squeeze enough money out of a defective and inadequate social security system, until the next surge of concern.'[26] On this occasion, the EC did commit, in May, about half the extra food aid needed. It moved with

unusual speed to mobilize and deliver the food, thanks to EC
civil servants breaking the complicated Community rules.[27]

Oxfam is probably the most sophisticated publicist among
British relief NGOs, aiming its multi-pronged national and
international campaigns at politicians, public servants and
the media while also mobilizing its own committed supporters. Lobbying and media work are planned together as a
concerted endeavour. 'Don't Forget Africa' was launched at
the beginning of March with a five-month timetable. By the
end of April, the campaign coordinator could announce a
turning-point where 'we are last beginning to see a shift in
attention by both the media and politicians towards the
famine in Africa.'[28] During May, Oxfam arranged a well-
publicized tour of Africa by its then Director, Frank Judd, as
the focal point of 'Don't Forget Africa'.

Christian Aid, which has no overseas staff but works with
overseas partners, cooperated in particular with the Eritrean
Relief Association to truck supplies to remote regions of the
northern province of Eritrea, which was previously independent and has never accepted its federation with Ethiopia
in 1962. Christian Aid's aim was to try to prevent mass
migration. With CAFOD, they also organized emergency
airlifts to southern Sudan, the scene of another grim civil war.

The crises in several African countries are so chronic and so
complicated by civil strife that even the quality Western press
finds difficulty in covering them adequately. But there are
occasional television series such as the Yorkshire TV/
International Broadcasting Trust's *The Dispossessed*, concerned
with world refugee problems and screened in 1991, which
dwelt effectively and in some detail on the problems of
countries like Malawi, where food shortages (with nearly two
million people in need of immediate help) are aggravated by
the people's generous and hospitable reception of refugees
from neighbouring Mozambique.

The Gulf war
The British agencies had raised substantial earmarked sums
for African famine relief during the winter of 1990–1, thanks to
skilful and experienced public relations, but in January 1991
they were faced with a new challenge, the Gulf war.

The Gulf crisis had been simmering since news of the invasion of Kuwait in August 1990 disturbed the beaches and swimming-pools of Europe and America. In Britain, the DEC launched its Gulf Crisis Appeal in September 1990 on behalf of some 600,000 refugees, mostly from Arab and Asian countries, who flooded across the Jordanian border, and a small number who took refuge in neighbouring countries. Conditions in the camps were grim; the worst ones in Jordan were quickly closed and new, better organized temporary camps were opened with relief inputs from overseas agencies.

Until late December 1990, most people believed or hoped that there would be a peaceful settlement with Iraq, but it was not to be. The intense international interest in the Gulf meant that every agency had to have a prominent presence there. But the threat of famine to 20 million lives in Africa is more serious in terms of numbers than the threats, however grave, to the people of Iraq and Kuwait who in all number only 18 million. For this reason, no agency wanted to reduce its commitment to Africa.

During the war which started on 17 January, the ICRC's privileged status enabled it to play a key role. Its delegation of nine people in Baghdad was cut off from the outside world during the initial phase of the war, but the first relief convoy from the ICRC's rear base in Iran reached Baghdad on 30 January. Convoys continued to be sent into Iraq from Iran until early March, when regular access to Baghdad from Amman in Jordan became possible. (In addition, the ICRC carried out its traditional role of protection for the prisoners of war on both sides.) The ICRC under its established policies was unable to pass on any information to the media about the bombing of Iraq, and indeed it would certainly have been expelled by the Iraqi authorities if it had done so.

After the end of the ground war and the risings of the Kurds and Shiites, which were ruthlessly suppressed by Saddam Hussein, it was probably the reports by journalists which saved the Kurds from being hideously treated. The US government, stung by criticism that its actions had encouraged the Kurdish uprising, set up a safety zone on the Turkish border, and there was a great deal of international relief

activity, most of it poorly coordinated. After a few weeks the
Kurdish leaders negotiated a settlement with Saddam. The
media did not attract as much interest to the Shiites in the
south of Iraq. Yet Basra, for instance, had endured eight years
of the Iran–Iraq war, then within one month in early 1991 the
American invasion, the revolt against Saddam, and reprisals
by Saddam's troops. For some reason hardly anyone in the
West wanted to know about the Shiites – probably it was their
reputation for sectarian political terrorism and their association with the Iranian regime. The Kurds – though their
oppression had been virtually ignored by the West for years,
and they were at first spurned after the war by President Bush
– suddenly became the object of fashionable concern (with
consequences in Britain considered later in this chapter).

World Vision of Britain (the British arm of an international
agency discussed in Chapter 5) raised nearly £270,000 for
Kurdish relief, and spent it on plastic sheeting, aluminium
poles and nylon cord bought in Turkey, special light-weight
blankets bought in Britain, and oral rehydration salts to help
prevent deaths from diarrhoeal infections.

In July 1991, a UN mission went to Iraq to report on
humanitarian needs in Iraq itself, under the headings of water
and sanitation, health, food supply and energy. The report's
conclusion[29] was that the magnitude of these needs 'requires
funding which exceeds international aid and short-term
palliatives and can only be met from the country's own
resources. How this finding is to be reconciled with the
Security Council's imposition of sanctions is a determination
which is not ours to make . . .' In the event, the Security
Council decided to allow Iraq to sell oil to meet humanitarian
needs but Saddam Hussein refused to do so, and in the
autumn of 1992 the predicament of the Iraqi people remains
desperate.

British agencies were specially concerned not only by the
direct impact of the Gulf war on the people of Iraq, Kuwait
and neighbouring countries, but by the serious cost which it
imposed on the world's poor through the flight of hundreds of
thousands of guest-workers (leaving behind their savings and
possessions), loss of remittances, temporarily higher oil prices
for the six months preceding the war, and loss of aid.[30]

The Bangladesh cyclone

The third major disaster to occur in early 1991 was the cyclone in Bangladesh on 30 April.[31] The low-lying Bangladesh delta is particularly vulnerable to cyclones, as well as to tidal surges and annual floods; in 1970, a cyclone caused the deaths of half a million people. The country is one of the most densely populated in the world (some 110 million people live in an area of 55,000 square miles) and people are forced to try to make a living wherever they can, even on the intensely vulnerable offshore islands. The main rice crop is in fact dependent on 'normal' levels of flooding, and the country's main export industry, jute processing, also depends on plentiful water supplies.[32]

The 1991 cyclone is thought to have killed up to 340,000 people and left millions of people homeless. Those in the disaster zone who survived lost their crops, livestock and all their possessions. The salt water ruined the rice harvest and the seed beds for the next planting. Cholera is endemic in Bangladesh, but contamination of tubewells increases the risk of its spreading.

The Bangladesh Government is relatively experienced in providing relief for victims of natural disasters, and they have a well-developed health information service. A Western agency like Save the Children was able to supply such provisions as shovels for burying dead bodies and animal carcasses, to reduce health risks; soap and bleaching powder; and containers for collecting clean water. They also helped to install deep tubewells, and gave shelter and building materials and emergency food supplies. SCF also provided mobile medical teams to supplement government facilities. Supplying cash-in-hand to victims of such a disaster is also a practice sometimes favoured by SCF.

By contrast, dropping food supplies by helicopter (as the American Government did) is extremely expensive and of questionable use when there is no proof of a food shortage. Relief of this kind – displaying the West's superior technology – is sometimes deplored by experienced agencies as a visual stunt.

Later, SCF helped to rebuild primary schools, using a design to withstand strong winds and with a first-floor flood shelter for families. Tubewells in the schoolgrounds help ensure that clean water is available. These are more attractive to families during a cyclone than shelters three or four miles away, since they fear that if they leave their homes and land they will be taken over by someone else. SCF also funded the work of a local agency, Unnayan Shahojogy Team, which rehoused 1,000 families using local contractors and locally available materials, so helping to strengthen the community's economy.

It is the instructive policy of WHO to try to use the emergency phase, when interest from donor governments is still lively, to work on preparedness for the next cyclical disaster. Not enough was done after the last major disasters in Bangladesh, a cyclone in 1985 and a major flood in 1988, to build raised shelters, and the post-emergency phase gives an opportunity to invest for the future in precautions of this type before media fatigue sets in. This will help, but Bangladesh's problems are rooted in deep poverty and aggravated by overpopulation: they constitute a chronic and apparently permanent emergency which only comes to the attention of the media at the time of occasional cyclical peaks. Even then, the Western media in 1991 were much less interested in Bangladesh than in other disaster zones.

CRUCIAL ROLE OF THE MEDIA

The importance of the media is clear. Perceived humanitarian needs are increasing. There is no reason to assume that Africa is doomed to famine, but it is virtually certain that AIDS in Africa will be a major scourge leaving millions of orphans and a 'demographic hour-glass' with the loss of productive adults; in many other countries, too, HIV-related sickness and death will escalate. There is no decline in the incidence of civil strife, with some 13 civil wars in progress in Africa alone in 1991 (a few of them fortunately now more or less resolved), and atrocities in former Yugoslavia which have shocked even hardened observers. Fewer countries remain closed to the media than during the 1970s and 80s, so that journalists have more opportunities to cover emergencies. Enterprising reporters are becoming adept at gaining access to closed countries through contact with guerrilla forces, for instance in Afghanistan and Burma.

In countries prone to food shortages, the agencies' early warning systems are improving, so that there is no excuse for lack of preparedness. Poverty and poor public health are clearly seen to be factors which aggravate all kinds of emergency. WHO statistics show that the mortality rate for disasters in rich countries is far less than that in poor countries (48 times higher per square kilometre, 27 times higher per each disaster, 3.5 times higher per 1,000 inhabitants).[33] This brings the problem back to long-term economic and health planning.

Is the generosity of donor nations – the public purse and private charity taken together – increasing to meet these needs? Apparently not. Most of the major Western nations have endured a serious recession for the last two to three years. Many other demands for public and private spending pile up. In Britain, we are asked to dip into our pockets to support domestic institutions which were formerly the undisputed financial responsibility of the State, such as the Royal Botanic Gardens at Kew, or the universities. Countless new and genuine needs for charitable giving arise: from child psychotherapy to saving the chimpanzee. Civil unrest in the inner cities of some industrial nations alerts their politicians to the need for investment in the social fabric at home. The liberation of the Soviet Union and Eastern Europe has resulted in many urgent demands for development funding, in countries whose rulers used to make a virtue of not asking for charity.

As if this were not enough, there is competition within the humanitarian agencies themselves. Though the major NGOs that I discuss in this book on the whole behave correctly towards one another, in a spirit of friendly rivalry, and cooperate as much as possible, competition is ever present. There are also quite significant differences of emphasis and principle between agencies. For instance, whereas the mainstream Christian churches cooperate freely and reciprocally with non-denominational agencies, an evangelistic agency like World Vision, whatever its technical competence and financial success, can generate disagreement and resentment. However, if evangelistically minded donors want to support World Vision – and they do so to the extent that it has a worldwide budget of US$260 million, making it one of the largest NGOs – that is their right, and competition no doubt acts as a spur to effectiveness. Competition has certainly benefited the NGOs, for standards of management have had to improve and consequently governments such as Britain's have tended to recognize their ability to target programmes sensibly and manage them with minimum wastage. Emergency relief operations were characterized by a World Food Programme expert in 1984 as 'the last bastion of unprofessionalism',[34] and there have been a number of bad cases since then (particularly the late UN response in Somalia in 1992), but on the whole this judgment would now be out of date.

Competition has spurred the formerly reticent ICRC to be more communicative – a process which has affected UN agencies, too. WHO was formerly run by a director-general who never saw journalists, but it is now one of the most media-conscious agencies and seems intent on making its contribution to disaster relief an even more focal part of the total UN effort than, at this point, it actually is. But competition also threatens to reduce the size of everyone's cake.

The British public is generous to charities in general and relief and development in particular. All the major agencies' annual incomes rose considerably in 1991, but British Government aid to the Third World is not keeping up in real terms with inflation. The British Government's aid spending has fallen to about 0.3 per cent of Gross National Product (GNP), far short of the UN's aid target of 0.7 per cent and well behind Norway, Netherlands, Denmark, Sweden, France and Finland, where the proportion is over 0.6 per cent. Aid spending by British NGOs increased in 1990 from £150 million in the previous year to £184 million, an increase of 13 per cent after inflation. However, this figure is dwarfed by the net flow of money from developing countries to Britain, which was about £25 billion.[35] Third World aid is at best an insignificant election issue between the political parties.

The only way to reverse the downward spiral is to find new ways of using the media to generate a more informed public knowledge of disasters and emergencies, including chronic disasters. This knowledge should in turn generate both a higher degree of pressure on national politicians to support UN agencies and others such as ICRC[36] which depend on government donations, and also a higher revenue for the NGOs from individuals. (It is, incidentally, by no means unknown for substantial individual donations to go to government bodies. For instance, readers of the *Independent* in London donated £500,000 for reconstruction after the Iranian earthquake in 1990. WHO acted as intermediary between the newspaper and the Iranian government, and the money was spent on building more secure structures.)

There are two possible approaches to adopt in pursuit of this objective. One is to ride with the media's own way of doing things. The other is to try to discover how the media function, and to devise alternative routes. Both approaches must be tried. The first is the more realistic, the second the more radical.

'Compassion fatigue', 'donor fatigue' and 'appeal fatigue' are expressions frequently heard in the aid agencies. Some of them, pointing to their expansion of revenue and expenditure from year to year, deny that such fatigue exists. There is some opinion-poll evidence that the British public, especially the 18–24 age group, is increasingly supportive of constructive aid to the Third World and sceptical about government policies.[37] But the expansion of tangible revenue is only achieved by means of marketing campaigns whose persistence *Time* magazine or the *Reader's Digest* would not be ashamed of. £30 million raised from the public for British agencies to relieve famine in Africa in six months may seem a large sum, but it is a small figure both in relation to governmental budgets for, say, military spending, and in relation to the need, which is to avert the risk of an avoidable holocaust. There is increasing evidence that repeated or long-lasting emergencies do sap donors' goodwill. We are all as individuals able to think of good reasons for *not* responding to needs; and the same is true of governments. When the media, too, get the impression that a chronic disaster has become a normal way of life, it thereby ceases to be news.

Public disasters are like the private disasters affecting our individual lives. Even the gravest of sudden accidents or misfortunes are made a little less difficult to bear because of the atmosphere of high drama that surrounds them, rallying support from relatives, friends and neighbours. It is the chronic, gnawing affliction which is most difficult to manage and assuage, and which too often fails to hold friends' attention. This is true on the domestic scale, where we communicate as individuals one-to-one; it is no different on the public scale, when communication is through the mass media.

Western and non-western media

It is well recognized by this book, and indeed by the policies of the more far-sighted Western agencies, that one should not overestimate the impact which these agencies can have in solving the difficulties of Third World countries. Perhaps, it may be argued, I am falling into the same trap by laying too much emphasis on the international, largely Western-dominated, media and agencies – as if the press and television, and humanitarian agencies, did not exist in Third World countries too.

There is no need to apologize for examining these Western organizations and processes and their interactions, which have been relatively little studied although they directly or indirectly affect the lives and deaths of many millions of people. It is equally necessary, however, though largely beyond the scope of this book, that national media and agencies in Third World countries should be studied within the bounds of each particular nation-state, where they can participate actively in helping national policies to evolve progressively, or, alternatively, collude with the oppression of minorities.

In a collection of papers on the political economy of hunger, Drèze and Sen argue that, to prevent hunger in countries prone to famine,

> an active newspaper system can lead to early and effective intervention by the government. One of the

roles of the press is to make it 'too expensive' in political terms for the government to be callous and lethargic, and this can be decisive since famines are extremely easy to prevent by early intervention. Indeed, it appears that no country with a free press *and* scope for oppositional politics has ever experienced a major famine.[38]

They adduce the relative success of India as against China in preventing major acute famines since the Second World War, for some 23 to 30 million are estimated to have died in China in the famine of 1958–61; in Africa, moreover, the development of a free press to combat hunger and distress has been, to put it politely, uneven. A valuable article in the same collection, by N. Ram, a leading Indian journalist, does much to substantiate this claim, but he also argues that journalism in India is so prone to sensationalism, dilettantism and other vices that, while quite successful in preventing open starvation and famines, it is less competent to supply the sustained analysis necessary to understand and mitigate endemic deprivation.[39]

Sen's argument that a free press is the key factor in preventing famine has been criticized as over-simplified. Alex de Waal,[40] for instance, recalls that the press coverage of the 1986–9 war-induced famine in Southern Sudan was relatively low-key as opposed to what was written about the famines in Ethiopia. It was the Western relief agencies and concerned politicians who eventually, in February 1989, forced the Sudanese government to agree to a ceasefire, by means of threats to suspend the USA's regular food aid. Such threats would have provoked public outcry if the media coverage had been more intense; 'political space', argues de Waal, was created for political initiatives by the relative silence of the media.

The 'Band Aid factor' distracts attention from the need to address the political causes underlying the famines in Ethiopia. The press tends to misrepresent famines and the misrepresentation grows as the media coverage increases. Press attention to famines in Ethiopia and Sudan is essential. However, it is also essential that the coverage is politically informed. Over-hyped naively 'humanitarian' reporting can be as bad as no reporting at all.

De Waal concludes that, though government censorship in both Ethiopia and Sudan has condemned thousands of their citizens to premature death, and international bureaucracies are also partly to blame, the international media needs to accept the challenge of 'accurate and timely portrayal of famines'.

THE DISASTERS EMERGENCY COMMITTEE

Britain has an almost unique system of cooperative fund-raising between the major relief agencies with the support of the broadcasting authorities. Examining the history and functioning of this system will suggest some features – such as a preference for solving problems discreetly behind closed doors, and a commitment to regulatory authority in broadcasting – which are perhaps characteristic of the British 'Establishment' but which must be recognized as impressively effective. An analysis of the DEC will give insight into the fund-raising and operational aspects of the major British agencies as they interact with the media. We will also examine a recent episode which has probably enabled the DEC to perform better in future through learning from mistakes.

How the DEC works
In 1963 a cyclone hit Sri Lanka. The High Commissioner in London for Ceylon (as it then was) appeared on television, and said that any British citizens who would like to help should send donations for relief to War on Want. War on Want was at that time one of Britain's most innovative and farsighted agencies working in and for the Third World.[41] The broadcasting authorities had uncomfortable visions of rival agencies exerting pressures on them that they would find it painful to refuse. A solution was discovered: the Disasters Emergency Committee. Originally it was founded merely to exchange information, with the agencies still issuing appeals

separately, but it soon became an influential force in the channelling of appeals by television and radio, and arrangements were made with the clearing banks and the Post Office for special publicity and in-payment facilities. Since the first joint appeal, for the Turkish earthquake in 1966, the DEC has launched 35 appeals and raised over £96 million.

This is an institution that is in principle hard to fault, within its admittedly narrow fund-raising brief – which is not to deny that some adjustments to its way of working may from time to time be justifiable. The DEC is not a costly 'quango'[42] presided over for a large salary by some hack politician put out to grass by his party. It has no corporate constitution of its own, but is merely a committee of leading relief agencies which meet as and when necessary with a Secretary who is employed by one of them.

The DEC has seven members – British Red Cross, CAFOD, Christian Aid, Oxfam and Save the Children, recently joined by two former 'associates', ActionAid and Help the Aged. War on Want was one of the original five, but it left the DEC by mutual consent in 1978 at a point when its emerging role as a 'political' pressure-group had made the Charity Commissioners uneasy. CAFOD, whose interests had previously been represented by Christian Aid, replaced War on Want. The broadcasting authorities, according to the DEC handbook, 'accept that the charities composing the DEC are the leading British Charities concerned with the provision of aid and relief overseas. . . .'

The full members each have a vote. There are a chairman and an independent member, both distinguished public servants in retirement, appointed to advise and monitor, but with no voting rights. The function of the DEC is 'to provide British aid agencies with a channel of cooperation for emergency relief overseas after large-scale disasters'. Through this channel, the member agencies jointly launch appeals to the public from time to time. The Committee may co-opt *ad hoc* other charities capable of contributing to the relief effort. The Committee has a permanent arrangement with the BBC and the Independent Television Commission (ITC, formerly Independent Broadcasting Authority or IBA) regarding air time for television and radio appeals, and with the banks and the Post Office regarding the collection of donations. The Overseas Development Administration of the Foreign and Commonwealth Office pays 40 per cent of the costs of the secretariat, and is an observer member; as are also the Refugee Council and the Office of the UK Representative of UNHCR.

Operational staff from all these organizations meet regularly to exchange information, and the Chief Executives of the seven member agencies meet twice a year to hold a policy review. When a major disaster breaks, meetings of the agencies' operational staff take place first, but key decisions are always taken by the Chief Executives.

During the period of decision whether to launch an appeal, no member charity may issue an individual appeal through the media, and the Broadcasting Authorities withhold air time for appeals by any organization. If the decision is made to launch an appeal, a 'cut-in date' is agreed from which the period of joint action begins. Both the BBC and Independent Television broadcast their appeals during this period, normally on a weekday at peak time (with facilities for credit card payments), and there is also an appeal on BBC Radio 4. The appeal period continues until an agreed 'cut-off date'. Press advertisement appeals are also published, and arrangements are made with the banks and the Post Office for automated credits.

The following is a summary of the results of the 36 appeals launched by the DEC up to November 1992, including £13.8 million raised for 'Africa in Crisis' in 1992.

	No. of appeals	£m raised[43]
Mainly 'natural' disasters		
Earthquakes	7	3.07
Floods	4	6.89
Cyclones/hurricanes	6	8.11
African drought/famines	9	68.72
Mainly 'man-made' disasters		
Conflict/refugees	9	9.88
Total	35	96.67

The DEC's agreed 'criteria for launching appeals'[44] state that the purpose of the DEC is to 'bring to the notice of the public the extent and needs of any particular disaster and to offer a reliable channel for giving aid if it believes the disaster to be on such a scale that the public might wish to subscribe to the help of the victims.' Any decision taken by the DEC must be based on a study of the facts 'and should not be influenced unduly by the amount of publicity which has been given to it by the press'.

The criteria for considering whether to launch an appeal are as follows:

1 scale;
2 the amount of effective resources available in the country concerned;
3 the 'existence of effective co-ordinating machinery available at the national level';
4 ease of access to the site for material access and supervision, including the time factor in getting aid to remote and far distant countries;
5 the amount of inter-governmental assistance known to have been given or expected to be given;
6 the likely degree of involvement possible at each phase of the disaster (immediate relief, survival relief and rehabilitation);
7 the degree of response which can be expected from the public.

Each of the full member agencies normally took a one-fifth share, but when the two associate members joined in they took one-twelfth each and the full members one-sixth each. If an agency decides not to join in a particular appeal, it may turn its share back into the pool, or else give it to other member agencies of its choice. Agencies are allowed to pass on their take to overseas partners if they wish, in accordance with their normal practice (this is how Christian Aid and CAFOD always operate).

BBC television appeals always bring in more money for the DEC than do ITV appeals, probably because their viewers are on average more affluent and/or more inclined to support

Third World causes, but also perhaps because their appeals tend to be more carefully produced and presented. ITN usually uses its newscasters, who are well-known to viewers and easily available. The BBC now rules that its newscasters should not present appeals (though they used to do this), adhering to a sharp distinction between news, where 'pure' journalistic values should prevail, and asking their viewers for cash. For the same reason, they strongly deprecate the planning of DEC appeals by the agencies in anticipation of the screening of news stories.

How well the DEC works

At the highest levels in the BBC, there is general satisfaction with the way the DEC works, but an awareness that potentially the system puts the agencies in a strong position to exert moral pressure on them. The Chairman and Governors are conscientious in asking the awkward questions that the public will ask (Why this part of the world again? Will the money get through to the victims? What steps are being taken to avoid a recurrence of such-and-such an emergency?) Sometimes a BBC appeal will incorporate an interview with an agency official who has recently visited the disaster site and can reply to questions. Direct statements by agency workers who speak with authority and passion[45] are more effective than a bland presentation by some immaculately dressed newscaster.

The history of the DEC has not yet been properly recorded, partly because the discussions between the agencies, and between agencies and broadcasters, are confidential. But it is clear that during its seemingly unruffled 29 years, disagreements have been aired within the structure and procedures of the committee, which were expressly designed for such ventilation. It would be most improbable that all the agencies agreed with one another on every topic. Most, but not all, are committed to campaigning and public education; some are proudly 'operational', others not; some have royal patronage, others not; some are religious, others not; and so forth. There are tensions, too, *within* each agency. Individual disasters inevitably provoke emotional responses from time to time among field staff, executives or fund-raisers. The broadcasting authorities have to coordinate their duties to the DEC with much broader responsibilities. Everyone is aware that whereas an appeal for a given 'minor' disaster may be justifiable in itself, it may also cheapen the currency of a DEC appeal for a 'major' disaster – according to the criteria – which on average seems to happen perhaps every two years. The account given in this chapter of the workings of the DEC is necessarily fragmentary, based on conversations with various agency workers and the BBC, and on press reports.

Occasionally disagreements have focused on natural disasters: for instance, some agencies were initially opposed to the appeal to help Jamaica following the hurricane in September 1988, within two months of two large and successful appeals for floods in Bangladesh and also in Sudan. But 'man-made' disasters are more controversial. The DEC has always supported relief for these, and indeed three out of the first five appeals were for conflict in the Middle East in 1967, war in Vietnam in early 1968, and war in Nigeria in late 1968. In the early 1980s, the agencies thought for a time that they perceived a change in attitude on the part of the broadcasters, both the BBC and the IBA. Tensions between broadcasters and agencies flared up as a result of a particular crisis in Central America. The broadcasters expressed fears that man-made disasters with political implications could cause concern to a large section of the public, and jeopardize all appeals, not just those made by the DEC. The counter-argument was that if only non-controversial natural disasters and selected man-made disasters were chosen for appeals, the DEC's impartial concern for humanitarian needs would be destroyed. The clearing banks, too, had their reservations, but this appeal went ahead, and brought in a reasonable if not spectacular take. In 1982, crisis in Lebanon provoked similar disagreement, which was again resolved.

In November 1989, disagreement between the Committee and the broadcasters was publicized in the press. The country concerned was Ethiopia, at a time when the crops had failed because of lack of rain, but also when (as the *Financial Times* put it) 'the response to the needs of some 4 million Ethiopians may well be blunted by a sense of futility and frustration about a tragedy which owes more to the destruction wrought by man than the vagaries of nature.'[46] The civil war waged by Mengistu against the Tigréan and the Eritrean People's Liberation Fronts was devouring about 60 per cent of the country's GNP, and the government's policies, for instance in prohibiting inter-regional migration, were aggravating the effects of drought and war. 'There are those who declare', commented the *Daily Telegraph*, evoking memories of similar debates about Biafra and Cambodia, 'that much international relief work in Ethiopia simply releases resources for the prosecution of a cruel war. Mercifully for the innocent victims, and in our view rightly, this line of argument has not prevailed on this or the United States Government. In the relief of human suffering, we have never observed a differential between natural and man-made disasters, and to that principle we should hold.'[47]

A spokesman for one of the agencies complained to the press that the BBC and the IBA were dragging their heels in not consenting immediately to an appeal.[48] The *Independent* made this its lead story the following day.[49] The agencies were keen that the appeal should coincide with the extensive television news coverage, rather than losing its impact through delay. The IBA's spokesman was reported as saying that 'There has not been a lot of press coverage and we have to be convinced that the public are clamouring to send money.' Senior BBC executives were reported as uneasy about asking for funds which might be seen as assisting rebel movements, or which could not help food to reach those who needed it.

Aggrieved by the press coverage, officials of the BBC and IBA published a joint letter in the *Independent*[50] denying that they had been dragging their feet. They were, they said, concerned about problems of distribution, but what appears to have upset the BBC particularly was that the DEC member agencies, in applying for an appeal, had wished to *anticipate* television news coverage which they knew was due to be screened. This drew the BBC's attention to the awkward fact that it is hard for them to resist the collective pressure of the DEC member agencies; and understandably they insisted on maintaining their editorial control over their channels.

Though this is not made explicit in the *Independent* letter, the BBC feels it must give priority to protecting the journalistic integrity of its news services from any possible manipulation, even in the most impeccably humanitarian cause.

The appeal went ahead, breaking DEC records with £10.24 million.[51] The press did note, however, that DEC appeals do not approach the scale of mass fundraising in the style of Bob Geldof in the mid-1980s; by 1989 Geldof had decided to return to his profession as a singer and songwriter, though he did organize 'Band Aid 2', a re-recording of the original fund-raising disc with new singers that raised nearly £500,000 for DEC agencies.

These problems of adverse publicity for the DEC system need not have arisen if proper confidentiality had been observed. All that seems to have happened is that the broadcasting authorities, who are not specialists in disaster relief, were not fully up-to-date with the facts and needed to satisfy themselves as to the merits of an appeal. Journalists have a nose and taste for indecision and are able to make a 'story' of what is actually a normal process of debate and negotiation.

There have been disagreements within the agencies about the timing of appeals. Sometimes, it is argued that a disaster is creeping rather than urgent, that it is too early to assess the contributions of major donors, or that there are summer holidays and various political distractions. Indeed some of the agencies have even been accused of not playing with a 'straight bat' – a cricketing reproof which may seem tame compared with the polemics current among the Paris voluntary agencies, but is strong language in London. However, the member agencies do agree that they should work together during emergencies and not indulge in rivalry, which could put other agencies in a difficult situation *vis-à-vis* their supporters.

The 'Simple Truth'

In May 1991, an episode took place, at a time of intense emotion in the country as a result of the Gulf war, which should cause concern to those responsible for the DEC. It will be recalled that in March the Kurds and the southern Shiites in Iraq rose against Saddam Hussein, partly at the instigation of the US Government, but the Coalition negotiated a ceasefire with Saddam and gave no military support to the rebels. President Bush initially showed indifference to the plight of the rebels, but in response to media coverage of the Kurds (though the Shiites were neglected) and political pressure from Europe, a massive effort was launched under US leadership to bring them humanitarian relief.

The betrayal of the Kurds (as it seemed to many observers, as well as to the Kurds themselves) was a matter of embarrassment to the British Government which had laid stress on the morality of the war against Saddam, gaining the implicit support of leading British churchmen who had argued that the war was just or justifiable. With hindsight it would seem clear that, following the DEC rules and custom, the five member agencies ought to have proposed a joint appeal to the broadcasting authorities, covering the emergency needs of the whole region, including the southern Shiites – and possibly, indeed, all the defenceless peoples of the region without distinction of ethnicity or religion. Probably it was felt that an appeal would be premature, or that the provision of effective relief could not be guaranteed; and that the DEC had already launched an appeal for the Gulf crisis in September 1990, shortly after the invasion of Kuwait. At all events, the DEC decided not to launch an appeal.

The British Red Cross had launched a unilateral appeal for the Gulf, with the agreement of the other DEC members, on 18 January. A final total of £4 million was raised, partly for the work of the ICRC in the Gulf and partly to allow for the contingency of British casualties being repatriated. The other member agencies decided in effect that they should concentrate on their African commitments, having launched a DEC appeal for 'Crisis in Africa' on 8 January just before the war broke out. This opened the way for what happened. Jeffrey Archer – the well-known popular novelist, former MP and former deputy chairman of the Conservative Party – proposed a huge appeal for the Kurds, to be coordinated through the British Red Cross Society.

What appears to have taken the agency world by surprise is that hitherto the British Red Cross had had a reputation for being the most conservative (with a small 'c') of the major agencies. But a new director-general, Michael Whitlam, had taken over on 1 January. With a base of experience in Save the Children's UK department and the Royal National Institute for the Deaf, Whitlam is both dynamic and ambitious. He admits that the Simple Truth campaign appeal, as it came to be called, was 'media-driven' but he argues that it would have been wrong to turn down such an opportunity. It caused friction not only with the other DEC agencies but also with his partners in the League of Red Cross Societies, who had plans of their own.

Archer had a promise of £10 million from the British Government towards the appeal. Mrs Lynda Chalker, the government minister, was pressed in television interviews on the wisdom of earmarking large sums of money for the Kurds only, and at one point it was suggested that the funds could be available for other ethnic groups as well; and that the government's direct contribution to this appeal would some-how release other moneys that were lying available to be spent on other urgent causes such as the African famine. (This 'argument' was soon dropped.)

In the event, the DEC agencies agreed to associate themselves with the Simple Truth appeal, and a huge pop concert was held at Wembley stadium, with the television authorities' cooperation and in the presence of the Princess of Wales. The concert itself covered its expenses and some £3 million was raised from donations in the UK, plus an extraordinary £43 million said to have been raised from governments and individual and corporate donations from overseas. Archer was photographed for the press holding a huge placard above his head with the figures '£57,042,000', which included the British Government's £10 million.

It later emerged, in October, that large balances of the UK-raised funds were lying in the accounts of British agencies, while many thousand Kurdish refugee families were still without adequate shelter. This in itself should not provoke criticism, for it was no doubt difficult in civil war conditions to bring effective humanitarian aid to the Kurds, and it is normal for agencies to hold earmarked balances in reserve when they cannot spend them responsibly at once. Oxfam had injected £400,000 of aid into the Kurdish refugee areas, mainly on water purification, but their press officer was reported as saying that 'We cannot move a muscle without the UN getting us visas, work permits and escorts, and the harsh reality is that the Iraqi people have been fired up by Saddam to treat us all as enemy spies when we work under UN auspices.'[52]

The *Evening Standard*[53] raised the question of what had happened to the £43 million which Archer claimed had been raised or pledged from overseas. It appeared that, whereas many governments had made large grants for Kurdish relief, and some might have been encouraged to be more generous as a result of the efforts of Jeffrey Archer, it was hard to correlate sums actually received by UN agencies with this large sum. The *Standard* reporter described Archer as a 'highly likeable man of prodigious energy and talent' who was now suffering from 'personal embarrassment and deep hurt'.

In the months that followed, Archer to his credit visited the Kurds to try to follow up his efforts on their behalf and plead for their interests. But the 'Simple Truth' has not made fund-raising easier for future large-scale appeals in Britain. The BBC, which on the whole has an excellent record of standing up to government political pressure, ought to have declined to adopt a humanitarian appeal spearheaded by such a prominent party-political personality. The DEC and all its member agencies should surely have taken the same line. The tradition of the relief and development agencies in Britain is to be rigorously non-party-political, as indeed is required under charity law. This chapter has illustrated how, on previous occasions, the DEC structure has enabled differences of opinion to be debated and resolved in a frank, orderly and civilized way. The DEC was set up precisely to avoid muddles such as the Simple Truth appeal occurring.

It would, of course, be naive to pretend that humanitarian action can be kept entirely free from political considerations, but it is essential for the reputation and self-respect of the agencies that they hold the line as far as possible. On this occasion, the British Government's £10 million, presented in the way it was, bore too strong an aroma of detergent at the end of the allied military campaign which, though arguably necessary for the wider security of the Middle East, was extremely dirty in its unintended effects on defenceless civilians.

The DEC member agencies have probably learnt from this lesson, and in fairness it should be added that the aftermath of the Gulf war, which coincided with major appeals for Africa and Bangladesh, was probably the most testing time for them collectively since the DEC was formed in 1963. The episode is now tactfully referred to as a 'one-off', not intended to set a precedent.

Should the DEC in future resist any pre-emption of its normal initiative in disaster situations, especially by influential party politicians like Archer? Its future standing in such crises must depend on the quality of leadership in the member agencies, which is to a great extent a matter of personalities. But the DEC system as such is currently being reviewed by a retired senior civil servant, and some adjustments are likely.

Problem areas and the DEC's future

The principal problem areas are as follows:

1. *Quick versus creeping disasters.* The natural/man-made distinction is now generally regarded as less useful than that between quick and creeping disasters. The DEC was set up at a time when techniques for disaster prediction were less advanced than today. Famines, in particular, can be predicted with reasonable accuracy several months in advance through such techniques as tracking the price of grain or patterns of population movement. The BBC is quite willing to break its schedules at short notice (the practice with all DEC appeals at present) in order to respond to a quick disaster such as a hurricane or earthquake. They question whether it is appropriate to present such an urgent message when the agencies have been aware that a famine has been building up for six months.

In defence of the present system, the forecasting techniques are far from perfect and it may make sense to leave a disaster appeal until it is fairly certain that local efforts have been unsuccessful in staving off the emergency. In practice, it must be acknowledged that one or two of the agencies are now such sophisticated fund-raisers that they tend to use DEC appeals to top up revenue which they already have coming in from other sources.

The suggestion has been made that in order to respond to long-term creeping disasters, such as famine or HIV in Africa, there should be one or two appeal days per year, still organized through the DEC but on a somewhat different basis.

2. *The membership of the DEC.* The members of the DEC are the blue-chips of the agency world, but it is seen from outside, with some justification, as having some of the characteristics of a cartel. Much of the innovation in sponsoring relief and development comes, however, from smaller agencies which are not well-known, do not have such prestigious boards of trustees and may perhaps be more error-prone because of relative lack of management and field experience. (In the field of disaster relief, experience does count for a lot, but large organizations can become ossified.) Should the smaller agencies be allowed a say in the DEC's deliberations and a slice of the cake?

By the same token, there are other relatively large agencies such as World Vision and CARE Britain which would like to be included. So would Médecins sans Frontières, no doubt, which has recently opened a UK branch. In defence of the present system, it is argued that all the existing agencies are not only British-registered charities, all dependent for a very large proportion of their funding on private donations, but also of British origin. A more workable and less insular criterion for excluding unwanted agencies might be to impose a maximum permissible ratio for administration and fund-raising expenses as against total revenue.

INTERNATIONAL PRESSURES

The DEC is an influence for cooperation and coordination, to balance the growing competitiveness and marketing sophistication of the big agencies. The only other country with a similar system is the Irish Republic.[54] We may contrast the difficulties of the ICRC, which has a large communications department, in getting adequate coverage from the Télévision

Suisse Romande with a potential audience of not more than half a million. The DEC fund-raising model is in principle widely applicable elsewhere within national boundaries.

Yet the DEC, representing an élite of the British independent voluntary sector but backed by government endorsement and statutory powers over the airwaves, harks back to a more self-assured era when the perceived need was more measurable and manageable. The scale of need and of opportunities for prevention and relief of disaster is now so enormous that creative thinking at an international level is called for.

Of all the NGOs (outside the UN and the Red Cross systems) which operate in the relief sector, it is World Vision, the Christian agency (to be discussed in Chapter 4), which has established the most genuinely multinational network; yet this agency has been informally blackballed in Britain from membership of the Disasters Emergency Committee. Some of the objections advanced against World Vision by certain other agencies are understandable, but maybe the issues at stake are now too serious to be settle behind closed doors.

The world is changing so quickly that a root-and-branch reform of the UN, however implausible it may seem in 1993, might become a real political possibility by the end of the century. What is certain is that the media regime is becoming more global. If Bob Geldof in the 1980s could single-handedly mount an international fund-raising campaign that dwarfed the DEC's, it should not be beyond the capacity of organizations like the European Broadcasting Union to cooperate on fund-raising with the voluntary relief agencies on an international scale. If this is done, priority should be given to agencies with long grassroots experience and short lines of vertical reporting.

2   Ambivalence within the Agencies

Even a large organization can appear from outside to have a clear and homogeneous character. Modern image-building has established the task of positively building up 'corporate identity' as one of the management's principal duties. Yet any organization from the inside is, we all know, an arena for competing interests and points of view, sometimes for more or less bitter micro-political battles. Successful institutional directors are generally those who are able to understand the principal tensions within their organizations and 'internalize' them, so that they maintain the loyalty of all departments.

The most stressful tension in a Western humanitarian agency is between, on the one hand, the need to campaign and raise funds within the domestic context, and, on the other, the need to maintain an institutional ethos appropriate to the organization's 'deprived' clientele and the professional practice of the field personnel directly concerned with them. In this chapter I look at the effects of this internal tension or 'ambivalence' within the agencies, that is the co-existence within a single organization (or indeed a single office-holder) of conflicting attitudes.

CHARITIES IN A MERCHANDISING ENVIRONMENT

Charities in all fields have to balance with sensitivity the wishes and aspirations of donors against spending priorities. This balancing is the task of the governing body and the senior directors. In English charity law, the governing body are 'trustees' for the interests of the beneficiaries. In the case of humanitarian charities, these are anyone who might benefit from the charity's work – sometimes narrowed down to a defined category, which can cause problems of interpretation. (At what age, for instance, does a 'child' cease to be a child?)

In a typical large agency today, fund-raising has become a highly professional operation. A well-managed agency seeks to diversify its sources of income so as to limit its dependence on any one source. Donations from the public through the post in response to major appeals are therefore just one means of raising money: there are also shops, branches, flag-days, house-to-house collections, payroll giving, corporate membership schemes, legacies, special events such as benefit concerts, and so forth. Many British charities also receive earmarked grants from central or local government for specific projects, though their 'trade association', the National Council for Voluntary Organizations, recommends that consideration be given to the consequences of any excessive dependence on government grant-aid.

Arguably, all British charities receive an indirect government subsidy since they are entirely exempt from income tax, corporation tax and capital gains tax (though not from Value Added Tax). Agencies that decide to engage in full-fledged political lobbying have to forego the privileges of charitable status. Some charities have formed associated companies without charitable status to which politically sensitive work is hived off (a practice open to the criticism that it allows the trustees' true intentions to be fudged). Associated companies are also formed to undertake commercial activities, such as running chains of shops, for the benefit of the parent charity; these companies are allowed to covenant their profits back to the parent charity so that tax is largely avoided.

Direct mailing has been practised for many years but it is now very different from what it was 20 years ago. In the 1960s, Oxfam used to send out two mailings a year to its circulation list, one at Christmas, and it was considered impolite to ask for money in the same letter as saying thank you.[1] Nowadays the letters from such agencies are still written with the printed signature of the Director-General, complete with mock blue ink and a P.S. The letters usually go into some detail about the needs they are setting out to satisfy, arguing a close relationship between the act of sending in a cheque and the tangible benefit to a particular category of individuals.

But the whole process is now highly planned and systematized. Oxfam were the first to use commercial mailing practices in the late 1970s. At that time, they were the only charity in their field to do so and the result was a surge in income. Now, every large charity uses direct mailing and there are diminishing marginal returns. The success rate in securing donations is currently 1 per cent at the most for 'cold mailing' (i.e. to a list of names with no prior contact) and less than 1 per cent for 'inserts' included with, for instance, a magazine. Direct mailing continues as a major part of fundraising, but boom-time is over and the economics are now finely balanced. A recent survey found that 60 per cent of a British sample said that the number of postal appeals was increasing, and 40 per cent said that this annoyed them.[2] One expert told me that large-scale cold mailing is becoming a money loser. Agencies regularly swap their lists on a carefully controlled basis. But each agency's donor base is highly confidential, and so are the statistics and research data extracted from it. Some agencies refuse to swap or rent their lists.

For every major charity, its 'donor base' is its lifeblood. Mailings to recruit new donors are sharply distinguished from those to existing supporters. These are divided into committed givers who pay regularly under 'covenant' (a tax concession in the UK for regular donations to charities), and one-off cash donors who respond to specific appeals. The key problem is maintaining the donor base because a large proportion of names and addresses 'drop off' every year on account of death, moving house, changed loyalties, financial pressures or for other reasons. Hence the pressure to recruit new donors. Lists of names and addresses can be rented to access the lifestyle group the agency is targeting. Considerable research is undertaken to identify a particular agency's 'donor profile' – including average age-group, preferred newspaper, political persuasion – and sometimes an agency may try to modify this through emphasis on recruiting a particular category of donor. For instance, despite its original strong links with the universities, Oxfam lost ground in the 1960s through altruist-ically sponsoring other organizations to spread their message among students; it is now campaigning to strengthen its student support again. Though it does not have the longest list of regular donors, Oxfam is able to extract a high-value annual average covenant which other agencies would envy.

Press advertising is important in raising revenue, though perhaps less so now than in the past. All the relief agencies invest in some press advertising to maintain their public presence, and it is an effective, if expensive, way for new agencies to establish themselves. The agencies also publish posters, information packs and brochures in support of their fund-raising. Very few use open-air posters on hoardings: Christian Aid is an exception. Christian Aid is also one of the few British agencies that sometimes buys advertising time on television, which in the USA is a standard practice. They have recently switched spending from posters to television, having found that television achieves greater 'penetration'. The aim of two of their television advertisements was to support the annual Christian Aid Week and in particular house-to-house fund-raising during that week. Some of the poster companies are willing to make arrangements to provide spaces free to charities, because they always have a proportion empty, but the charity does not know where they will be.

'Skip lunch. Save a life'

Outside advertising agencies are used regularly by the larger NGOs. The relationship is sometimes a difficult one because the 'product' that is being sold is much more complicated than, say, a consumer brand: a strong personal commitment from one or more of the 'creative' staff is usually required. Advertising agencies are used particularly for the specialized task of donor recruitment rather than for keeping in touch with the existing donor base.

SCF used an outside agency in March 1991 to attract attention to Africa, when the media appeared to be locked into the Gulf war.[3] They invited four separate agencies each to spend an hour with them, explaining its suggested strategy. One of the agencies – which had been responsible not long before for a shocking picture of a pile of dead dogs to boost the

Royal Society for the Protection of Cruelty to Animals – favoured a picture to horrify, and this was ruled out. All the other three decided not to focus on the tragedy itself but on something people could do as an everyday response. The slogan chosen was 'Skip lunch. Save a life'. The tricky and topical problem of imagery (one we will explore at some length in Chapter 5) was thus bypassed. For the first time, SCF took an advertising slot on television and their advertisement, which included a shot of sizzling eggs and bacon, was successful enough to be a news item in its own right. The TV ad was used as a small component in a bigger campaign in which the Princess Royal, SCF's President, had a central role. Thanks to her intervention, pictures of Africa were on the news for every news bulletin over a 24-hour period – the first time this had ever happened – and they were in every newspaper. The campaign brought in millions of pounds earmarked for African food aid, surprising both the advertising agency and the Fund.[4]

The idea of 'skip lunch' dates back to War on Want campaigns around 1960 when university staff and students would regularly pay for a bread and cheese lunch, with the profits going to this charity. SCF's professionally inspired slogan was a refinement of the old concept, for it plays on the connotations of eating and over-eating which are deeply embedded in Western upper-middle-class culture. For the upper middle class in Europe (but even more so in America), social status is widely expressed by being slim, thus showing that you have enough food available to you not to have to parade it. It is easier for many to aspire to slimness than to achieve it. The 'Skip lunch' campaign deserved to succeed because it carries in a few words the following implicit messages:

1. We could nearly all remain healthy even if we were to eat less than we do.
2. The Princess Royal is fashionably slim, and prefers not to eat lunch anyway, therefore by skipping lunch to help SCF, one is taking a step in the desired direction.
3. SCF as an efficient and conscientious agency can justifiably

claim that the donor's sacrifice will contribute to saving lives.

But the problem is not so simple. At a Unicef meeting in 1991, Peter Adamson – former founder of the magazine *New Internationalist*, which was initially financed by Oxfam and Christian Aid, and more recently author of a Unicef report 'The State of the World's Children' – sharply criticized all charities (including Unicef) which claim that a few dollars can bring a person safe water, or prevent a death from dehydration or measles, or save a child's eyesight. 'It raises funds. But it is not true. Oh, I know, only too well, that it can be argued that it is true, or that the statements we make are not technically incorrect. But if we ask ourselves not "what we say" but "what is the received message?", then we know that much of what we say is simply not true.' Adamson argues that 'many of the advertisements put out by organizations which raise money for development *would not pass the advertising standards test which we rightly insist on applying to commercial products*.'[5] It is easier for a Unicef official to take this demanding moral line, however, because this agency depends for only 26 per cent or so of its total revenue on non-governmental funding.

An article in the American *Forbes Magazine* published in 1986[6] criticized Save the Children (USA) for publishing allegedly misleading advertisements – giving the impression that funds raised were to be used for sponsorships of individual children whereas their actual policy had been changed to community uplift. 'Is a little deception okay for a worthy cause?' said the headline. In fairness to SCF (USA), the advertisement did say in small print that they had given up individual sponsorships and were committed to using donors' money 'in the most effective way possible – by helping the entire community'. But the visual image showed two screen celebrities, Paul Newman and Joanne Woodward, with a scotch terrier and framed photos of individual children with their names – Pedro, Gustavo etc. – and the caption 'We share our love with seven wonderful children we have never seen.'

SCF (UK)'s new slogan, 'Skip lunch. Save a life', attracted

some criticism both within and outside the Fund, but arguably it is merely an elliptical expression which the public does not take literally. In any case, SCF has repeated the slogan in its 1992 campaigning, and one press photograph showed the Princess Royal holding her hands up in mock protest to dissuade 'Manuel' (the Spanish waiter in a well-known television comedy series) from serving her a steaming dish. Actually, there is no certainty that it was the advertising campaign, rather than general publicity for SCF's work, which brought in such large donations in 1991. The follow-up campaign in 1992 was less successful.

Oxfam: 'To hell with sympathy'

The leader in applying modern marketing techniques to fund-raising for overseas relief and development was Oxfam. I interviewed Harold Sumption, who has spent all his career as an advertising consultant and was Oxfam's chief publicity expert from the early 1950s when Leslie Kirkley was its innovative Director. Now retired, Sumption still advises other charities. He is a Quaker, as were some of the other early leaders of Oxfam, and his methods are underpinned by a strong sense of moral obligation. (The first chairman of the Oxford Committee for Famine Relief, founded in 1942, was Canon T. R. Milford, minister in charge of St Mary's Church, Oxford.)

Oxfam's rapid growth was originally based on the national press. It was not until about 1973 that television superseded the press as the principal medium in Britain. Thinking back to the campaigns run by Oxfam in the 1960s, one recalls how innovative they were in hitting hard and tugging at the heart-strings. Earlier advertising by Oxfam had stressed the appeal by a famous person, such as Lord Birkett the jurist, and one of its earlier broadcasts in about 1950 was by Professor Gilbert Murray, the classical scholar, in aid of relief for Greece. Oxfam gradually made more use of pictures and enlisted the support of prominent journalists and photographers. A classic example from the beginning of the 1970s is this statement by the great journalist James Cameron, quoted here in full:

Obscenity is a six letter word
This is said to be the Permissive Age, in that it is almost

impossible to shock normal people into what used to be called moral outrage. Four-letter words abound. Probably not a bad thing either.

Yet there is a six-letter word that is the real obscenity of our time and that shames us all: it is spelled *hunger*. It is the disgraceful challenge to a permissive age.

People have been saying this for long enough, to be sure. One grows impatient with regret. To hell with sympathy; indignation is something to be used. We live in a world where, quite simply, most people are poor, in the sense that they just haven't got enough to eat. There are a hundred reasons for this, political and sociological. And while we debate them, people die. It is extremely easy to die.

Some things are hard to say without sounding pretentious or smug. I have spent much of my life in places where a handful of rice meant survival. If that sounds like journalism I am sorry but it is true. If it sounds like Oxfam promotion I am equally sorry and it is equally true. The provision of that handful of rice is vital in the short run; the provision of the means to make that handful grow into a store is more important still.

Less than two hundred years ago the existence of slavery was accepted, almost without question, as something probably unpleasant but inevitable, until a man called Wilberforce made nations stare it in the eye and realize that it was needless, wrong and *capable of change*. Today there are more people fettered with hunger than there were slaves fettered with iron.

If people are fighting a war we can join in the battle. If they are making a revolution we can join them on the barricades. But if they are hungry we cannot usefully join them in hunger. We can only help them to get out.

I know it should not be left to charity. I know that a rational human society would make all that I am writing irrelevant. But we have not got there yet. I wish with all my heart that there were no need for Oxfam, but there is. I have seen it at work for years. It is, I assure you, a lot more than handouts.

I never wrote a commercial before. It asks a very simple thing: Help.

In the 1990s, Cameron's 'commercial' would probably be criticized as too pessimistic in tone. Peter Adamson has attacked 'the oasis mentality', the impression among Westerners that 'the developing world is exclusively a theatre of tragedy in which poverty and human misery figure prominently in almost every scene.'[7] If this is the case, the relief agencies led by Oxfam are now largely the victims of their own success in propagating its message. Yet there probably are more dying babies in the 1990s than twenty years ago.

Oxfam at that time deliberately abstained from crawling to prospective donors, but played instead on feelings of responsibility and conscience. At one point, Harold Sumption introduced a motivational researcher who advanced the argument that guilt was the key emotion to play on. According to Sumption, Oxfam never consciously tried to generate guilt or exploit it, though some readers of Oxfam's advertisements may have felt guilt already and Oxfam was aware that guilt was one motivating factor. A typical Oxfam advertisement of 1982 shows an emaciated old woman in a barren landscape with the caption 'What has to happen before you give to Oxfam?'[8]

No one, it seems, wants to take any credit for having introduced the theme of guilt into Oxfam's advertising policies – perhaps because those who have played on our guilt (or conscience) feel guilty themselves about having done so. However, it does seem in retrospect to have been a crucial innovation. Since the 1960s, advertising for Oxfam and similar agencies has oscillated between playing on guilt and playing on compassion. Guilt is associated with the fear that despite one's own apparent good fortune one may be struck down at any moment by a punitive Providence. Compassion is the straightforward recognition of a suffering fellow-human, breaking down barriers of culture, language, skin colour. One experienced fund-raiser tells me that he considers the appeal to guilt to be the most effective style with which to recruit *new* donors. In 1988, a leading advertising agency handled all the advertising for the United Nations Association (UNA) in

London, which was appealing for Sudanese refugees at a time when one per hundred was dying in camps every day. The account manager was quoted in the press as saying: 'We have tried to make advertisements far more positive, and to get away from the usual "starving baby" image . . . But no one dipped their hands into their pockets. The only thing that does it is guilt: you have to shock people.'[9] On similar lines, the chief executive of a major British NGO has been heard in private to comment sardonically, and only half-seriously, that it is mainly a safety-valve for the guilt of the middle classes. A north-east African activist in London has recently argued at a conference that funds raised through appealing to guilt are morally tainted, however urgent the need for relief aid may be.

But Oxfam's achievement was not merely to bring in the money. Sumption contends that the great advantage of 'direct marketing' is that it generates a relationship between individual members of the public and the advertiser. An appeal to compassion and generosity was certainly the priority of Leslie Kirkley and his colleagues, but this was closely followed by a call for commitment (Cameron: 'to hell with sympathy'). From the 1950s Oxfam sponsored campaigns to help first the European refugees, then Koreans, then Africans and other countries as the need arose. It realized from an early stage that the 'fire-brigade' or 'soup-kitchen' role was only part of the answer. The real answer must lie in helping poor people to develop their resources. Clearly it was relatively easy to generate an emotional response; the great need was to educate and inform those people warm-hearted enough to help in an emergency. In the 1960s Oxfam saw that the most tragic sufferers from disease and lack of food were children, who are among the first to die during a famine. The surest way to get an immediate response was to show the truth about those children. Oxfam's fund-raising yardstick at this time was that it must get £5 back in the near future from every £1 spent on publicity (still the rule of thumb under which it works); but the actual sum, according to Sumption, could be as much as £30.

This led to an important debate. In the late 1960s people were already saying that the style of this publicity, especially the focus on children, was simplistic and obscured larger needs. As a result, in the early 1970s Oxfam developed a policy which it called 'the educated pound' (the phrase was Leslie Kirkley's),[10] seeking to enlarge people's understanding of the problem they set out to tackle. They carried out a number of tests to see how to maintain a sensible and honest balance between short-term fund-raising and educational/developmental goals. Sometimes they went too quickly, trying to enlarge understanding in a way that was not financially viable, but in general the strategy worked well.

The method employed by Sumption and his colleagues was first to open people's hearts, because donations, like commercial decisions, are not based simply on rational analysis of a situation; and, second, to open their minds because they would then commit themselves to opening their cheque-books regularly. Oxfam was a pioneer of committed income through covenants that allow the receiving charity a tax credit for each annual payment. Sumption contends that charities have obligations to their donors as well as to beneficiaries. The Disasters Emergency Committee is thus (in his view) a splendid idea, except that when the incoming money has been parcelled out among the agencies, the donors get nothing in return. After every disaster there must be a long slog of rehabilitation and reconstruction, not to mention improving preparedness; donors to DEC appeals are not involved in understanding those needs and contributing to them. Similarly, a 30-second TV advertisement for a specific charity cannot possibly communicate anything worthwhile about its work or the needs it sets out to meet.

From Oxfam's concept of the educated pound sprang the 'development education' movement, which was encouraged by the Labour government of the late 1970s. A number of charities now specialize exclusively in this field, such as the Centre for World Development Education, while every major relief and development agency in Britain has its education department. Significantly, this is usually associated structurally in the organization with 'public affairs', hardly ever with fund-raising.

Some of these departments, like SCF's, have remained fairly low-key, publishing teaching packs on such topics as poverty and debt as well as regular newsletters for supporters.

In recent years, CAFOD has spent about 5 per cent of its budget on development education, Christian Aid about 10 per cent. These and other agencies developed their educational policies against the background of lively educational debates in the 1980s.

ISSUES IN DEVELOPMENT EDUCATION

The right-wing Conservatives who achieved ascendancy in the 1980s tended to see the proper role of charity as ministering to those unlucky enough to be left out of the 'trickle-down' benefits of a surging market economy. Hence they regarded most development education as covert left-wing political propaganda. The way the agencies saw it, however, they were merely drawing out the logical conclusion of their practical experience, which was that making cash donations alone was a wholly inadequate response to disasters and underdevelopment.

On some points, such as the need to draw attention to the underestimation of women's roles in virtually all human societies, or the need to challenge stereotypical thinking about other groups, there was general agreement in educational circles. But much energy was spent in debate between the 'multi-culturalists' and the 'anti-racists' – an argument over domestic issues which spilt over into consideration of the Third World.[11]

Some agencies came close to breaking, and were occasionally rebuked for allegedly breaking, the Charity Commissioners' rules about how far a charity may go in 'political' campaigning.[12] In Britain, charities may not engage in party politics, or in large-scale lobbying to put pressure on the British or any other government; however, they are allowed – as a function ancillary to their main objectives – to take advantage of their special experience to bring issues to the attention of the public. SCF has always kept well within these limits, but Oxfam has at times been pilloried by the Right for alleged leftist bias. From 1985 to 1991 its Director, Frank Judd, was generally deemed to have left-of-centre sympathies, being a former Labour minister, and in 1991 he resigned from

Oxfam to take up a seat on the Labour benches of the House of Lords. However, the Charity Commissioners have never gone further than mildly rebuke Oxfam, and its loyal public never seems to have lost confidence in it. Indeed there is anecdotal evidence that organizations like Oxfam and Save the Children are respected and admired as much as any other institutions in the country.

Oxfam still aims at a rather less broad spectrum of opinion than SCF. Its current campaign for 'A Fairer World' is carefully reasoned and in no way strident, but SCF would not allow a politically aggressive term like 'structural violence' – the notion that inequitable distribution of power and resources is itself responsible for civil strife – to creep into any of its briefings.[13] An Oxfam slogan like 'solidarity with the poor' would never have fitted in with the more pragmatic, less politically engaged culture of SCF. The differences are now largely a matter of style: Oxfam's call for a 'Marshall plan' for Africa – including debt reduction, increased aid, modification of economic adjustment programmes,[14] and better terms of trade – would be broadly supported by all the major aid agencies.

Christian Aid, like Oxfam, has come up against the limit of the charity laws, for instance in recent campaigning to draw attention to the Third World's debt, but has perhaps been rather more careful in scrutinizing its promotional material before it is released. Christian Aid is strongly committed to its education and campaigning work, which it has always approached with boldness and innovation, while recognizing the need to do it carefully.

For instance, in May 1988 it published *Mozambique: Caught in the Trap* by Derrick Knight. Christian Aid had been working with the Christian Council of Mozambique since 1977, assisting them with training, health and agricultural programmes. A decade later, the civil war – specifically, attacks from Mozambique National Resistance (MNR) – had resulted in the suspension of most of these programmes. MNR was supported and supplied by South Africa. Christian Aid shifted its support towards supplying relief and rehabilitation assistance – food, seeds, blankets – but even that was subject to attack. The agency saw six million people suffering gravely as a result of the war, and another million forced to take refuge in other countries because of MNR attacks on their homes. Christian Aid was urged by its partners in Mozambique, Zimbabwe, Malawi, Zambia, Swaziland and South Africa not only to provide aid, but also to do what they could to make people in the UK understand the degree and nature of the suffering taking place, and the factors which caused the war to continue. It came to the conclusion that if MNR operations were to cease, a great deal of horrific cruelty and suffering would be prevented and the prospects of Mozambique's people greatly improved. Hence the book it published was not a political tract so much as an exercise in educational campaigning, securely grounded in the charity's direct experience of Mozambique.

In 1988, Christian Aid printed a card headed 'Stop the Killing' for circulation to their supporters; the idea was that they would tear off one portion of the card, sign it and send it to the South African Embassy in London. The returnable portion of the card originally read:

SOUTH AFRICA
Please stop supporting the MNR in Mozambique.
Give the people a chance to live in peace

and the explanatory text included the words:

. . . The Christian Council of Mozambique, seeing the terrible effect of these attacks on their country, has called upon the British People to help in whatever ways are possible to eliminate those forces working for the destabilization of Mozambique.

After discussions with the Charity Commissioners, a new card was published in which the returnable portion said:

FROM A SUPPORTER OF CHRISTIAN AID
SOUTH AFRICA
Please use your influence to end support for the MNR in Mozambique. . . .'

In the explanatory text, 'Christian Aid supporters in Britain' was substituted for 'the British People'.

Similar specific campaigns emerged from Christian Aid's work in South Africa and Cambodia. Christian Aid's present director, Michael Taylor, considers its more general campaigning for fundamental political change to be at least as important as anything else that it does. He argues strongly against any suggestion that the operational agencies have a better way of working: 'indeed, we believe that fostering and supporting indigenous organizations is the more respectful and appropriate approach.'[15]

Christian Aid and Oxfam have both been attacked from the right. Neither agency has identified itself with the kind of thinking which blames all the world's ills on Europe and North America, though such thinking is widespread in many Third World countries and has keen sympathizers everywhere.[16]

One of the earliest critiques of Oxfam from a conservative source (in this case, a high-minded disciple of the literary critic, F. R. Leavis) was written in 1973 by Ian Robinson.[17] From this point of view, 'to help relieve famine can at least be to remind oneself that there are human needs, that life is precarious, and that we should bear one another's burdens.' Robinson's text notes that Oxfam is coming to attach importance to the education of British children in the needs of and problems of the developing nations. He satirizes an English teacher who has recently published 'a disease-poem for menacing voices' which goes:

'Kwashiorkor ... Kwashiorkor ... Kwashiorkor ...
    Kwashiorkor
Marasmas
Marasmas ... Marasmas ... Marasmas ...
Pellagra ... Pellagra
Pellagra ... Pellagra ...
Beri-beri   Beri-beri   Beri-beri
[etc.]'

According to Robinson, 'The further you get from the simple feeling that people ought not to starve, now, in this or that particular place, the further Oxfam drifts from what it can be sure of. That is why it is inherently difficult for Oxfam to maintain its goodness as a permanent institution: between famines it has some of the difficulties of a standing army during a long peace, and when there *is* a famine the appeal to charity rightly comes with fresh force.' Such a complaint seems dated now because it avoids any consideration of prevention and preparedness, as opposed to relief, and it assumes naïvely that famines either exist or do not exist, whereas it is also possible for a famine to exist but not to be publicized through the media. In the 1990s it seems that far from there being any prospect of a 'long peace', with no disasters and the relief agencies trying to justify their existence, the extent of grave human needs is overwhelming. A commitment to development education is now shared, in varying degrees, by nearly all the major relief and development agencies.

Development education today

Within an often highly confusing context of debate – about poverty, cultures and races, neo-colonialism, inequality – the agencies have had to formulate educational policies. In so far as their packs for teachers are either purely factual or scrupulously non-partisan – stating both sides of every argument – they run into little difficulty.

To take a typical example, Oxfam's teaching pack for 11–13-year-olds, *Disasters in the Classroom: Teaching about Disasters in the Third World*,[18] would probably be regarded as left-wing propaganda by right-wing Conservatives, but there is nothing in it which a member of the Liberal Democrats or a 'wet' Conservative could not accept, and the emphasis is on dialogue within the classroom. For instance, in an exercise called 'Making the news', a news clipping from the liberal *Observer* and one from the right-wing populist *News of the World* covering the same 'story' are contrasted. The *Observer* reporter is criticizing the British government for appearing to be meaner than the other Western nations in its contributions to an aid fund to prevent African famine and economic collapse; the right-wing populist *News of the World* portrays Margaret

Thatcher (then Prime Minister) as 'moved almost to tears by the plight of starving Ethiopians' and personally exerting 'massive pressure' on EC partners to match Britain's generosity.

In another exercise, 'Brainstorm', the teacher is asked to set small groups of students to write down words or phrases which express their view of, or reaction to, the disaster being studied. Initially all ideas are accepted without comment, and a discussion follows. The teacher is told not to devalue any students because of the ideas they hold, yet equally to challenge those that devalue or stereotype other people – for instance, the assumption that black people are poor or helpless, which might be transferred to black people in the school or the local area. Since the students' images often derive from the media, the images can be criticized without criticism of the students who pass them on.

An agency such as Christian Aid is able to draw on biblical encouragement of commitment to poor people, but this can be interpreted to fit various different concepts of charity – for instance, the old-fashioned 'soup-kitchen' approach which is now discredited except for acute cases of deprivation. Christian Aid takes its faith seriously, allowing it to sustain and inform all their work. But, in practice, religious teaching does not exist in a vacuum and is constantly reinterpreted in accordance with current secular educational principles. The secular agencies would find little, if anything, to disagree with in Christian Aid's 1992 campaign to help 'strengthen the hand of the poor, often against overwhelming odds, for a decent and dignified life'.

The non-denominational agencies base their educational material on fundamental principles of human rights. SCF's founder Eglantyne Jebb was instrumental in drawing up the 'Rights of the Child' in 1922, a document which anticipated the 1990 UN Convention on the Rights of Child, sponsored by Unicef. Contentious issues such as family planning are addressed with subtlety and a degree of circumspection, with the varying opinions of its supporters in mind. For instance, SCF's 'Famine Myths: setting the record straight', an informative 'briefing paper' primarily intended for adults,[19] challenges as a 'myth' the proposition that overpopulation is the root cause of famine in Africa (since India and China, with far higher population densities, have had more success in overcoming acute famines) while conceding that 'population does become a critical issue when there is a mis-match between the rate of population growth and the development of complementary resources such as irrigation, transport, and health services.' SCF considers it both simplistic and impracticable to propose family planning as a strategy to relieve the strains faced by developing countries, but supports family planning as an essential component of Maternal and Child Health programmes.[20]

This coincides more or less with Christian Aid's policy statement on family planning. Christian Aid, like SCF, opposes coercive population programmes of any kind but goes further than SCF in deploring the 'racist stereotypes behind some calls in the North for control of southern population growth'.[21] This reflects standard teaching of the main non-Catholic churches on contraception. CAFOD, by contrast, supports the Roman Catholic teaching that mechanical contraception is wrong. CAFOD's policies on underdevelopment come close to those of many Third World governments which regard with suspicion the insistence of the West that they should control their population growth, arguing that the priority should be to reduce the West's excessive consumption. The general trend is for aid agencies to address the population issue more squarely than in the recent past, but 'in a new framework – by stressing its links with environmental issues and poverty'.[22]

In 1980, some 60 NGOs, including all the big relief and development agencies, formed the Fourth Channel Development Education Group, renamed the International Broadcasting Trust (IBT) in 1982. The IBT lobbies the broadcasting authorities to maintain and enhance their coverage of development issue, and produces its own television programmes accompanied by substantial educational back-up. Up to now, Christian Aid and Oxfam have supplied its core funding.[23]

The difficulty with educational material of this kind is that it tends to reflect the current liberal consensus in the agencies, and to be subject to intellectual fashion. What is known as PC

– 'political correctness' – can sometimes sway decisions. Even SCF's books on Africa,[24] published a few years ago to present a positive, upbeat image of the continent, hardly touched on the problems of corrupt governments, self-serving elites and unscrupulous arms dealers. On the whole, instead of speaking out publicly against governments, SCF has sought accommodation with their more acceptable elements. Some of its trustees argue that the more repressive a government, the more children under its dominion are in need of SCF's care and services.

With regard to Africa, in the 1990s it is certain that increasing pressures will be exerted from both within and outside the continent for more rigorous observance of human rights, and that aid from Western governments will increasingly be conditional on movement towards democratic institutions, on the pattern of Eastern Europe and the ex-Soviet Union. The NGOs may well follow this trend to some extent; and some of them will also, probably, become more accustomed to providing humanitarian services in areas where governmental authority is disputed or defunct, as in southern Sudan today. Their education departments will lay more emphasis than before on the natural environment, and on the restrictions which the First World places on free trade and labour migration – restrictions whose gradual removal would greatly ease problems of world hunger.[25] But sharp criticism of Third World governments will probably be seen by the agencies as beyond their brief and potentially damaging to race relations at home – as well as to their charitable status. Significantly, a recent popular television programme about poverty in Africa, broadcast on Good Friday 1992 by the BBC in association with Comic Relief, did include bad government as *one* of the heavy burdens that bear down on poor people in Africa.

Scholars who study economic growth in comparative perspective are by no means unanimous about solutions to underdevelopment. Economic growth and inequality often march together – for instance, in Taiwan and South Korea, and in the earlier industrial history of Western Europe – so a reduction in inequality though fairer distribution of benefits is unlikely to guarantee economic growth. Even if relative equality is accepted as a political priority, it is not proved that democracy necessarily promotes equality. One analyst[26] argues that authoritarian regimes are more likely to pursue egalitarian development policies than are democratic regimes, and can do a better job of protecting the interests of the poorest. In this view, the poorest cannot take advantage of the available electoral rights and gain political influence. An example to support this point of view would be India. If, on the other hand, democracy is chosen as the priority, we must consider the argument, advanced by another scholar,[27] that democratic governments cannot tolerate the degree of restraint in consumption necessary for maximizing the rate of growth in a developing country, whereas an authoritarian government can foster the accumulation of capital to finance industrialization by squeezing surplus from the working class.

None of these viewpoints may be correct, but all are tenable, and all conflict with the comfortable view that observance of human rights, democracy, egalitarianism and economic growth can proceed hand in hand as the rest of the world gradually models itself on Western liberalism. Indeed, some Third World intellectuals dismiss Western liberalism and philanthropy as a cover for a neo-colonial domination likely to culminate in military intervention.

It is also true that technological advances – even when planned with due consideration of their social and environmental impact – can bring disadvantages in their train. For instance, low-lying land in overcrowded Bangladesh may be rendered more resistant to floods by storm defences and shelters, but this may also encourage more people to take the risk of living in marginally safe areas.

'Development education' as undertaken by the NGOs has most integrity when it is closely tied to their practical work, emerging as a result of their own institutional experience. This is in fact strictly in keeping with British charity law. The NGOs can get out of their depth when they make it seem, as some of them have in the past, that there are easy solutions to underdevelopment. Educational texts of this kind can 'date' very quickly when the jargon of a particular developmental theory passes out of favour. And the public is able to discern that only a few humanitarians who are willing to *live* with poor people, like Mother Teresa, actually have the right to claim 'solidarity with the poor'.

FIELD OPERATIONS

The field staff of the major agencies tend to be more practical than the educationists, for obvious reasons, and with the authority of harsh experience they are now and then sceptical about high-sounding statements by Head Office. It is a universal problem of large organizations that workers in the field – relief officers, soldiers or computer salesmen – feel misunderstood by the Head Office desk people. But the major agencies are successful in attracting field staff of high calibre and qualifications, and such people cannot be expected to be content in a 'fire brigade' role. This is probably one reason why most of the major British NGOs, except the British Red Cross, give precedence to long-term development (or disaster prevention and preparedness) over short-term relief. In 1989–90, SCF devoted two thirds of its overseas budget to long-term development projects. However, these were all hard-headed projects with demonstrable pay-offs: primary health care, terracing schemes to prevent soil erosion, water conservation, tree planting, livestock feeding when fodder is scarce, and the supply of seeds and tools.

Much attention is given at present to the potential of a given project for 'replication'. An agency increases its influence by providing models of excellent practice. Agencies have emphasized 'scaling up' (that is, increasing their impact) in reaction to growing pressure from Western governments who use NGOs as large-scale service providers. An international workshop on this subject was organized by SCF with Manchester University in January 1992. There is now increasing awareness that 'NGO impact' can be increased by pursuing policies other than service provision; this indeed is the settled policy of Christian Aid, CAFOD and to some extent Oxfam.

For instance, in the mid-1980s SCF (UK) funded the Villa El Salvador Health Project, designed to reduce mortality, morbidity and malnutrition among newborns in a squatter settlement near Lima, Peru, which is short of water and vulnerable to cholera epidemics. In 1986 the project was handed over to a Peruvian NGO. The intention is that the Peruvian agency should be able to develop policy proposals to pass on to government, and should also build up a strong relationship with the local people to enhance 'community capacity' in a democratic and participatory way. According to a British researcher who has studied the project, it is not yet established that this Peruvian scheme has actually succeeded in involving the poorest strata of the district in participatory decision-making, but evidence is growing that the general strategy is sound since in principle it offers a way for NGOs to influence government policy reforms on the basis of community support.[28]

While some of the small operational agencies may justly be criticized for naïveté (see Timothy Morris's *The Despairing Developer: Diary of an Aid Worker in the Middle East*,[29] about a health project in South Yemen) a well-managed agency encourages a culture of self-criticism, humility and 'institutional learning'.

Obviously, mistakes are not always avoided. One Oxfam veteran, Guy Stringer, told me that he 'never gave a talk without including a failure. It is a vital part of the "educated pound" idea.' But it is still unusual for agencies to give external publicity to their mistakes when they are dependent on private fund-raising.

Serious mistakes have certainly occurred in recent years, even in the best-run NGOs, but they are greatly outnumbered by unsung successes. The danger to the larger NGOs, perhaps, is that when any organization grows beyond a certain size it becomes difficult to accommodate the charismatic leaders who are able to make smaller organizations flourish.[30] Any large corporation risks being run more for management's benefit than for anyone else's.

FUND-RAISING VERSUS OPERATIONS

If there is likely to be tension in an NGO between the field departments and development education (usually a comparatively small department), this is of little account compared to the potential strain between both of these and the fund-raising department.

Agencies which depend mainly on loyal individual donors stand the strain best: Oxfam with its strong base among the liberal *Guardian-* or *Independent* -reading intelligentsia, Save the Children with its extensive branch network, and Christian Aid or CAFOD with their church collections. Shops and trading operations create little ideological difficulty as they are relatively straightforward commercial enterprises under the direct control of the charity. It is true that ethical problems can arise from time to time, for instance when there is a call to boycott a particular company such as Nestlé some of whose policies (in this case, on marketing powdered milk in the Third World) are under public criticism. Appeals to the public, either for the charity's general purposes or for specific projects, can generate considerable tension. All donors, large and small, tend to be governed by emotion as much as by reason.

As we have seen, a great deal of market research, much of it confidential, has been done on who donors actually are. But for purposes of analysis we may imagine the ideal private donor as an abstract utopian type. He or she, having stated general guidelines for the selection of charitable objects, would set up a committee of disinterested, qualified people, assisted by a secretariat, to invite and process applications for funds and make decisions on the basis of pure merit, helped by the advice of independent referees. Only thus can the element of personal bias be reduced to a minimum. There are in fact a number of foundations that operate in just this way, and it is the norm in the academic world. However, except for specialized activities such as academic research, a trust fund has to be rather large to make it worthwhile for a secretariat to be set up in this way. Even when a foundation is large, the trustees may frequently prefer to run it in a more personal and consequently biased way.

The reality is that donors, whether large or small, are mostly not impartial but emotional and idiosyncratic. We should not complain about this, for it is one of the advantages of living in a free and plural society. But fund-raisers have to woo donors, play on their feelings as well as their thoughts, channel their concern into a particular commitment and loyalty to a particular 'label'.

Meanwhile, the spending departments of the major agencies have become bureaucracies. There is almost no room left for volunteer helpers (though these are still the mainstay of much fund-raising). These departments are assisted by advisory committees whose members include development specialists, medical doctors, engineers, social scientists, parliamentarians and other experts, to provide an outside view and keep the departments in touch with trends in other organizations and the country at large.

Misunderstandings are likely to arise between spenders and fund-raisers, which it is one of the jobs of the chief executive and governing body to clarify and resolve by negotiation and leadership. Children's charities are an obvious example. Children are obviously a marketing expert's dream and they tend to be played for all they they are worth. The special importance attached to the protection of children can be justified morally on intellectual grounds: children are thrown into a world for whose evils they have no responsibility, and they represent the hope of a better future. A name like 'Save the Children' carries resonances of the tradition which dictates that, when a ship is abandoned, the first available space on lifeboats is reserved for women and children. However, a moment's thought about the needs of any society in acute crisis suggests that it would be misguided to set out to save a generation of children with no one to care for them and no viable source of economic sustenance.[31] WHO guidelines explicitly say that in case of food need after a disaster, it is wrong to think of priority being necessarily given to young people.[32] If priority *has* to be given, they argue, it ought to be to those who are taking part in rescue work and urgent reconstruction of the economic fabric.

Fieldworkers are, of course, motivated by the compassion which the plight of a particularly helpless human being can elicit. From a professional point of view, however, their job is to help restore health and self-reliance not only to individuals, but also to a social system which has undergone a profound shock. A children's charity like SCF, while sticking resolutely and correctly to its legal objects, concentrates on helping children *in the community*, and finds much common ground with Oxfam in its actual response in the field to an acute emergency – as with the joint trucking operation in Ethiopia. Yet a new donor who has not studied Save the Children's literature carefully might imagine from its name that it was still engaged in programmes of evacuating children from war and disaster zones – a remedy which today is hardly ever practised by the major children's agencies.

Pressures of fund-raising

The pressures of modern fund-raising can distort an agency's identity in another way. Raising money for charity is deeply embedded in the middle-class and upper-class leisure activity of Britain.

It would seem that, though lower-middle-class and working-class people do give to charity, and often give generously, the charities they support are mainly domestic ones. The pattern has been changed radically by the advent of telethons and televised pop/rock concerts, but these are a highly specialized form of fund-raising which does not affect people's ordinary day-to-day giving.

The coffee morning, bring-and-buy sale, or sponsored swim are a staple source of revenue for some of the big overseas charities, and they often have an extensive country-wide branch network. But they also have to target high-income donors and this is often done – in Britain and Italy, but especially in the USA – through glamorous 'black-tie' events – auctions, balls, concerts or opera performances, organized by means of committees of volunteers. When a prominent classical pianist forgoes her fee and the ticket proceeds go to Unicef, what could be more straightforward and natural? However, now that fund-raising has become a sector of the marketing industry, arrangements for a typical gala concert may include a lavish and glamorous dinner sponsored by a commercial company from its public relations budget (not its charitable donations budget). Cultural institutions such as art galleries and opera companies could not survive without this kind of 'special event', and it is quite usual for the proceeds to be halved between an artistic cause and a humanitarian charity so as to maximize the event's attractiveness to a wide public. The fund-raiser's dream is for all the costs of the special event to be met by commercial sponsorship, so that all the ticket proceeds go to the charity without deduction. The ticket prices are often set extremely high, though recently the recession has caused this whole sector of fund-raising to contract.

Some overseas charities such as Oxfam are strong enough to be able to do without events of this kind, which is as well for their left-of-centre image. The nearest which Christian Aid gets to such fund-raising is the film première. Many other charities, however, are happy to use whatever fund-raising clout they can, such is the pressure on their budgets. What is wrong with combining conviviality with charitable giving, as is the custom in many affluent countries? In a nation like Britain, where the Conservative government has cut the rate of personal income tax in order to stimulate the economy, there are still, despite the economic problems, many affluent people to be wooed and correspondingly less available money in the national exchequer for meeting human needs.

The only point against such galas is that they pander to conspicuous consumption. Ritual events of this kind, like the well-publicized munificence with which a millionaire makes a huge gift to 'save' a painting for the nation, belong to what one anthropologist has called the luxury or prestige modality of social action.[33] The potential contradictions of the 'charity ball' were satirized by Byron, in a short poem of that name, some 170 years ago.

It seems likely that the industrial countries are now entering a period of austerity – which they would have been more prudent to embrace rather earlier, around 1980. Some of the major voluntary agencies feel they should be leading public opinion towards accepting such austerity and making a virtue – or an aesthetic – of necessity, and some of them are. Buckminster Fuller summed up this new ethic/aesthetic many years ago with his apophthegm 'More with less'. Encouraging conspicuous *under*consumption emits a signal that the agency is doing what it can to promote a 'fairer world' (a current Oxfam campaign slogan).

Oxfam has a large and profitable recycling depot in

Huddersfield. Christian Aid, alone among the UK relief and development agencies, co-sponsored the Tree of Life initiative in 1991, calling on its supporters to pledge to plant trees, recycle glass and paper, and so forth. Oxfam America has found a way to combine glitzy fund-raising with recognition of the process's inherent problems. In November 1991 they invited a number of celebrities in Los Angeles to a 'hunger banquet' in Sony Studios, designed to dramatize imbalance in world food distribution. 'Banquet participants drew numbers to see if they were among 15 per cent who dined on a gourmet meal, 25 per cent who shared a simple meal, or 60 per cent who sat on the floor vying for rice and water.' This was reported in *USA Today* (22 November) under the headline, 'Behind the scenes with the famous and the fascinating: Some celebs have a taste of hunger'. The hunger banquet would appear to be a reprise of the 'rich man/poor man' lunches put on by a number of British agencies in the 1960s and 1970s, when tickets were drawn from a hat, resulting in four courses with wine for a few, rice and water for the majority.

'Special events' give a charity a high profile with the more affluent public, but for a large charity they raise only a tiny proportion of total income. In recent years, attempts have been made to secure more substantial support for the charities from commercial companies, which can set off charitable donations against tax, or run sponsorship campaigns out of their publicity budgets. This part of the charity system functions extensively through networks of patronage. However, a supermarket chain or a credit card company can make tangible commercial profits for its shareholders out of a deal whereby a small percentage of certain purchases is remitted to a charity – because public support for the charity can actually boost overall revenue.

Corporate sponsorship is also an important way of diversifying an agency's sources of support. Charities must avoid the support of companies that might compromise their reputation, for instance those in ethically dubious industries. As the recession bites, many major companies in Britain are reporting heavy drops in profitability and cutting back on charitable sponsorship. The tobacco industry is still ready to offer sponsorship but no reputable agency in the humanitarian or medical field would accept it. Cash donations, however, are normally accepted from any legal source provided that there are no 'strings' attached.

The response of the British public to 1991's spate of emergencies has given the agencies cause for confidence in the future, and revenue growth during a deep recession disproves any simple theory of 'compassion fatigue'. However, this is not the case in all other industrial countries. In the Toronto *Globe and Mail* (15 November 1991), an article by Sheldon Gordon, a relentlessly tough-minded financial journalist, is headed 'Give us a break from giving'. In Canada, citizens are becoming less generous to their 63,000 registered charities (donations as a proportion of pre-tax income declined to 0.81 per cent in 1987 from 1.06 per cent in 1969, compared to a rising trend of 2.5 per cent in the USA). Gordon complains that three quarters of his daily mail is made up of solicitations, and that the charities which he donates to have passed his name to the computerized mailing systems of other ones. He questions the ethics of this practice. Telephone selling has become the norm in Canada (it has only recently reached the charity field in Britain), with salesmen taking large proportions of each donation realized. The author concludes his article:

Not only does charity begin at home: these days it barely waits for me to enter the door first. As I arrived at my house recently with a draft of this article, footsteps quickened behind me. It was a canvasser for the Arthritis Society in hot pursuit. 'If everyone gave $5 . . .' she began. I thought of a recent conversation I'd had with an official at the Canadian Centre for Philanthropy, which advises people to plan their donations systematically rather than giving spontaneously, 'then you won't feel guilt about turning down the others'. Oh yeah?

In Britain too, donations to charities as a percentage of gross income appear to be on a declining trend as a result of the recession, and the value of larger individual donations is dropping.[34]

Fund-raising post-Band Aid

Bob Geldof did not invent the charity telethon,[35] but he did manage to change the fund-raising scene in Britain decisively – almost single-handedly, it seemed at the time. Geldof conceived of Band Aid as a direct result of British television coverage of the Ethiopian famine in 1984. Paul Harrison and Robin Palmer have shown in their book *News out of Africa*[36] how arbitrary and fortuitous were the processes whereby earlier, in 1973, Jonathan Dimbleby had filmed *The Unknown Famine* in Ethiopia for Thames Television. For equally arbitrary reasons again, in October 1984, a Visnews film, shot by Mohamed Amin and narrated by Michael Buerk, was shown first on BBC Television news and then around the world.

According to legend, it was this Amin/Buerk footage filmed in Korem and Makalle in northern Ethiopia, and screened internationally on 23 October 1984, which broke the story of the Ethiopian famine to the West. In fact, a number of films had been made over the previous months, notably Charles Stewart's *Seeds of Despair* for Central Television, screened on 17 July, and there had been extensive press and radio coverage. The major agencies were desperate to get the crisis more widely recognized. The position was rather similar to that relating to the southern African drought in summer 1992, when alarming projections of death from starvation were being published but the world's attention was distracted by the civil war in former Yugoslavia.

The Amin/Buerk footage was nearly not shown at all. But it did turn out to be 'one of those exceptionally rare moments in television history'.[37] It was followed up two days later by a political documentary made by Peter Gill for Thames Television, *Bitter Harvest*, its screening delayed by a union dispute in London.[38] Amin's intensely moving portrayal of the feeding centres in the Visnews film, and Buerk's underlining of its biblical associations, are what everyone now remembers: 'Dawn, and as the sun breaks through the piercing chill of the night on the plain outside Korem, it lights up a biblical famine, now, in the twentieth century. This place, say workers here, is the closest thing to hell on earth.' It is easy to understand how the words and images opened pockets and generated political pressure for relief.

Bob Geldof was at the time known only as a young Irish rock singer, leader of the Boomtown Rats, and former music journalist. With remarkable speed, he galvanized the pop and rock industry, raising huge sums of money from a new audience of young people, and commanding the attention of the media. A record of the song, 'Do They Know It's Christmas?' was brought out and became number one in the charts. Six million copies were sold at £1.30, almost all the proceeds going to Band Aid, so that about US$8 million was raised. In July, Live Aid, the 'global jukebox', took place simultaneously in Wembley, London, in front of 70,000 people and in Philadelphia in front of 80,000, and was seen on television via satellite by 1.5 billion people, raising over $80 million. Sport Aid '86 – 'Run the World' – contributed about $30 million. Initially, Geldof believed that the relief agencies were fuddy-duddy bodies that spent too much on administration and were too competitive with one another, and he tried to bypass them. However he soon recognized that it would be wiser to benefit from their experience. He and his trustees set up a highly qualified advisory panel to advise the director, Penny Jenden, an anthropologist, on which agencies or individuals in Africa to support with grants. The grand total raised was $144 million, of which $71 million was spent on short-term relief (mainly to Ethiopia and Sudan) and $70 million on long-term development and rehabilitation, only $2.5 million (taken from bank interest) being spent on administration and travel and field costs. Geldof eventually wound up Band Aid and retired from the scene, having gained an Honorary Knighthood in 1986. In his parting statement he wrote:

> Seven years ago I said I did not want to create an institution, but I did not want the *idea* of Band Aid to die. I did not want the potential of it to cease. There are a few dozen aid agencies, and they do great work, but that was not our function. Our idea was to open up the avenues of possibility. The possibilities of ending hunger in Africa are there. There can be other Band Aids, there *must* be

others, in new times, in different ways. I said once that we would be more powerful in memory than in reality. Now we are that memory.[39]

Geldof's bluntness, directness and charm enabled him over a short period to change the face of fund-raising, drawing on networks of people who had never before played a major part in charitable giving, and brilliantly exploiting the possibilities of the media on a global scale. He never pretended to be politically or diplomatically sophisticated, nor to make a lifelong commitment to Third World causes.

The television audience for the 1992 Wembley concert, in memory of Freddy Mercury ('Queen') and in support of AIDS charities, was estimated to be in the billion range. Britain is a centre of competence in organizing such events, partly because of the example of Geldof but also because of its favourable time zone for worldwide coverage (a late-night concert in London can be screened live in North America during the day-time, but not vice versa), technological sophistication, and prominence in the pop and rock music industry (partly associated with the dominance of the English language).

Charity Projects / Comic Relief

Another organization, Charity Projects/Comic Relief, founded in 1985, has greatly stimulated the relief and development scene in Britain over the last six years or so. The basic concept predates Band Aid, though aid to Africa came in later. Of the original co-founders, Jane Tewson is still the director and Richard Curtis is a trustee. They wanted to generate new money for the voluntary sector with all their administrative costs covered by commercial firms through either sponsorship or goods and services provided in kind. For example, different advertising agencies take it in turns to frank their mail every day, and all their office space and furniture are donated. Their aim is to campaign for social change in both the UK[40] and Africa and to share their knowledge. They are not operational themselves, holding that there are enough operational agencies already and preferring to act as the 'charity's charity', a generic fund-raiser for the sector, allocating their funds after careful research. To date about £65 million has been raised over six years.

Comic Relief is best known for its Red Nose Day every two years, now well established, which mobilizes the support of Britain's best-known comedians to dedicate one day in the year to raising funds for the charity (the comedians originally came to Charity Projects because they were impressed by the way it was set up). Red noses may be bought for 70p from Woolworths, Oxfam, Save the Children shops and elsewhere, and the nation is urged to do things for the fund like getting local councillors to wear red noses, setting up a human shooting gallery with custard pies and porridge as ammunition, or eating peanuts with boxing gloves. The BBC gives Comic Relief consistent support in its programming and in the *Radio Times*. Charity Projects has recently created an education/information department which has published impressive teaching resources under the title 'Teacher Relief', repackaging in video cassette form a number of short films originally made for television transmission on Red Nose Days.

Comic Relief has emphasized education of the British public, but also the importance of spending money wisely, especially through 'empowering' people to help themselves. Will Day, their Africa Grants Director, argues that *raising* money for disasters is as easy as selling sweets to children. They have indeed made it seem easy, though they have done so on the back of years of effort by Oxfam and Save the Children, whose projects were used as a basis for their initial fund-raising. Having annual grants of about £11 million to distribute, about two thirds of which is earmarked for Africa and about a sixth for acute rather than long-term African needs), they are now a substantial and controversial force in the charity world. Trying to help others, they contend, is not incompatible with having fun. This poses a viable alternative to the evocation of guilt which Oxfam made its hallmark in the 1960s.

Above all, Comic Relief has access to a superb communications machine and is determined to keep Africa in the front of people's minds, whereas other agencies tend to preach to the converted. It has benefited from the talent of Lenny Henry, Griff Rhys Jones and a few other remarkable British comedians who speak to camera in places where African communities are actively finding solutions to problems. Many commentators, before it happened, were sceptical as to whether letting loose British comedians in stricken areas of Africa would have fruitful results, but they have on the whole admitted they were wrong. Success is achieved by placing familiar faces in unfamiliar settings, paying close attention to the performer's scripts and not allowing anyone to have 'platforms'. These visiting comedians are able to make local people laugh, making them seem real and close to the Western viewer. No charity had achieved this before.

Kevin Cahill, Director of Information and Education, argues that Comic Relief is inverting the moment in Shakespearian tragedy when the porter comes on in *Macbeth* to relieve tension. They are leading the public from the comic to the serious. The difficulty inherent in the idea is that, whereas a certain kind of basic humour is undoubtedly international, the things which make people crease themselves with laughter are usually specific to in-groups; and even the national sense of humour, catered to and moulded by television commercials for lagers or jeans, may be seen as that of an in-group. Really understanding other people, whether Africans or others, should mean trying to understand *their* humour, and this Comic Relief has not yet attempted to do.

The 1990s will show whether Comic Relief can develop its winning formula to combine education with fun as a durable policy, or whether it will be looked back on as a wizardry that worked for a time but lacked staying power. At all events, the parent concept, Charity Projects, is recognized as one of the most innovative organizations in the voluntary sector, and it is likely to come up with many new ideas to challenge and enrich – especially in trying to resolve some of the tensions and ambivalences within the agencies.

INDEPENDENCE VERSUS SERVICE PROVISION FOR GOVERNMENTS

Whatever the drawbacks of the free-market charity system, it has great advantages over systems where agencies depend largely on governments. SCF and Oxfam, for instance, are able to accept funds for overseas relief aid from the Overseas Development Administration (a department of the Foreign and Commonwealth Office) with a clear conscience, but only because they are not dependent on state funds. Oxfam's rule, for instance, is that government and EC funds should never exceed 10 per cent of total income.[41] They are hence able on occasion to ask critical questions about government policy, for instance in letters to the press, by having their staff speak on television or radio, or by seeking an interview with a minister. They are able to say 'no' when the government seems to want to take advantage of them.

For instance, the British government has tried to persuade some voluntary agencies to endorse the principle of mandatory repatriation of Vietnamese 'boat people' from Hong Kong, and to associate themselves with monitoring the screening procedures which set out to distinguish so-called United Nations refugees (those with a 'well-founded fear of persecution') from mere 'economic migrants'. The agencies have understandably refused to bring on themselves the odium which such political actions would inevitably attract, and they confine themselves to bringing what short-term succour they can to the detained boat people in Hong Kong, and pressing for long-term development aid to Vietnam which, if effective, would eventually make dangerous emigration less attractive.

Oxfam and SCF are further distinguished from those relief and development agencies, especially some of the American ones, which are primarily service contractors for Western governments, lacking their own independent voice and distinctive constituency.

THE FLAME OF CHARITY, AND ITS COLDNESS

There is an old, ironic English catchphrase, 'as cold as charity', which has sometimes been taken up by those who want to underline how vulnerable to degradation is the charitable ideal. Bernard Kouchner, whose work in co-founding both Médecins sans Frontières and Médecins du

Monde we will discuss in Chapter 4, has been particularly articulate in criticizing the conservatism and 'technocratic retention'[42] to which NGOs can be prone. Though he is now a senior minister in the French government, Kouchner as a young man was a Parisian leftist with leanings towards Maoism, and his approach to NGOs retains some of this influence.

The great relief agencies do not build up large capital reserves. SCF (UK), for instance, observes a financial principle that it should maintain only enough capital assets to allow, in theory, the orderly run-down and termination of all its projects, if the need should arise. However, the prestige of any major charity does result in a proportion of donations coming in without fund-raising effort, assisted by regular bankers' orders and testamentary bequests. Marx, in one of his most striking insights, alluded to the 'congealed labour' which is stored in the machine or industrial capital, and sucks living labour dry. There is a risk for any NGO of becoming congealed charity.

In the smaller agencies there is much energy and inno-vation to be found. Yet with so much now known about the pitfalls of ill-considered relief and development aid, the experience and sophistication of the large agencies are now indispensable. The challenge for them is to keep alight the flame that animated the early founders of humanitarianism.

At a more profound level of analysis, originated by Marcel Mauss in his classic essay *The Gift*, it has been said that the unreciprocated gift 'wounds' whoever accepts it. The 'unconscious and injurious patronage of the rich almsgiver'[43] aggravates social divisions rather than cementing bonds and obligations as gift exchange does. This kind of perception was one of the motives for the setting up of the Welfare State, which recognizes citizens' *rights* to education, health, old-age pensions and so forth. However, in practice the Welfare State cannot even look after all the citizens of advanced industrial societies to a reasonable standard, let alone those who live outside them.

Organized charity must find ways to warm rather than wound. Though the distinction between commerce and charity is particularly entrenched in English law, and on the whole for good reason, it is currently being questioned. The Body Shop, a remarkable international commercial empire based on toiletries and cosmetics, has taken a lead which caught the imagination of investors and customers, but which also provoked controversy because their commitment to environmental and other good causes is combined with relentless corporate and also personal publicity. This risks reducing the beneficiaries of their concern to counters in a media game. Gordon and Anita Roddick's policy of 'Trade not Aid' – entering ethical trading relations with Brazilian Indian communities over such products as brazil-nut oil – comes into the scope of the present book since they aim to enable these threatened Amerindian groups to avert economic and cultural disaster. If the efforts of the Body Shop and a few other similar companies are successful in breaking the mould of Western business, their brashness will eventually be more than forgiven.[44]

3 Parables of Disaster

This chapter presents two extended case studies of individual disasters: the first, man-made and lasting for some years during the late 1960s – the Nigerian civil war; the second, 'natural' and sudden, from the late 1980s – the Armenian earthquake of 1988. Many of the central issues explored in this book are pointed up by the study of these two disasters and the efforts to relieve the victims. The stories may be regarded, then, as real-life parables of disaster and relief, charged with moral implications for consideration and debate.

I. THE NIGERIAN CIVIL WAR

Chronology of the War

1960	Nigeria becomes an independent member of the Commonwealth.
January 1966	Ibo-led coup in which the veteran prime minister Sir Abubakar Tafawa Balewa (Hausa-Fulani) and other politicians are killed.
January-July 1966	General Ironsi (Ibo) is head of state.
May 1966	Riots and massacres of several hundred Ibo in the Hausa-dominated North.
July 1966	Counter-coup by Northerners. Ironsi and his staff are tortured and killed.
July–September 1966	Civil disorder, (?) 6–8,000 Ibos killed in the North. Colonel Gowon (Northern minority tribe) becomes head of state, but is not

	recognized by the Eastern Region under its governor Colonel Ojukwu (Ibo).
January 1967	Gowon and Ojukwu meet for negotiations in Aburi, Ghana.
February 1967	Eastern government hires American PR firm.
May 1967	Eastern government declares Republic of Biafra.
July 1967	Fighting breaks out between Biafran and Federal troops.
August 1967	Biafran invasion of mid-West, repulsed in September with heavy massacres.
October 1967	Enugu, capital of Eastern Region, falls.
end-1967	Churches make first appeal for food and vitamins for Biafra.
February 1968	First press release by Markpress.
April–May 1968	Tanzania, Gabon, Ivory Coast and Zambia recognize Biafra.
May 1968	Last proper airport (Port Harcourt) falls. Starvation begins.
June 1968	*Sun* and ITN *News at Ten* reports stir concern for Biafra in Britain.
1968	Peace talks in Kampala, Niamey, Addis Ababa.
1969	Military stalemate, intensive relief operations.
June 1969	Ahiara Declaration by Ojukwu.
January 1970	Biafra falls. Ojukwu flees to Ivory Coast.

The Nigerian civil war lasted from 1967 to 1970. It was a war to defend an unstable federation against secession by the Eastern Region, which gave itself the name of Biafra until its leaders were defeated after much bloodshed and suffering. The war is a useful historical reference point for examining the relationship of the media to disasters and relief; the politicization of disaster, especially food shortage, and its use as a weapon; the emergence of propaganda and public relations to further war aims; State interference in the distribution of humanitarian aid; resentment against the West; the power of visual imagery.

This war was a landmark in the evolution of some of the major NGOs. Oxfam, for instance, took an independent position at an early stage in the war when its director, Leslie Kirkley, flew to the Biafran enclave in the west of the federation in June 1968 and said on his return, 'Unless we pull out all the stops . . . we will have a terrifying disaster by the end of August. By then two million may have died.'[1] Soon afterwards, however, Oxfam acceded to the British government policy that relief must be coordinated with the International Committee of the Red Cross, and refrained from going in without the Nigerian Federal Government's permission. For the ICRC itself, the war was a major drama, in its own view the 'gravest emergency'[2] it had handled since the Second World War, resulting in a steep increase in its budgeting (from £0.5 million per year before the civil war to £1.4 million per month at its height)[3] and in a good deal of controversy and soul-searching. French voluntary aid, too, was the origin of the 'French doctors' movement (Chapter 4) which was in due course to transform the international NGO scene.

The Nigerian civil war hardly involved the superpowers. In this respect it differs sharply from, say, the Cambodian crisis of 1979–80 and many other conflicts of the Cold War era. It was a conflict founded almost entirely on ethnic and economic rivalry with little ideological content. Hence this war has analytical interest for the purposes of the present book; it may also be seen historically as a precursor of some of the post-Cold War ethnic conflicts which plague the world today.

Without falling into the trap of drawing crude historical analogies, one cannot escape noting that the role of starvation as a weapon of war is again a major military issue today, and that the relief agencies and the media alike risk being manipulated. In the winter of 1992–3, influential observers and even some relief agency workers are heard to speculate privately that the quicker the victory of the Serbs in Bosnia, the shorter will be the agony of the Bosnian Muslims. Such arguments are anathema to the whole ethos of humanitarianism and are always based on unreliable projections into the future, but the Nigerian civil war provides evidence that they cannot be simply brushed aside. Likewise, the support of professional publicists for particular ethnic factions is one of the less well studied aspects of contemporary conflicts.

Origins and development of the war

Whether the eruption of the war was foreordained by administrative mistakes made by the British towards the end of colonial rule in 1960 is a matter of historical interpretation.[4] There can be no disagreement about the long-standing difference between the Muslim North and the Christian Ibos in the East which underlay the massacre of Ibos in 1966 and their consequent secession; though it was as Ibos, not as Christians, that they were massacred, for Yoruba Christians in the same towns were left unmolested, as in earlier riots in the northern town of Kano in 1953.[5] Muslim (as well as several non-Muslim) African countries backed Federal Nigeria throughout the conflict. The Federal leadership did their best to downplay the religious element, choosing a leader, Yakubu Gowon, who was Christian, and setting out to unite the sympathies of all denominations within the Federation against the rebels of 'biafra' (Federal newspapers axed the capital letter in references to the breakaway state). The Biafrans played their Christian, and specifically Roman Catholic, card heavily to win sympathy from Europeans, with considerable success; and towards the end of the war their leader, Emeka Ojukwu, tried to introduce an element of Christian utopianism in his 'Ahiara Declaration' – but this was a tired, desperate throw. The conflict thus had some religious content, including a certain amount of anti-Muslim prejudice,[6] but religious ideology hardly figured in it and there was no element of fundamentalism.

For these reasons, the particular question of the relationships between disaster, relief and the media in wartime can be examined clearly in the Biafran example, relatively unclouded by the fog of doctrinal controversy which envelops any conflict where one or more of the parties is a Communist State or faction, or a State where religion has major political sway.

The Nigerian civil war was not of course the first war in which the media and propaganda were crucial factors, but it challenged the world with a new combination of vivid visual reporting, professional 'public relations' and the politics of famine. The war provoked much debate about these issues in the press, in parliamentary assemblies and within the NGOs.

The war of secession resulted from the fears of the Ibos that they would become victims of at best expropriation and oppression, or at worst genocide. The Ibos were a sophisticated and economically successful people, which suggested at the time a comparison – however inexact – with the Jews of Europe. The secessionist state which called itself Biafra won much sporadic sympathy all over the world, but the British government took the view – in a devious rather than a straightforward manner, sometimes claiming to be neutral rather than partisan – that it must help the Federal government to defend Nigeria's territorial integrity. The Eastern Region's richness in oil was undoubtedly a critical factor both in its original secession and in the determination to crush it.

In the end, after the Biafran republic had been in existence for two and a half years, gradually weakening but yet maintaining till the last much of the apparatus of bureaucracy and law courts, the Federal government recovered military control, and Ojukwu fled to the Ivory Coast by air. Though there was great suffering in the enclave both during and immediately after the war, the fear of genocide which had fuelled the Biafrans' resistance – reasonable in itself but intensified, as we shall see, by calculated propaganda – was not, in the end, realized, and the victors behaved with considerable magnanimity. This might have been lacking if the spotlight of media attention had not held them over the previous two years. They ordered no victory celebrations or parades and built no war monuments. Throughout the course of the war, the main causes of death were not massacres – though these did occur – but starvation, fighting and accidents.

The siege of Biafra, 1968–9
Between half a million and a million Nigerians died as a result of the war (the figure of two million was mentioned at the time). My concern here is not with the wider genesis and ramifications of the war, outlined in the chronological table, but with the period 1968–9, during which Biafra was under

siege. Ojukwu's territory was greatly reduced by the fall of a number of key ports and airfields, so that it was cut off, blockaded by sea and encircled on land. It was finally left with but one makeshift airport, Uli, where planes were allowed by Ojukwu to land only at night, when they could not easily be intercepted. The airlifts brought arms and relief supplies. As the ICRC delegate said at the time, 'At night all cats are grey and one cannot tell which cat carries the Red Cross.' Some ardently pro-Biafran agencies – not the ICRC – acquiesced to the sending of mixed cargoes (arms and relief supplies). The Federal commander, Gowon, was ready to allow relief supplies to be brought into Biafra by a land corridor under his control, but Ojukwu rejected this offer on military and political grounds.

The Eastern region, occupying no more than an eighth of Federal Nigeria, was densely populated: some 13 million at the start of the war, out of a total Nigerian population of 47 million. It had always been prone to starvation and malnutrition. Though self-sufficient in some foods such as fruits, it depended for staple food and protein on the import of wheat and Norwegian dried cod. War devastated its agricultural and industrial production, so that it became almost completely dependent on food aid – a 'relief economy', as one historian has called it.[7]

The Federal army had considerable superiority, and many observers in mid-1967 predicted it would gain a swift victory in a straightforward 'bush war'. The aim of Federal propaganda was to treat the war as a domestic affair, so that they could buy arms on the open market without difficulty. The aim of Biafran propaganda was to widen and diversify foreign intervention. Biafra succeeded in securing recognition from four African countries and varying degrees of support – generally for reasons of *realpolitik* – from Portugal, which was still a colonial power (Biafra's main communications link with the outside world was through a telex connection in Lisbon) and also France, South Africa, Israel, Rhodesia (as it then was) and China. An articulate and emotional pro-Biafran lobby sprang up in Britain, the USA and a number of other countries. At one point even Richard Nixon, speaking as Republican candidate in the 1968 United States presidential campaign, claimed that 'genocide is what is taking place right now – and starvation is the grim reaper', though the American government, following the British lead, never gave political recognition (as opposed to relief aid) to Biafra.[8] If Britain had had a Conservative government at the time, its policies might well have been effectively challenged by the Opposition. However, a Labour government following the Commonwealth Office line was in fact supported by most Conservatives and opposed only by an *ad hoc* cross-bench coalition in which the hard Left joined forces with some eccentric voices on the Right.

With hindsight, that Biafra held out against the Federal siege for as long as two and a half years was a remarkable achievement, due in large part to the skilful manipulation of public opinion. A directorate of propaganda was formed right at the start of the war, staffed by displaced young university lecturers, with close attention given to village-level contact. 'Nigeria was accused of presenting a religious vendetta or *jihad* [Muslim holy war], and while the image was intended to stir sympathies among foreign missionaries inside Biafra and among Christians around the world, the first objective was to arouse the Biafran masses.'[9] Within the enclave, Biafrans were urged to make every personal sacrifice to avert genocide. 'Genocide', said Ojukwu, 'cannot be proven until it is done.'[10] Internationally, extensive pressures were applied by various actors in the drama to keep the war, and particularly the conduct of the Federal armed forces, in the spotlight. The Federal forces were continuously scrutinized by the media, and, for a time, by an international observer team admitted by Gowon to the war zone. Who were the agitators of overseas opinion that kept up this pressure?

How overseas opinion was swayed

First, there were the relief organizations and in particular the churches. Most of the Biafrans were Catholic, or Christians of some other denominations (as was most of the west of Nigeria, which supported the Federal cause). The first agency to fly relief into the enclave without Federal permission was Caritas Internationalis, based in the Vatican; soon after, Protestants and Catholics combined to form Joint Church Aid. Of Biafra's

Christian supporters, the Irish Catholics were the most unequivocal and politically committed – for reasons of religious sympathy, hostility to Britain as the Federal government's backer, and probably also their atavistic memories of famine. The Order of the Holy Ghost, for instance, had a hundred priests and nuns in Biafra, some of whom saved thousands of lives. Pope Paul VI took a personal interest in the fate of Biafra, having previous experience of Africa when as Cardinal Montini he had served in the Vatican State Department.[11] The Order of Malta's French association sent extensive supplies of food and medicine to the enclave, and evacuated children to safety until the war was over, stating at the end of the war that the Biafrans' hope for freedom had 'a resonance which made the heart of French people vibrate.'[12]

Church organizations agonized over the morality of sending relief, aware that

humanitarian and political actions were inextricably entangled. Those who carried food into Biafra by breaking the Federal blockade were accused of supporting Biafra's resistance and prolonging the war; those who respected Nigerian sovereignty were accused of assisting the Federal side to commit genocide by starvation.[13]

The churches raised large sums of money. Some of it certainly helped to contribute to Biafra's foreign exchange reserves through payment of landing fees and purchase of local food, and these were a regular and major source of the foreign currency out of which Biafra had to pay for weapons, spare parts, transport, mercenary soldiers and overseas representation – and it does seem that the practical military support received from friendly states was never substantial. Later, Ojukwu in exile told an interviewer 'The only source of income available to Biafra was the hard currency spent by the churches for yams and gari.'[14] As for the actual food that was imported, inevitably the Biafran government gave priority to feeding their army. 'The international humanitarian organizations denied feeding anyone but the most desperate –

pregnant women, nursing mothers, the very young, and the aged. While one cannot doubt their noble intentions, their own records reveal that conditions were beyond their control.'[15] In any case, some of the churches explicitly defended their policies, claiming that they were using the only means available to save innocent lives. In September 1969, four months from the end of the war, the churches announced their 3,500th flight. The International Committee of the Red Cross had formerly been intensely active – on one occasion an ICRC plane had flown five trips into Biafra in one night – but early in 1969, tied by its unique mandate under the Geneva conventions, it decided to comply with the Nigerians' ban on night flights. As a historian of the ICRC's role during the war writes:

> After having helped the Biafrans to strengthen their resistance, the ICRC contributed to their defeat. Not only because it categorically suspended its flights, but also because it allowed Nigeria indirectly to claim for itself a certificate of good conduct without great cost, leaving all the weight of failure to fall on Biafra.[16]

A second channel for extending the international propaganda front was Biafra's official information service. Biafra was not the first warring state to engage a private PR service: that distinction is held by Katanga, which in the early 1960s seceded from the Congo, supported by Belgium and the copper companies.[17] But Biafra certainly opened up new horizons for the manipulation of public opinion beyond the traditional practice of 'war by communiqué' which is itself as old as the Peloponnesian war of the fourth century BC recounted by Thucydides.[18] The Eastern Region government hired a New York PR firm as early as February 1967, three months before secession. Later in the year, William Bernhardt, a Geneva-based PR specialist, was asked to open the Biafran Overseas Press Service, which he did under the name of Markpress (short for Marketing Press, an existing section of his business).[19] Markpress sent out hundreds of press releases to journalists, politicians and other opinion-formers, and was in charge of arrangements for them to visit Biafra. 'They used to vet people who were trying to go to Biafra. Unless you were wholly pro-Biafran you didn't get in.'[20] However, the information which Markpress itself circulated was often exaggerated and incorrect, and it has been claimed that Markpress's most significant effect on the progress of the war was to give the Federal side's supporters, especially the British government, a stick to beat the Biafran cause with.

Nonetheless, Markpress's impact disturbed the Federal authorities enough for them to engage their own British and American PR firms for a while. Bernhardt himself became an unofficial ambassador for the Biafrans, represented them in negotiations with the Red Cross, and attended a number of peace talks. Whatever moral judgment one may form of the Biafran leadership's intransigence near the end of the war, one has to note their quick perceptiveness at an earlier stage in recognizing that the siege of Biafra had no chance of being raised except through the projection of their new nation as a 'consumer product' for the West. The fact that about one million people in territory 'liberated' by the Federal army were also in desperate need received hardly any international press coverage.[21]

A third major channel was that provided by Western journalists, both press and television, and photographers – with the cooperation of the Biafran authorities and their advisers. A number of journalists – perhaps the majority – became committed to the Biafran side, though some experienced and influential Africa specialists were consistently sceptical. In London, 'the handling of the war by Fleet Street was to result in something like a subordinate war in its own right.'[22] The *Sunday Times*, for instance, was split between the staff of the main newspaper who were mainly pro-'Fed' and the magazine section which was pro-Biafran.[23] A few Biafran intellectuals such as the novelist Chinua Achebe, or the chief justice and leading churchman Sir Louis Mbanefo, had international reputations and personal friendships which enabled them to speak directly and personally to Western colleagues. But there is no doubt that it was Western, particularly British but also Swiss and French, journalists who in an important sense 'created' the Biafran war in the eyes of the world at large.

Journalism during the war

It must be remembered that Africa in the 1960s was much
more in the news than today, when there are hardly any
Africa correspondents left in European newspapers, and on
average a tiny number of column inches is given to African
stories, other than racial politics in South Africa or starvation
in the north-east and more recently the south. As Harrison
and Palmer write, 'The journalists and others – economic
planners, career diplomats, businessmen and academics –
who thought about Africa in the early 1960s tended to share
an optimism which now [1986], with the wisdom of hindsight,
appears tragic, misplaced and naive.'[24] Nigeria was perhaps
of all newly independent African States the one in which the
most generous political hopes were vested. It was especially
the country's prospective wealth in oil, and its already healthy
exports of cocoa, groundnuts and rubber, which gave it such
prominence; similar conflicts in countries such as Sudan have
attracted much less attention.

The Biafran war was the last in which traditional
newspaper reporters were able to scoop television.[25] Some
might condemn out of hand this way of discussing their
professional goals, but competition is an essential spur to
journalism as we know it, as it is to most other Western
professions; and competition does not necessarily exclude a
deeper seriousness about the issues at stake. Television was
still dependent on huge film cameras in chests, and tins of film
which had to be flown home for chemical developing and
cutting; so that it took about two days for a piece of new film
from west Africa to appear on the evening news. Press
reporters, though dependent on still primitive telex and
telephone links, had the edge – before the development of
satellite communications. Television did bring starvation in
Biafra to the full attention of millions of viewers, but black-
and-white photographs of starving children, published in
newspapers and magazines, were probably more important.

Of the photographers, Romano Cagnoni took the opportunity to document all aspects of Biafra under siege, from the
worst atrocities to the population's heroic achievement in
keeping up the normality of civilized life.[26] Don McCullin, the
great war photographer, describes his visits to Biafra as

among the most harrowing experiences in his career. His priority throughout this career has been to galvanize public opinion with shocking images:

> No heroics are possible when you are photographing people who are starving. All I could do was try to give the people caught up in this terrible disaster as much dignity as possible. There is a problem inside yourself, a sense of your own powerlessness, but it doesn't do to let it take hold, when your job is to stir the conscience of others who can help.[27]

These and other photographers filled the press with portraits of *marasmus*, the wasting away to a living skeleton, and *kwashiorkor*, the result of extreme protein deficiency in which the body burns up the fuel reserves in the liver, fatty tissues and muscles. Typical images were the skeletal 2–3 -year-old, seated alone with imploring eyes, holding up wasted hands in an appeal for help; or the nursing mother with terribly emaciated breasts. The ethics of such photo- graphy are considered elsewhere in this book: here it will suffice to point out that McCullin's apologia quoted above includes an apparent slip of the pen, for the dignity of victims of starvation cannot be 'given' by the photographer, as he says; it must inhere in their own stoicism or defiance, and it is, in a sense, their gift to us. To say that dignity is the gift of the photographer is to take away from the dispossessed even that which he has. And yet the work of such photographers as McCullin has done more, maybe, than anything else to drive home to ordinary people the human reality of remote wars and famines.

A *Daily Express* journalist was first with photographs of starving Biafran children, but his editor spiked them thinking that the public would not be interested (it was not the last time this would happen). Michael Leapman's story in the *Sun* appeared on 12 June 1968, scooping Ian Hart's ITN programme that same evening. At that time, the Biafran authorities were reluctant to publicize the famine lest it contradict their claim that they were winning the war (a presentational dilemma which they remained trapped by till the bitter end). It was these reports which triggered an overwhelming wave of concern, fuelled thereafter by atrocity photographs taken by a flood of itinerant reporters with no special knowledge of Africa. Late in June, Markpress played the famine card for the first time, and indeed the martyrdom of the Ibo people became the only trump card held by the Biafran leaders as they clung to the fiction of a sovereign state. Frederick Forsyth's strongly pro-Ojukwu *The Biafra Story* came out as a Penguin Special in 1969 and sold out quickly. Auberon Waugh also wrote a book and named one of his sons Biafra.[28] We must remember, however, that interest in Biafra was only intermittent because of competition from the Middle East, Czechoslovakia, Vietnam and other trouble spots which were in most ways more central to the great ideological and political issues of the late twentieth century.

Moral issues
Both sides, naturally, criticized Western agencies for their relief policies. Biafra maintained that sympathetic governments were withholding recognition and military assistance, and giving money instead to relief operations, and Ojukwu summed up his position in a speech to the Biafran consultative assembly in September 1968: 'Those governments motivated by humanitarian considerations have a responsibility now to ensure that Biafrans are enabled to defend themselves by providing them the wherewithal so to do.'[29]

From the other side, too, the 'fat white cats' of the West were criticized for seizing on Biafra as a means of assuaging their guilt.[30] A Nigerian civil servant claimed in July 1969 that 'Starvation is a legitimate weapon of war and we have every intention of using it against the rebels.'[31] The Federal authorities were torn between military toughness and humanitarian decency. After the war, Gowon refused relief aid – 'Let them keep their blood money' – from all countries that had supported Biafra, and from the church organizations and the ICRC.[32] Priests, do-gooders and journalists were lumped together as responsible for having prolonged the war, the airport at Uli was destroyed, and all relief aid had to be channelled through the Nigerian Red Cross.

Issues that haunt us today – in ex-Yugoslavia and

elsewhere – were foreshadowed in the Nigerian civil war. Several ardent pro-Biafrans in Western countries changed their minds at one stage or another during it or just after the end. Don McCullin was one. He was repelled by the flight of Ojukwu in a plane to the Ivory Coast, and by his own observation, on the evidence of the Biafran leadership's abandoned headquarters with its 'mountains of empty winebottles', that they had not shared the terrible sufferings which they had put their people through.[33] This was certainly fair comment, and the élites on both sides had a high survival rate throughout the war. 'Our young men are dying for our survival.'[34] Ojukwu's statement in October 1967 to the Biafran assembly has an unfortunate ring to it – at least to the ears of Europeans who remember similar pronouncements during our own wars. It is probable that, on at least one occasion during the war, Ojukwu refused to allow moderately inclined Biafran officials to negotiate a settlement. His powerful personality and quick wit had a lot to do with the way the Biafrans conducted the war, and some weight of blame is bound to rest particularly with him for taking the risks he did at the expense of hundreds of thousands of innocent people. If he himself had fallen like Che Guevara, or even been humiliated by the victors like Dubcek, he would probably have remained an effective symbol of devotion to his people's cause. As it is, some who lived through this period contend that Ojukwu and his fellow-secessionists felt genuinely close to the sufferings of their people, and genuinely feared genocide.

Both Gowon and Ojukwu were called on to exercise their responsibilities while still in their mid-30s. Another, still younger man, a British relief worker in Biafra for Save the Children shortly before the end of the war who afterwards joined the diplomatic service and now heads SCF's Overseas Department,[35] was impressed by Forsyth's pro-Biafra book 'for about a fortnight'. Then he decided that apportioning blame for such a catastrophe is a waste of effort. This is perhaps a more sophisticated viewpoint than one which seeks a culprit, and it is one which many historians would adopt. If there are lessons to be learnt to avoid recurrence of such a conflict elsewhere, these might well focus on processes of conciliation as technical ends in themselves. Processes of conciliation can be both assisted and impeded by the intervention of the media.

The dilemmas of relief agencies in many other wars that have followed have been similar. Their overriding aim is to save lives and alleviate suffering. Yet what if the cost is prolongation of the conflict when their food aid or foreign currency buttresses the position of the weaker party? Relief agencies should not make a policy of supporting the militarily stronger side purely on the grounds that it will win and bring the war to an early conclusion: plainly, such a policy would be the opposite of humanitarian. Yet in some cases it might, theoretically, be the most hardheaded policy if minimization of suffering and death to individuals were the *only* consideration. It is not, of course, for agencies do not operate in a political vacuum, and they must be alert to questions of principle and justice and example, as well as to a purely statistical morality. Similarly, it is generally accepted that a humanitarian agency must try to provide medical aid for all wounded people, even if some of them are soldiers who, when healed, are likely to go back to war and kill others. Inevitably, the agencies are also responsive, ever since the Biafran war, to the consequences of the fickle embrace of the media.

Humanitarian action has been compared by a cynic to war, as being another 'continuation of diplomacy by other means', and the Biafran war gives some plausibility to this claim, even though much of the relief aid for Biafra came from private as well as from government sources. Even the ICRC, which appears at first sight to suit its actions as nearly as possible to an apolitical ideal, is constrained by its neutral status which one disaffected former delegate has likened to 'a protective glass screen of neutral humanitarianism, deprived of all moral judgment' that disposes its representatives to take refuge in statistics and rules, rather than break the screen and take in the toxic gases of human suffering under oppression.[36]

It was, as we shall see, dissatisfaction with the restrictions on the ICRC's role in the Biafran war that impelled Bernard Kouchner to found Médecins sans Frontières.[37] The ICRC did little during the Second World War (until the very end) to try to save the civilian Jewish population from extermination, despite knowing what was going on in the death camps.[38] Kouchner has drawn an exact parallel with the ICRC's self-imposed restraint during the Nigerian civil war:

> I came across the same limits in Biafra, in 1968. We were in the field with my friends who were to found, with me, Médecins sans Frontières. The Biafran people were dying, we knew it, we were not allowed to talk about it. We were allowed to cure, but not to prevent. We resisted this position by forming the International Committee against Genocide in Biafra, where people from the Red Cross were to be found together with doctors, journalists, witnesses, people who knew what they were talking about.

Many of the same themes cropped up again in the Cambodian crisis of 1979–80, which was complicated immeasurably by extremist political ideology and great-power involvement: the impact of photographs and the reports of journalists and aid officials; the analogy between an oppressed people and the Jews under the Third Reich; the generation by the media of the image of a whole country as a charnel-house; the raising of large sums of money; the focusing by the media on one region for a limited period at the expense of other needs including the need for long-term development; the conflicting political pressures on agencies. William Shawcross's sad conclusion is that:

> One question that we must surely ask ourselves is whether the brief attention given by the international community to some peoples in distress really alleviates their condition as much as it assuages our consciences, or whether it sometimes actually reinforces the underlying causes of their despair. In this regard the case of Cambodia is not necessarily encouraging . . . one of the effects of humanitarian aid was actually to reinforce the political stalemate.[39]

The Cambodian stalemate is only now, at the time of writing, beginning to be broken, with the endorsement of a realistic plan for the country by the rival factions, in the face of many obstacles including the unspeakable record of the Khmer Rouge. The Biafran case would have been a simple siege but for the defenders' ingeniousness in opening up the propaganda front, and it ended in a brisk checkmate after which the King was suddenly whisked off the board, to the chagrin of his many Western admirers.

Every war is different, but study of the Biafran war should warn us against the danger of 'taking sides' too naïvely when each side is conducting a propaganda war as well as a shooting war, and when the achievement of truly skilful propaganda may be to disguise itself as impartial news.

II THE ARMENIAN EARTHQUAKE, 1988

A great earthquake struck Soviet Armenia at 11.41 a.m. on Wednesday, 7 December 1988, for about 40 seconds – a main shock and an aftershock. The epicentre was at a village called Nalband, at an altitude of 2,000 metres, but several large towns were also gravely damaged. Many people were caught inside poorly constructed buildings of six to nine storeys, where they were working or eating. The population was swollen by refugees from Azerbaijan and the autonomous region of Nagorno-Karabakh. At least 25,000 people died (probably a serious underestimate) and the USSR suffered a loss of more than 2.5 per cent of its GDP in 1988.[40]

One eye-witness wrote:

Because of its size, this catastrophe is henceforth part of the history of the world, like Pompeii. It is a historic event which people will argue about, and I was there, I trod the ground of history as an astronaut walks on the moon. For the first time in my life, I saw a historical moment and I was an integral part of that instant, crossing the tragic destiny of humanity.[41]

This is an essentially external view which would not have rung true with the survivors who were buried for hours or days and had to be dug out; or with the parents of schoolchildren who, if the quake had struck a few minutes later, would have left the school buildings for their lunch break and not been trapped. The most tragic destiny for human beings is that of senseless loss, the loss of meaning itself which a major disaster can inflict on a community.

The historical momentousness of the Armenian earthquake is indeed inescapable, but it is of a kind dependent on refraction of realities through the technically sophisticated modern media. We shall therefore trace the narrative using the perspective not of local Armenian people (well drawn by other writers),[42] but of remote 'consumers' of the disaster who learnt about it through the press and television. We shall see how the clash of continental plates a few hundred feet below the ground set off extraordinary political and social repercussions, both internationally and within the USSR. Our media trace will also follow the rhythm of the classic 'big story' which breaks suddenly, swells to a climax, keeps going for a time with the help of new journalistic angles, and finally peters out.

No attempt is made here to trace reporting the earthquake by the Armenian and Soviet domestic media, except where such reporting was picked up, for quotation or comment, by the international media – the domestic coverage of the tragedy becoming part of the international 'story'.

A media trace of the relief operation

The story breaks
The first news of the earthquake was given out by the Islamic Republic News Agency of Iran. It was then confirmed to reporters by Soviet seismologists. Photographers from Tass, the Soviet news agency, in Yerevan – the capital of Soviet Armenia, 75 miles south of the epicentre, which suffered only slight tremors – reached the distressed area by military helicopter while correspondents were stuck on the blocked highways and all telephone lines were down; so the agency had pictures but no story.[43] Even in Yerevan, it was not till about 4 p.m. that the extent of the earthquake was learnt.[44] Not until eight hours had passed did Tass describe it as a disaster.[45]

The leading Paris newspaper *Le Monde* (8 December),

which goes to press the evening before its publication date, said that about a hundred people were dead. In London *The Times*, going to press in the middle of the night, estimated 'at least 200 dead' after a severe earthquake. It added that there was no question of General Secretary Gorbachev, who was in the middle of an important tour of the USA, returning from New York. According to *The Times*, the Soviet state-run television, in an unusually prompt and detailed report from the scene in its evening news bulletin, had shown film of crumbled buildings in Kirovokan, Armenia's third largest city, and Spitak, a regional centre.

Le Monde's next issue (9 December) estimated 30,000 dead, and also included a petition 'For the Armenians' protesting against recent murders of Armenians by Azeris in connection with the disputed territory of Nagorno ('mountainous') Karabakh, already an Autonomous Region but part of the Azerbaijan Republic.[46] (In February the same year, Armenians in Sumgait, a dormitory suburb of the Azeri capital Baku, had been massacred, and the worldwide publicity had stirred memories of earlier anti-Armenian pogroms.)

The story swells to climax
In London, ITN's 10 p.m. news bulletin for 8 December showed the following (much of the footage acquired from Soviet television):

- rescue workers searching in the rubble of Leninakan (a big town 30 miles west of the epicentre), with shots of survivors, cranes, a stretcher case, an army convoy;
- Soviet Prime Minister Nikolai Ryzhkov arriving in Yerevan;
- An Armenian radio monitor reporting that construction in the area is so poor that houses (of up to nine storeys) simply collapsed 'like a house of cards' when the quake struck; he refers to intense cold (plunging to −20°C overnight) and a people without shelter;
- a Young Communist emergency centre in Moscow;
- a scientist in a Moscow seismic laboratory;
- an excerpt from Soviet news;
- Gorbachev explains to Reagan why he must cut short his US trip.

The Times for 9 December estimated a death toll of 100,000, and announced that Gorbachev had postponed his planned visit to London. The Soviet Embassy appealed for help 'in a move almost without precedent', setting up a disaster fund and opening the embassy to receive gifts. In its first reminder of ethnic conflict in the region, *The Times* noted that many Soviet troops had already been deployed there because of civil unrest earlier in the year. It also recalled that the Armenians had suffered from a series of genocides in their history, and in 1920 accepted the Bolsheviks' protection against the Turks. Leninakan was estimated to be 75 per cent destroyed. According to the leading article, 'A national disaster is an occasion not for politics but for charity, and Moscow's recognition that help is needed is the first step to receiving it'. The Home Office was sending specialist firemen with thermal image cameras and vibrophones to assist in the search for survivors; and the British-based International Rescue Corps, which can exist self-sufficiently for 14 days, was also sending volunteers.

The ITN bulletin for 9 December showed Ian Glover-James, their correspondent in Moscow, saying, 'No one understood the true scale of this tragedy until today, and as the hours pass the rush to get men and medicines to Armenia is becoming acute.' We were shown rescue workers, hampered by lack of equipment, pulling at the rubble with their bare hands, listening for signs of life. The first foreign rescue team to arrive was Swiss, followed by the French, then the Finns. Gorbachev's motorcade carried him from the airport into Moscow. Muscovites gave blood. There were interviews with an Armenian leader in London, then the Soviet ambassador (who said that 2.5 million people were homeless), and the British minister for overseas aid. An American student at Yerevan University spoke by telephone of the devastation. The British ambassador in Moscow greeted the firemen who had arrived from London. Rescue workers described the horror of not being able to reach people only centimetres away, whose voices can be heard. Archive film of the mountainous landscape was screened, and the difficulties of bringing relief to such a remote area, with some of the roads destroyed, were explained.

On 10 December, *The Times* reported that hardly anyone in the region of Spitak, close to the epicentre, was alive. The relief effort was involving both governments and ordinary citizens across the globe, and ideological barriers were being set aside. The British government had given £5 million, the first aid it had given to the USSR and the largest it had contributed in response to any national disaster. The US had revived its CARE packages, which were stopped twenty years ago, as a means of sending emergency food supplies.

New angles: the climax sustained

A columnist in the same issue wrote of '*glasnost* [openness] in action'. Formerly scant attention had been paid to disasters, and the news was reported in 'the flat monotones for which the Soviet media was at one time renowned'. Now, *Pravda* was telling of 'our pain and tragedy': for the first time, Soviet television viewers were being shown footage from the disaster zone, relief appeals, the reactions of foreign governments. Ryzhkov appealed for cranes and lifting gear. Injured Armenians were crossing borders into Azerbaijan, the ethnic conflict temporarily suspended. Turkey was opening its border to allow in relief supplies (the quake had rippled over the border and left 1,000 Turks homeless). According to *The Times*, some reports suggested that Muslim rioters had set fire to the houses of Armenians in Azerbaijan, taking advantage of the absence of troops who were called to the earthquake area. Soviet families had offered to adopt orphaned Armenian children, but Armenian women had protested against this proposal in front of the Communist Party headquarters in Yerevan. (In fact, there were few orphans, as so many schoolchildren were killed.)

Le Monde recalled that Gorbachev had not left Moscow at the time of the explosion of the Chernobyl nuclear reactor in the Ukrainian SSR in 1986. The main new elements in ITN's evening bulletin for 10 December were Mikhail and Raisa Gorbachev's visit to the disaster zone, and the declaration of a 'national day of mourning' throughout the USSR – usually declared only after the death of a national leader. Robert Maxwell's private jet had left for Moscow.

Le Monde of 11–12 December emphasized the grave organizational difficulties in providing effective relief. They quoted an Agence-France Presse report that groups of young people in Baku, the capital of Muslim Azerbaijan, had gone into the streets congratulating themselves on the 'punishment inflicted by Allah on those who killed and drove from Armenia their brother Azeris'. Among those testifying to this provocation was a Ukrainian resident in Baku, interviewed by telephone from Moscow. Meanwhile Soviet television was putting out that Azerbaijan was at the head of the republics showing solidarity with the Armenians. The Karabakh Committee in Armenia, which with immense popular support had been spearheading the nationalist movement to seek autonomy for the enclave of Karabakh, had asked the Soviet media to 'put an end to this cheap and totally ineffective internationalist propaganda', denying that they knew of any Azerbaijanis who had come to help the Armenian victims. Meanwhile, Armenians were fleeing from Azerbaijan, and Azeris from Armenia.

On 10 December Gorbachev attacked the Karabakh Committee for seizing the initiative in the organization of rescue work. In fact, the Committee had been for some months a kind of *de facto* opposition to the Armenian Communist Party, with large support from the people, and they were relatively well-equipped to organize relief. Indeed they were the first to appreciate the severity of the disaster and organize voluntary help.[47]

On 13 December *Le Monde*'s Moscow correspondent, Bernard Guetta, commented acutely:

Several dailies print simply 'pain', and everywhere, filmed, described and photographed, this Armenian pain is moving the USSR to its depths. For this country which has known civil war, forced collectivization, mass deportations, famines, wars and terror, this country which will have known all the horrors of the twentieth century, was quite ignorant until three days ago of the representation of human suffering and despair.

As for unhappiness, that existed only in the capitalist hell. The shock of a photo, the shriek of a headline, the

punch of a close-up, that was bourgeois sensationalism –
a loaf that one didn't eat. Suddenly, not only do they
announce that there has been an earthquake, not only do
they not hide its extreme gravity, not only do they say it,
but they let it be seen too.

Guetta concluded that, though there was a propagandistic
element in Gorbachev's policy of openness to Western
sympathy and aid, 'what is happening is much more
profound. For the first time since the 1917 revolution,
"solidarity" means no longer for Moscow geographic exten-
sion of the Soviet model, but human solidarity.'

On 11–12 December, there were two fatal air crashes in the
disaster zone involving relief planes, as a result of excessive air
traffic. On 10 December in Yerevan, a number of members of
the Karabakh Committee were jailed on a charge of having
appealed for gifts for emergency relief. On 11 December,
Gorbachev expressed on television his horror at what he had
seen, and exploded with anger against the Armenian
campaign for Karabakh. He said that there were admittedly
real roots to the problem because Armenians in the region had
been badly treated, but the 'political adventurism' of 'corrupt
and dishonest people' was leading to 'the edge of the abyss'.[48]

According to *The Times* of 12 December, US experts
estimated that only 1,000 would have been killed if an
earthquake of this kind had hit California, on account of the
cheap high-rise buildings that had been allowed in Armenia
since the Second World War. The buildings which had
survived were mainly older ones and traditional one-storey
buildings. 'Buildings, not earthquakes, kill people.' The extra
cost of simple anti-quake measures added only about 5 per
cent to building costs, but most of the countries most likely to
be hit by an earthquake were also those least likely to have
done anything about protection. About one third of those
trapped were likely to die. Untrained rescuers could unwittingly kill those they are trying to save, unless they know about
'crush syndrome', the clogging of the kidneys caused by severe
contusions of the limbs.

Western reporters were now allowed to visit the area. ITN's
Peter Sharp reported from Leninakan on 13 December that

Right. Oxfam appeal, 1968.

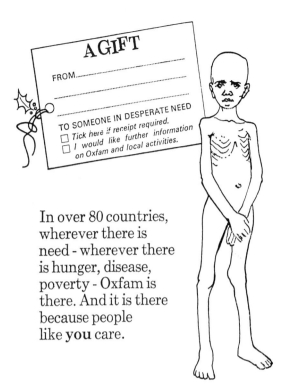

A GIFT

FROM...............................
....

TO SOMEONE IN DESPERATE NEED
☐ Tick here if receipt required.
☐ I would like further information
   on Oxfam and local activities.

In over 80 countries,
wherever there is
need - wherever there
is hunger, disease,
poverty - Oxfam is
there. And it is there
because people
like **you** care.

For a happier Christmas at this season of giving,
why not hang this envelope on your tree and let
your family and guests contribute to a New Year
of hope for those who have almost given up hoping.

Stick both sides of this section to
the flaps above. To send your gift
(cheque or postal order, please),
fill in your name and address
above, and stick down the top section.

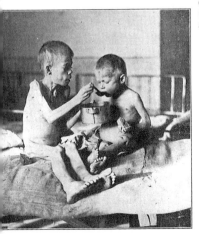

ve the Children Fund

Our Errand of Mercy into
:: the Regions of Death ::

TAGES OF STARVATION: SKIN AND BONE—BLOATED.
y of these photographs appear in the Film entitled "Famine," and give some idea
work of the Save the Children Fund in the province of Saratov, which covers an
ual to two-thirds of England and Wales, with a population of about 3 millions.

Left. Front cover of Save the Children
leaflet on the Russian famine, *c.* 1922.

Fresh food is now flying in to Biafra.

Good nourishing stuff it is, too.

Sausage-flies are full of protein.

So Biafran mothers feed them to their children. It's the only way to keep them alive.

And if they can't stomach sausage-flies, there are always rats and lizards.

But sausage-flies are the easiest meat. At night they flock to any bright light they see.

Which is more than can be said of relief planes.

They can't get through with food and medical supplies, because an air route can't be established.

And Nigeria and Biafra can't agree on the best way to set up routes overland.

So thousands of people die of hunger and disease.

Both in Biafra and Nigeria.

3,000 deaths a day is one estimate.

What can be done?

Why do we, Christian Aid, ask you to give us money when we can't immediately use it to help Biafrans?

At the moment, we're stockpiling non-perishable food and medicines on the island of Fernando Po off the Nigerian coast.

The minute we can get it into Biafra we will.

(We've already flown 1,400 tons of stockfish into starvation areas now held by Federal troops.)

But our main concern is for Biafra and Nigeria when the fighting ends.

Because that's when the biggest fight begins.

We need money to rebuild schools and hospitals.

To buy farmers seeds and equipment.

To fly in irrigation experts, agriculturalists, doctors, engineers, and teachers.

We need the money now.

We need the money now because we have to plan for the future now.

Christian Aid people will be working in Nigeria and Biafra years after the war is over.

The same as they are still at work in the Congo, the Arab countries, South America, India, and all over the world.

Of course helping the hungry will be our first thought.

But you can't plant next year's harvest with dried fish. **Christian Aid.**

Christian Aid appeal for relief in Biafra, 1968.
(*Agency: Doyle Dane Bernbach UK.*)

SENTENCED TO DEATH

INNOCENT

Save the ⋀ Children ⋏

Support our emergency aid programmes for the victims of disaster

Save the Children poster, 1981.

125 YEARS
ANS
AÑOS
سنة

PROTECTING HUMAN LIFE
A PROTEGER LA VIE HUMAINE
PARA PROTEGER LA VIDA HUMANA
لحماية حياة البشر

Poster published jointly by the ICRC and the League (now
International Federation) of Red Cross and Red Crescent Societies in
1989, to mark 125 years of the movement. (*Photo: Dany Gignoux.*)

Christian Aid Week 1991 Advertising.

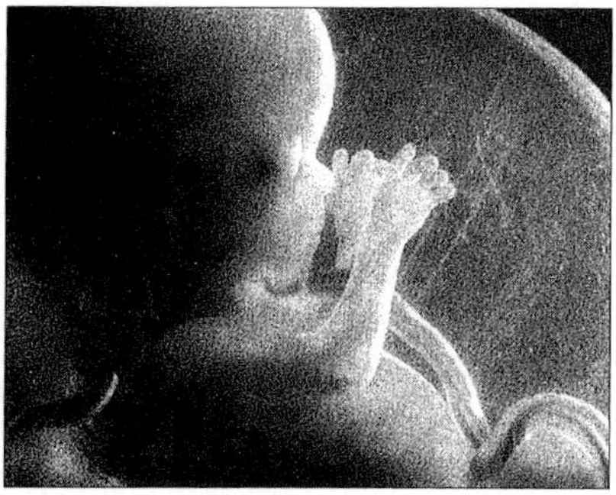

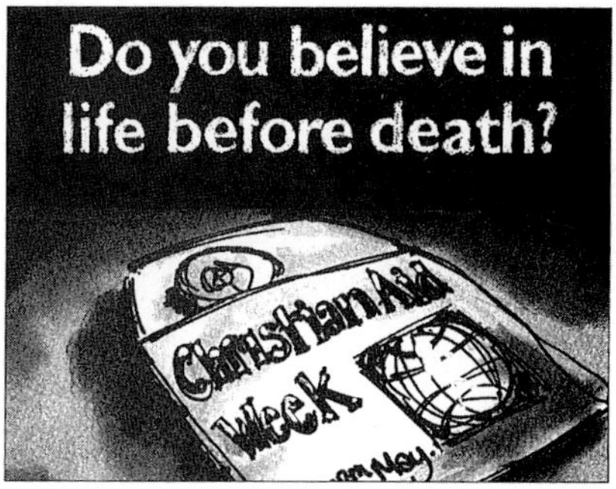

Do you believe in life before death?
Christian Aid
Week

Television. (To be on air 8-17 May.)

Voice over: For millions of people in the Third World, these will be the best months of their lives. Later on there is little nourishment, less shelter, and no comfort. We're working to give everyone the chance of a real life, because we believe in life before death. Do you?
Please help us in Christian Aid Week.

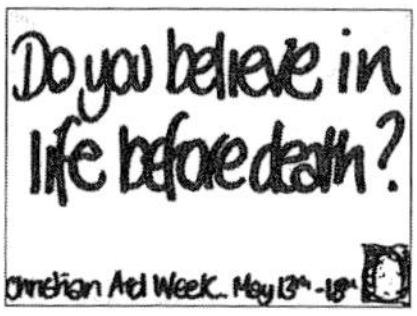

Do you believe in life before death?
Christian Aid Week. May 13th - 18th

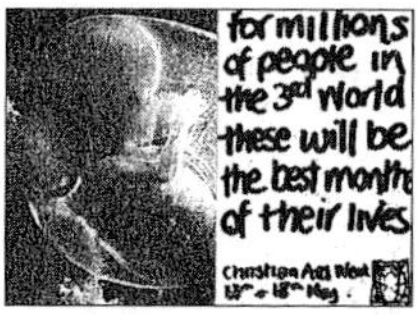

for millions of people in the 3rd World these will be the best months of their lives
Christian Aid Week
13th - 18th May

National Press. (To appear 7-17 May.)

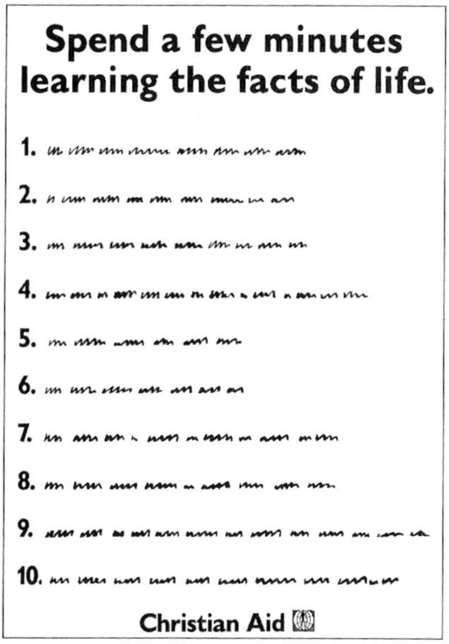

Spend a few minutes learning the facts of life.
1.
2.
3.
4.
5.
6.
7.
8.
9.
10.
Christian Aid

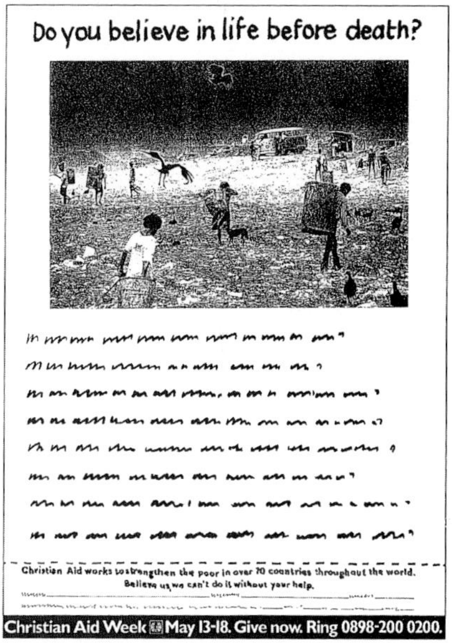

Do you believe in life before death?
Christian Aid works to strengthen the poor in over 70 countries throughout the world.
Believe us, we can't do it without your help.
Christian Aid Week May 13-18. Give now. Ring 0898-200 0200.

National, Regional and Church Press. (To appear 7-17 May.)

Christian Aid internal circular on forthcoming advertisements, 1991.

Penny Tweedie

Save the Children

Front page of Save the Children appeal leaflet, 1992. Photo (*by Penny Tweedie*), of children from Mozambique at a refugee camp in Malawi.

Médecins sans Frontières poster, 1993, depicting open-air surgery in Cambodia. (© *Sebastião Salgado, Magnum, for MSF.*)

1(a)

1(b)

2

3(a)

4

3(b)

3(c)

5(a)

5(b)

5(c)

5(d)

5(e)

6(b)

6(a)

6(c)

7

8(a)

8(b)

9

10

11

IGO and NGO emblems and logos

1(a). The red cross and red crescent.
1(b). International Committee of the Red Cross
2. Sovereign Military Order of Malta
3(a). MSF
3(b). Médecins du Monde
3(c). Swiss Disaster Relief Unit
4. Christian Aid
5(a). United Nations
5(b). Unicef
5(c). WHO

5(d). UNDRO
5(e). UNHCR
6(a). The first Save the Children Fund badge
6(b). Save the Children Fund c. 1959
6(c). Save the Children Fund today
7. CAFOD
8(a). Oxfam c. 1990
8(b). New Oxfam logo
9. Disasters Emergency Committee
10. World Vision
11. Care International

The use of the Red Cross and Red Crescent emblems is ruled by the Geneva Conventions.

'people are too numbed to notice even our intrusion into their grief.' He interviewed the distraught mother of a victim; a schoolteacher who called for more rescue equipment; an American fireman, on his way home, who described chaotic conditions with no interpreters, little transportation, no telephones.

On 14 December, *Le Monde*'s Moscow correspondent told his readers that the earthquake and its publicity had revealed that the USSR was the only modern country without a rapid deployment medical force. The national television service made no attempt to hide this superpower's lack of organiza-tion and indeed its 'profound underdevelopment'. There was a thoroughgoing lack of syringes, field hospitals, tents and shelters, artificial kidneys, and cranes. In a country of such vast natural riches, there should be no such crying need for international help. 'Consequently, this international aid is endlessly emphasized, by means of reports, televised images and statements of gratitude by the authorities to foreign governments.' Bernard Guetta reached the strong conclusion that 'in the six days following the earthquake, it seems that the country has changed more deeply than in four years of *perestroika*; carried by a wave that they are encouraging, Mr Gorbachev and his team are lending a hand to the truth.' *The Times* of 13 December also reported high-flown articles in the Soviet press alluding to nuclear war, nuclear winter, the apocalypse.

The story falls away

On 14 December, some light relief was generated by the British decision to send the Armenians one million eggs – unsold surpluses caused by a recent salmonella scare. It was reported in *Pravda* that some Armenians were receiving 'congratulatory telegrams' from Azerbaijan. Some individuals were commandeering cranes to mount private rescue efforts for relatives. The number of dead bodies recovered had risen to 21,775 and martial law had been introduced to curb looting.

In *The Times* of 15 December, its Moscow correspondent Mary Dejevsky praised Gorbachev for acting like a national leader and insisting that it was morally reprehensible to link the earthquake and territorial claims. She also noted that the Soviet civil defence system had been shown to be ineffective.

By 17 December, the last survivors were being dragged from the ruins. There were 1,500 foreign aid workers on the spot, with poor reception facilities for them. Rescue teams were now all asked to leave, though a number of agencies extended their involvement into long-term reconstruction projects.

Pravda accused the Karabakh Committee of being in league with the Armenian mafia. The Committee, it was true, had made contact with the French singer Charles Aznavour and the Governor of California, John Tokmedzhan, asking them to organize relief efforts and hand funds directly over to the Armenians, bypassing official channels.[49] A benefit concert for the earthquake victims was organized in London by the Russian cellist Mstislav Rostropovich, who was born in Azerbaijan. By 21 December, a disaster fund raised by voluntary donations in Britain stood at £7.9 million.

The story was now fading from the front pages, but on 20 December *The Times* reported the return of the British firemen to the UK. Though they had found a number of dead bodies, they could not report a single confirmed rescue. Nonetheless, *The Times* noted the evident superiority of Western disaster teams (from a number of countries that are not in earthquake zones). A leading article noted that the Armenians' long cultural tradition of openness towards and interest in the rest of the world, and the extensive and influential Armenian disapora, had made it easier for the West to respond.

In *The Times* for 20 December, the Soviet foreign minister Eduard Shevardnadze was quoted as saying that his country should be ashamed not to have joined in aid and disaster relief programmes in the past.

There was a time when we even voted against increasing the funds of the disaster relief operation [i.e., UNDRO]. This time the disaster has happened in our homeland, and the bureau has offered to help coordinate the international relief effort and assist the victims of the earthquake in Armenia. What, other than shame, can we feel about the shortsightedness of our former position?

In *Le Monde* on 21 December, Laurent Greilsamer explained the strength of feeling behind the Armenian territorial claim to Karabakh: 'the mother cannot be separated from the child.'

The Economist (17 December) estimated that one tenth of Armenia's industry had been destroyed. Whereas strife between Armenia and Azerbaijan seemed to be getting worse, 'simply by not trying to hide the scale of the Armenian disaster, and by letting the world's sympathy flow in, Mr Gorbachev has done more to get the Soviet Union accepted into the family of nations than by any number of speeches about "common homes".' Another London weekly, the *New Statesman and Society*, noted under the headline 'A grisly calculus', that only £262,000 had been given to Mexico to relieve the 1985 earthquake. 'The good side of the affair is its demonstration that, in Western eyes, the Soviets have finally become fully-fledged human beings. The bad side is what it says about our feelings towards the rest of the world's population.'

Extended reports on the earthquake appeared in both *Newsweek* and *Time* of 19 December. According to *Newsweek*, lessons had been learnt from the Mexico City earthquake three years before: the first 24 hours after a quake are crucial, and plenty of emergency doctors are needed on site; rather than use cranes to rescue survivors, rescuers should treat a collapsed structure as a natural cave and go in horizontally with light tools. *Time* noted that the earthquake registered 6.9 on the Richter scale and had resulted in a death toll of 40–50,000. The Mexico City quake in 1985 had registered 8.1 but fewer than 10,000 died. On 26 December *Time* gave attention to the long-term political consequences and the massive cost of reconstruction. Their reporter told the story of his harrowing flight on the first American relief plane to reach Yerevan, sent with a cargo of medical supplies by Ameri-Cares, an NGO based in New Canaan, Connecticut.

As frequently happens after a major disaster, sensational rumours were spreading and some of these were picked up and amplified by the media. Thirty-five days after the earthquake, Tass and Soviet television reported that a man had been rescued alive from a cellar after keeping himself alive with homemade jams and smoked ham. He turned out to be someone with a serious heart condition who wanted hospital treatment. Tass's story was generally believed because it had hitherto been so frugal in providing information of any kind. The incident, says Patrick Aeberhard, shows 'the importance of rumours in the aftermath of tragedies and the role of the press in spreading false information'.[50]

We shall leave our media chronicle here as the earthquake gradually receded from television screens and front pages, under pressure from such horrors as the PanAm plane crash over Lockerbie in Scotland. Later, in 1989, there were to be rumours that much of the foreign aid given to Armenia had disappeared, and that the reconstruction effort had been extremely slow.[51]

Some foreign relief missions

The leading non-Soviet agency by far was the League of Red Cross and Red Crescent Societies, in which officers of the British, German and other national societies worked together as a team. The Red Cross flew in substantial supplies (some twelve plane-loads from Britain alone before Christmas) and its presence remained for many months. The contribution of UNDRO was insignificant. Here we will examine the contribution of some of the other agencies as representative of the non-Soviet effort.

One of the first Western doctors on the scene was Patrick Aeberhard, president of the Paris-based Médecins du Monde, who arrived at Yerevan with supplies and a medical team of 20 (six of Armenian origin) in a Boeing 737 on Saturday 10 December. Dr Aeberhard had twenty years' experience of disasters and wars, but the sight of Spitak was the most shocking he had encountered – an open-air morgue, thousands of coffins, utter devastation, and little contribution to relief by the Soviet army. This improved rapidly after Gorbachev's visit to Spitak.[52] In Leninakan, by contrast, the Soviet army is said to have worked all through the first night after the quake.[53]

MDM was able to respond with its own plane so speedily because it received an appeal only a few hours after the quake from the Armenian church in Paris. On 8 December the

Soviet Embassy in Paris said that they could leave. MDM put together a budget of 1.35 million French francs (about £135,000) and on 9 December the head of the EC's disaster relief department, G. Molinier, authorized an immediate grant covering over half this cost. On arrival in Yerevan, the team found that the main medical need was for kidney dialysis, an emergency short-term technique to treat victims of crush syndrome (by artificially purifying the blood, which is circulated through a semi-permeable membrane that blocks the passage of waste products). Some of the team stayed in a hospital in Yerevan to help medical units there, and the rest went to help in six little villages near Spitak of which there was no news, including Nalband at the epicentre. It turned out that all the houses in the villages had been destroyed and in temperatures of −20°C the snow was beginning to fall.[54] Most of the Soviet relief effort went towards the four cities of Spitak, Leninakan, Stepanavan and Kirovakan, but in fact 58 villages were completely destroyed and more than 100 seriously damaged. (Some of the villages were not reached even by the end of the year because of weather conditions. It is reported that because of a market shortage of batteries for portable radios, in some instances villagers thought there had been a global catastrophe.)[55]

MDM sent further missions to Armenia. On 12 December they sent a dialysis team and medical supplies by air. On 23 December they landed two caravans at Yerevan, to cover rural areas near Spitak and Kirovakan, and medical teams stayed with the caravans for several months. They found little need to practise emergency medicine, but a high incidence of stress, insomnia, eating disorders and other psychological reactions to the disaster, as well as chronic pathologies of various kinds and a poor level of general health.[56] On 30 December MDM (in association with the French government and the EC) sent 103 prefabricated bungalows and sanitary structures by ship to the USSR, for erection in three villages near Spitak. These took some weeks to arrive but were installed during the second part of February. The MDM report speaks of 'astonishing administrative confusion and slowness'. Eventually 185 families were given temporary rehousing as a result of MDM's project, at a total cost of about 1.97 million French francs, averaging just over £1,000 per family.[57]

MDM's most important and ambitious project, also in association with the EC, was to re-equip a whole region of 100,000 inhabitants in the disaster zone with modern sanitary structures.[58] But MDM also sent psychotherapists to help children traumatized by the disaster, and later focused on training Armenian therapists.

Médecins sans Frontières (MSF), also based in Paris, sent its first relief plane on 9 December followed by several others. 175 doctors in all took part in their missions. MSF's longer-term work included kinesitherapy, plastic surgery, prostheses, and psychological help for children.[59] Notified of the need for a kidney dialysis team on 11 December, MSF was unable to provide treatment until 16 December. Xavier Emmanuelli, the team leader, writes of his travelling by convoy from Yerevan to the shattered city of Leninakan, only to find that half of the 'crush syndrome' patients had died of shock within two hours, and the others had been evacuated by military lorry to Yerevan. It was an appeal from the doctors in Yerevan which had triggered off MSF's mission. Other countries, too, had replied to the appeal and Emmanuelli records that he saw warehouses full of artificial kidneys of every design and origin.[60]

From the British end, similar experiences have been recorded. C. J. Rudge, a surgeon who was also expert in haemodialysis, left home under the auspices of the British Red Cross on the evening of 13 December but his plane did not leave Kent until the morning of the 16th and he eventually arrived 11 days after the earthquake. All patients with kidney failure were by then either receiving dialysis already or dead.[61] Another British team recorded that they treated 15 patients for acute renal failure, of whom 13 survived. The cost of the treatment was about £160,000.[62] Much the more pressing need was for syringes, needles, analgesics, plasma and even buckets. However, Armenian doctors are now using the donated haemodialysis machines on a regular basis and have updated their skills.

John Seaman of Save the Children has questioned the cost-effectiveness of this kind of mission, and comments that 'We have to decide why it is we think that injuries that occur after certain kinds of arbitrary events have a special category which means that we do not have to discuss the cost associated with them.'[63] The explanation must be that, as will be argued in Chapter 5, disaster relief operations as refracted through the media belong as much to the domain of magic as to that of reason and technology.

Whatever the relative efficiency of the foreign relief teams in Armenia, whatever the power of their symbolism for an ideal of fraternal cooperation between nations, their contribution could only be marginal to what was done by local people, despite the enormous logistic difficulties and lack of disaster preparedness.

The Armenian disaster gives the clearest warning that, despite technological progress, many earthquake-prone countries have such rapidly increasing populations that only drastic and low-cost improvements in construction practices will reduce the global mortality rate and economic devastation caused by earthquakes in future. Unlike some other types of disaster, earthquakes tend to have particularly serious consequences in middle-income countries.[64]

The seismic metaphor

If victims of mortal illness such as cancer or AIDS are sometimes offended when their disease is taken as a metaphor, the victims of natural disaster might well feel the same way. However, political cartoonists could not resist the opportunity. The *Times* cartoonist, Peter Brookes, drew for the 15 December issue a chasm in the form of a ruptured hammer-and-sickle in front of the Kremlin. In *Le Monde* of 13 December, Gorbachev in hat and overcoat surveys a devastated city, and a hand emerges from a crack in the earth bearing a placard which says 'Arménie libre'. In the next day's issue of *Le Monde*, Serguei shows a chasm which has broken through a thick brick wall that stretches to the horizon, but makes a road for ambulances to pass through. One bystander in a Russian hat is saying to another 'Eight degrees on the *perestroika* scale'. In another cartoon by Serguei, to illustrate an article in the 18–19 December issue on the ineffectiveness of the relief effort, Red Cross parcels are heaped to the left of the frame; a uniformed official wields a rubber-stamp with one hand and with the other he holds out a pen and a receipt to be signed; to the right of the frame a hand emerges helplessly from a jagged fissure in the earth.

The Armenian earthquake was not the only dramatic event in the lead-up to the destruction of the Berlin Wall and the break-up of the Soviet Union; but it was certainly one of them, especially in exposing the weaknesses and corruptions of a hitherto much feared superpower. Furthermore, it drew international attention to ethnic divisions in the Soviet Union and in particular to the 'Transcausian cauldron', in which Karabakh and Nakhichevan[65] could today potentially be the hotbed of a convulsion setting Islam and the Judaeo-Christian West against one another. It just happened that these major political fault-lines coincide with an area of the earth's surface which is 'jammed, like a nut between the jaws of a vice'[66] between vast continental plates performing their slow ballet.[67]

Whereas other earthquakes in living memory have registered higher on the Richter scale or the toll of lives and devastation, the Armenian earthquake of 1988 probably gained the most publicity – and was the most destructive in the USSR this century. The publicity resulted from the Soviet government's policy of *glasnost* and media manipulation; from the novelty of live news coverage of a major disaster in a hitherto closed society; from the international sophistication of the Armenian community; and from the coincidence of natural with political fault-lines.

4  The Cultural Styles of NGOs

With a few exceptions such as Shawcross's *The Quality of Mercy*, the literature on humanitarian agencies is rather thin. There is a tendency to idealize them – a tendency in which they sometimes collude. An aura of what has been called 'secular sanctity' surrounds them. Counterbalancing this tendency, an established charity can expect to be sharply attacked in the media on the rare occasions when it misappropriates funds, spends them incompetently or behaves shabbily. But serious sustained interest in the function and organization of NGOs is relatively new.

Yet they are social institutions as important in many ways as, say, the churches or professional associations. Those NGOs which are the focus of this book are active at the cutting edge of the schism between the industrialized world, where we agonize over the condition of the real estate market and the motor industry, and the developing world, where the accepted criterion of economic success is more likely to be the satisfaction of 'basic human needs'.

Of late, the NGOs are being examined more seriously.[1] Their value systems and policies, and their actions both 'in the field' and within their home constituencies, are likely to come under increasing scrutiny. The main emphasis of this book is on the British agencies concerned with disasters, but it is important to look at the scene from a broader perspective. In the last-chapter, I sought some time depth by means of case studies from the 1960s and late 1980s. The present chapter embarks on a lateral comparison with NGOs from other national traditions. For all the three cases chosen, relations with the media are of the greatest importance, but in different ways.

It would be trite to argue merely that national NGOs are embedded in the cultures of their respective countries. One can go further and show that the most effective humanitarian agencies to emerge in the last 20 years have been markedly 'mononational' in character. Their entrepreneurial spirit is at odds with the infighting, politicking, bureaucratization and lack of accountability which plague even the best of the large international or multinational organizations. In the UN agencies, for instance, it is not uncommon for the most dynamic fieldworkers to feel alienated from the '*seraglio* preoccupations'[2] of their administrators. Oxfam is so British, and Médecins sans Frontières so French, that neither formula is readily extensible into a federal scheme without difficulties. One of the challenges that will be faced by the NGOs over the next 20 years is to maintain their national strengths, while also developing the scale and vision to engage globally with global issues.

I shall look first at the distinctive characteristics of the well-known organizations of 'French doctors'; then at the Swissness of the ICRC; finally at an international agency which has its roots in American-style evangelical protestantism but is now growing to resemble the other Christian NGOs amidst an unusual degree of controversy. The emphasis in each section will be on relations with the media. The chapter concludes with brief notes on two major agencies which so far have managed to grow *without* any significant relationship with the media, and some reflections on how NGOs are seen from the South.

THE 'FRENCH DOCTORS'

The story of the 'French doctors' begins with the meeting of two groups of Frenchmen concerned respectively with the Biafran war and the floods in east Pakistan (now Bangladesh), which resulted in the foundation of Médecins sans Frontières (MSF).

A young doctor, Bernard Kouchner, was working for the

French Red Cross which was cooperating with the ICRC to run the airlift from the island of Fernando Po, one of the last Spanish colonies. The French Red Cross was at that time, though a large organization, as yet unequipped to provide wartime relief, but a small group of volunteer doctors had been assembled – probably as a political gesture by de Gaulle, then President of France, who hoped to extract some advantage for French interests from the war.[3]

Kouchner has described[4] the hair-raising drama of setting out for Uli airport, the beleaguered enclave's lifeline, in a Hercules loaded with dried fish, then having to return to base because of attack from the Federal airforce, and start again in a Finnish plane which landed successfully. The plane was met by Irish priests and mercenaries – and by Biafran immigration officials. Kouchner and his colleagues were then placed in charge of a hospital. Kouchner says that he and a half-dozen French colleagues in this hospital, Awo-Omama, first conceived the idea of MSF.

There were already 300 wounded in the hospital, but one of the fronts was only 15 miles away and the number soon rose to 800 – three to a bed and one underneath. The French team set to work with what Kouchner calls the 'terrible discipline of triage' – sorting out of patients according to their prospects of survival – and they carried out emergency surgery under enemy bombardment, sometimes not sleeping for 48 hours. Even more serious than the surgical emergencies was the famine caused by the economic blockade. Thousands of children were dying every day in Biafra. The French Red Cross team turned a school into a hospital. They found it intolerable to care for a child with kwashiorkor for three weeks, then send him back to his family, only to have him sent back a month later in a worse state. 'By keeping silent, we doctors were accomplices in the systematic massacre of a population.'[5] Drinking palm wine and smoking cigarettes in the sterilization room, Kouchner and his friends hatched their dream of an organization that would, unlike the ICRC, be able to act without the permission of governments.

In October 1968, the Nigerian troops advanced and the Awo-Omama hospital found itself only 500 metres from the front line. Colonel Adekunle, the Federal leader known as the

Black Scorpion, had threatened to kill Red Cross volunteers as if they were mercenaries; he already had a reputation for massacring doctors and patients in other hospitals. The ICRC asked the French doctors to stay at their posts as the troops advanced. They held a meeting and agreed to stay with their patients provided that a press conference were held in Geneva as soon as the Nigerian army arrived, to draw attention to this hospital. 'We were using the media before it became fashionable', writes Kouchner. 'We refused to allow sick people and doctors to be massacred in silence and submission.'

Kouchner tried to get to Geneva himself but was stopped by ICRC officials in Santa Isabel. There was no press conference, only a press release published in Switzerland, to which no one paid attention. He went back to Biafra. Wounded patients left the hospital in a panic and some of them died in the bush. The Biafrans repelled the Federal troops a few hundred metres from the hospital, but a number of patients were lost. To the north, another hospital had been evacuated by its patients; the Nigerians killed the Yugoslav doctors and British missionaries who stayed there.

When Kouchner had joined the ICRC teams as a volunteer, he had signed the usual contract, agreeing never to disclose what he might see in the course of his missions. He decided to break this agreement. Returning to France in early 1969, he started an International Committee against Genocide in Biafra. He drew a direct analogy between the ICRC's silence about Biafra now and about the Nazi murder camps during the Second World War. Kouchner argued that medical secrecy concerned only individuals, not peoples in peril or abuses of human rights. In the event, the ICRC did not object to Kouchner's actions, and indeed its reputation benefited from them. According to Kouchner, at that time the ICRC did not have permanent medical staff, or a medical division in Geneva,[6] though one was set up in 1976 and has proved itself many times over, becoming a particular centre of competence for war surgery.

Kouchner belonged to the then-fashionable Parisian Left and his close colleague, Max Récamier, was a Christian conservative. As the movement came nearer to constituting itself, Kouchner came to question some of the assumptions of the Left, and Récamier to move towards it. Among the leading French intellectuals who supported Kouchner were Sartre, Simone de Beauvoir, Michel Leiris and a number of academics. But some of the Left were less sympathetic.

At the end of the 1960s came the first gibes about mediatization and adventurism. But I had come from a terrible war, I was speaking of a people that had no access to the media, and obeying their order. I was bearing witness. The Biafran sufferers begged me to do so. I had seen their lives ruined and I was striving to give the alarm. I was a sort of look-out man. People accused me of speaking about myself. That is one of the characteristic treacheries of weak minds.[7]

Kouchner and his friends undertook three missions to Biafra in all, and were present at the time of its fall. After the war they formed the GIMCU (Groupement d'Intervention Médico-Chirurgicale d'Urgence). Members of this group went to the Peruvian earthquake in 1970 with Frères des Hommes, and later in the year with the ICRC to the Middle East after Black September, when Palestinians were massacred by the Jordanian Army.

Another landmark in the early history of MSF was the publication of an article about the floods in East Pakistan that appeared in 1970 in the medical journal *Tonus*, which also provided some logistic support. MSF was formally constituted in 1971, but not till the following year did it have an office, secretariat and funds of its own. MSF was from its beginnings highly media-oriented: 'Such a studied concept is a collective achievement, but to be as seductive as this it has to be a journalistic one. We [MSF] are the children of journalism and of medicine.'[8] Kouchner himself had worked as a journalist, and it seems clear that, with his vigorous and inspiring personality, and undoubted courage, he was the natural leader of the group.

Originally, MSF saw its role as providing a pool of doctors to assist established organizations such as the Red Cross,

Frères des Hommes, the Order of Malta, etc. Gradually, MSF began to plan missions on its own account, with the help of Air France and the French civil aviation authority. In 1976, a publicity agency enabled MSF to reach a nationwide public of doctors and the general public, and it began to concern itself with refugee problems. The first MSF poster bore the image of a little girl who seemed to be waiting for her paediatrician from behind the bars of her bed, with the caption: 'In their waiting-room: 2 billion people'.[9] From 1979 it became an established agency with the usual departments such as fund-raising and communications, and in 1980 new sections were founded in other European countries (Belgium, Switzerland and Holland). In 1985, following important nutritional work in Ethiopia, it gained recognition under French law as an organization 'in the public interest' and in 1987 it was nominated as a 'major national cause'.[10]

However, at the end of the 1970s there took place a classic French schism, when a rival organization called Médecins du Monde ('doctors of the world', MDM) was founded. It is hard to get a clear picture from the various protagonists as to exactly what happened. The MDM view is that issues of principle were at stake: they wanted to be free to ignore national borders and act independently of governments, speaking out free from impediment wherever they saw abuses of human rights. They wanted to be a church militant rather than a stuffy, do-gooding bureaucracy. Nearly all the original Biafra team joined Kouchner to break away from MSF.

The MSF view emphasizes the refusal of the schismatics to accept majority voting. A large majority of some 300, as opposed to the breakaway group of about ten, decided that their organization should accept its maturity and acquire the administrative and financial structures necessary to enable the volunteers to practise their emergency medicine effectively. Much of the initiative derived from Claude Malhuret, who had formerly worked with WHO on eradicating smallpox in India. (Malhuret later became a French government minister for human rights, and is now mayor of Vichy and a European *député*.) The *casus belli* was Kouchner's project to send a hospital ship to the China Sea to pick up the Vietnamese refugees known as Boat People. The old guard around Kouchner were particularly attached to the project's symbolism, for the boat happened to be named the *Ile de Lumière* (island of light).

In the debate that took place, the pragmatists argued that there was little to be done to protect the hundreds of little boats, which had already been leaving the coast of Vietnam for up to three years, either from pirates or from other hazards of the enormous China Sea: it was like looking for needles in haystacks. The true problem was political, and it was well beyond the capacity of a small French organization to intervene. The question was where to settle the refugees who were successfully saved or reached a safe haven, since merchant ships were refusing to pick them up and no country was willing to take many of them. Those refugees who survived their often terrible ordeal would for the most part recover from it rapidly, and the ones in need of medical care would be better looked after by the many doctors available on shore.

The schismatics, undeterred by the majority vote against the project, claimed that they represented the truly legitimate MSF. Personal rivalries and ambitions greatly contributed to the rupture. The symbolists remain triumphant about the role of the *Ile de Lumière*, despite its undoubted high cost in financial terms. Kouchner rallied support from a dazzling array of French celebrities, led by Yves Montand, and he persuaded the two grand old men of Parisian intellectual life, Jean-Paul Sartre and Raymond Aron, to shake hands in public after a thirty-year rift, in support of the boat.[11] But one of the leading MSF loyalists, Xavier Emmanuelli, a specialist in anaesthesia and resuscitation, published a stinging article in a journal, *Le Quotidien du Médecin*, in December 1978, entitled 'A boat for Saint-Germain-des-Prés', alluding to the street on Paris's Left Bank which is the heart of the intellectual Latin Quarter.[12] In fact, it does appear that the *Ile* did concentrate on picking up refugees who were already near the coast, though several thousand individuals were helped in one way or another. Emmanuelli now concedes that the boat probably did help to save some lives, but by means of 'instigating politicians to show themselves on the screen, outbidding one another in generosity, welcoming the survivors . . . The exodus did not cease, solutions were not found, but the scenario shifted to a new model – that of a mythological hospital-boat with its evocative name, so white, so luminous . . .'

At the most general level, the symbolism of the *Ile* may be defended. However, it may also have served as a 'pull factor', encouraging disaffected Vietnamese to leave their country – of whom a high proportion would have been murdered by pirates or drowned. The problem that *any* institutionalized aid can become a 'pull factor' is one which the large refugee organizations such as UNHCR, whose annual budget has increased enormously in the last twenty years, are only just beginning to come to terms with seriously.

Ten years later, the political context had changed completely. There is now no worldwide media interest in helping those refugees who are suspected of being merely 'economic migrants', as opposed to political asylum-seekers. Most of the Vietnamese migrants now in Hong Kong are refused the status of asylum-seekers, and this applies for the most part to other Vietnamese migrants and also to their Albanian, Haitian and Cuban counterparts.

Médecins du Monde was officially founded in 1981. Curiously, there does not now seem to be much difference of ideology or practice, as opposed to personalities, between MSF and MDM. MSF is the larger of the two, with an annual budget of about £22 million, mainly from its 700,000 private donors but also with substantial grant-aid from the EC and UNHCR. MDM is about two thirds the size, and considerably less formally structured. Every year it has some 30 missions in operation. As with other smallish organizations that pride themselves on an innovative and unbureaucratic approach, there is a proportionately high risk of funds being spent on projects that do not meet their objectives: in 1989 and 1990, Médecins du Monde had to write off about £900,000 invested in a scheme to promote the sale of handicrafts in deprived areas of the Third World. This gave useful employment to many craftspeople but was discontinued.[13] On the other hand, MDM has a well-designed and informative magazine, *Nouvelles*, which was nominated in 1991 for a French journalists' award, and the general standard of its communications is highly professional. The proportion of MDM's budget spent on administration, communications and fund-raising (about 34 per cent in 1990) is considerably higher than MSF's and by British standards appears to be very high. Yet one must remember that the 'French doctors' themselves give their services either for nothing, or for a small subsistence allowance, so the accounts of such associations are not strictly comparable with agencies that pay salaries to regular field officers.[14]

A third association, the smallest of the three, Aide Médicale Internationale (AMI), was founded in 1979 by Michel Bonnot, a close associate of Kouchner, and others. It differs from MSF and MDM in being deliberately less media-oriented, hence rather more like other agencies. Its hallmark is an insistence that nobody whom it sends on missions should be paid; its management costs are kept to a bare minimum. It is engaged in a number of clandestine, always strictly neutral operations in some of the world's most dangerous trouble-spots, with a discretion that is often appreciated by the people that it helps. Its watchword is 'Working for the Third World, not off the Third World'.

The three organizations were given the generic tag 'French doctors' by American journalists in Afghanistan who were unable to distinguish between the three agencies; and Kouchner has adopted the term. Emmanuelli, the MSF ultra-loyalist, holds that MSF should fight fiercely against this dilution of its image.[15] 'If everyone can be proud of being French, if everyone can recognize in MSF a manifestation of French culture or tradition, continuing to use the expression ["French doctors"] is to be the victim of manipulation.' MSF, he claims, is international: this is true, for there are now European sections in Belgium, Greece, Holland, Luxemburg, Spain and Switzerland, with local variations, and one has recently been founded in Britain. More seriously for Emmanuelli, the vagueness of the expression makes it possible for French politicians to take credit, in a covertly piratical manner, for an initiative originally undertaken by private individuals who subscribe to a universal ideal. According to him, the newer organizations of 'French doctors' merely mimic MSF's work, blurring its image with its donors.[16] The outside observer is likely to be struck, however, by how much the organizations of the 'French doctors' movement have in common.

Everyone is now aware how ready to crumble are national boundaries, but it has taken the French to coin the word *sans-frontiérisme*. Bernard Kouchner, still a flamboyant propagandist, is currently the French Government's Secretary of State for Health and for Humanitarian Action. He gives credit to the British for founding Amnesty International in 1961, but otherwise the initiative has been largely French. Their very language lends itself to florid expressions of humanitarian intent.

According to Kouchner, the ICRC limited its usefulness early in this century when it accepted that it could act only with the consent of national governments. Though the primary role of MSF and the others is to send medical and paramedical teams wherever they are needed – whether for spectacular war surgery or for more mundane jobs such as vaccination, sanitation projects or training of local staff – they all set themselves the task of *témoignage*, bearing witness, which the ICRC has traditionally forbidden itself out of obedience to its long-established rule of discretion (though recently it has become less reticent).

Since 8 December 1988, the UN's Resolution 43/131 has legitimized the crossing of national boundaries by NGOs in order to reach the victims of natural disasters and other similar emergencies. This is Kouchner's famous *devoir d'ingérence* (the duty of intervention) which has now become a *droit* (right).[17] With Kouchner's appointment as a senior minister, the idea has been incorporated in the structure of the French State, and its supporters hope that it will spread. The fact that aid to the Kurds after the Gulf war eventually took precedence over Iraq's national sovereignty is for Kouchner a clear sign of progress, even if effective relief was not extended also to the equally wronged Shiites in the south of Iraq. Whatever may be said against Kouchner by some of his detractors, his commitment to the idea that real historical *progress* is possible in humanitarian intervention has earned him admiration from a wide public in France which is normally sceptical about its politicians. He believes (probably wrongly) that the great massacres, such as those committed by the Khmer Rouge, are now 'behind us'.[18]

Kouchner endorses *la loi du tapage* (the law of hype)[19], seeing journalists and humanitarians as locked into a necessary if often testing partnership. He argues that it is necessary to 'popularize misfortunes and make use of feelings of remorse'. The latest Kurdish crisis was, he claims, 'probably the first time that information saved a people and forced the international community into a humanitarian intervention'. The same must be done tomorrow for other oppressed peoples.

Not unexpectedly, *ingérence* has come up against its critics in Paris and elsewhere, who accuse Kouchner of advocating a battleship diplomacy, of appropriating for the State – inevitably concerned by *realpolitik* at this stage in the evolution of human institutions, and in practice likely to be a White capitalist State – the humanitarian tradition which is better pursued by individuals and NGOs. Kouchner reassures critics that true *ingérence* can be pursued only in the name of UN agencies, the ICRC or NGOs. Against those bold enough to accuse him of neo-colonialism, Kouchner retorts that

> true colonialism is in the heads of white people who think themselves capable of judging as acceptable the woes of others which they would not tolerate in their own families. The worst is rooted in those who make a show of the misfortunes of others, the intellectuals of difference, the guides to the folklore of human perversions guaranteed to reflect perfectly. Misery is so much more attractive in the sun.

The opponents of intervention, a mixture of Right and Left,

> would not want us to help the Afghan women who shouted in our direction, because Muslim males forbade it. They are always on the side of the strongest, they give comfort to the received ruling ideology as an object of ethnographic study. They condemn Western moral attitudes, but admit distant oppressions quite readily.[20]

The difficulties over *ingérence* cannot be so easily dismissed. Who is to decide when and where to intervene? The ICRC is able to continue its quiet, generally unpublicized work of protection – which MSF never provides – and assistance just because of its unique, and constraining, role under international humanitarian law (though this does need to be amended to give the ICRC more power to intervene when governments kill their own people). The UN system is riddled with flaws and appears currently to be too dominated by Western nations, especially the USA, to be the credible basis for a 'new world order'. The First World War resulted, in part, from larger nations dabbling in the affairs of smaller nations. Again, if Hitler had been able to claim the *droit d'ingérence* to 'liberate' the Sudeten Germans, operating perhaps through some off-shore NGO, he might have chosen to do so. Furthermore, reasons of State cause certain regimes like Syria to become favoured by the West despite their flouting of human rights, so that they would presumably not be the targets of humanitarian *ingérence*. Nor would a very big country like China, whose leaders have done more or less as they wished in Tibet. And what of the West's own offences against human rights? In France, Muslim minorities are victims of racial violence from time to time but the Government would presumably not be friendly to 'ayatollahs without frontiers'[21] barging in. The United Kingdom has its own troubles in Northern Ireland. A French journalist has acidly pointed out that 'the Secretariat for Humanitarian Action can be seen as the after-sales service for the gun manufacturers who occupy the neighbouring ministries.'[22]

Some experienced agency workers argue that the cases where *ingérence* is justifiable are not all that common. The failures of the relief system are usually more critical than are the obstacles put in its way. In most cases, food and medical supplies can be brought in through careful negotiation with the sovereign government, however morally distasteful these authorities may be to the agencies. This way of working is made less feasible by the recent collapse of authority in so many nation states following the end of the Cold War (not only ex-Yugoslavia and Somalia but Haiti, Sudan, Liberia,

Afghanistan and others), so that *ingérence* is gaining more supporters.

The most prominent of the 'French doctors' seem to have something in common with Melanesian big-men jockeying for dominance, or Native American chiefs on the north-west coast who build up huge potlatches for the name-corporations that they control. Where Dr Kouchner is suave and worldly – one of the chapters in his *Le Malheur des Autres*, 'The high places of intervention', actually consists of memories of great hotels in the world's trouble-spots, such as the Addis Ababa Hilton, the American Colony in Jerusalem – Dr Emmanuelli in *his* book is like an angry old terrier recently unmuzzled, taking no trouble to conceal his personal hatred of Kouchner and resorting at times to juvenile abuse.

What Kouchner and Emmanuelli have in common is a grand vision of the role of the [white] doctor-humanitarian (Kouchner's 'aristocracy of risk', Emmanuelli's 'glorious mythological conquerors under the immodest eye of cameras the world over').[23] This recurrent theme in the narratives of disaster and relief aid (by no means confined to France) will be considered in Chapter 7 of this book, with special reference to television. Kouchner believes in the social force of the aggressive male hormone.[24] He is consistent in that he revels in the media. Emmanuelli recognizes that MSF owes its success to cooperation with the media, yet he despises television and in particular the reporters who zoom in on the sufferings of victims to give viewers the modern equivalent of a Roman circus. Rony Brauman, the current MSF president, notes that it is often said that humanitarian action is the principal expression today of collective values. There are dangers, he says, in this situation, but nonetheless it is important to recall that 'during its twenty years of existence, MSF has contributed more than anyone else to this phenomenon, by remodelling humanitarian action, by giving it inspiration, scale, in a word the letters patent of nobility. . . .'[25] No one doubts the genuine courage of the 'French doctors', and the record of deaths and injuries in the service of these agencies is testimony to the reality of the risks which they willingly run. During the Gulf war, MSF was running hospitals in northern Iraq before anyone else, and in

1992 was one of the handful of agencies which stayed in Somalia during the civil war and compensated for the ineffectiveness of the UN system.

The difference in style from that of British and almost all other agencies is marked. Few are flamboyant or macho, few ventilate disagreements in the national newspapers, for instance. Yet Save the Children's field officers are often courageous and nearly always work in difficult conditions of one kind or another; they are increasingly willing in special circumstances to cross national frontiers quietly, providing humanitarian aid to the victims of civil strife without the consent of governments. They are prepared on suitable occasions to bear witness against atrocities and also to follow it up with action. Though they live with the 'law of hype' as we all must, their fundamental belief is in trying unobtrusively to help people become self-reliant, serving the beneficiaries' long-term needs as a guiding rule. This requires defining needs with rigour, and staying with parts of the world that are right out of the news, as well as responding to 'glamorous' emergencies. Kouchner is not against this style, far from it, but he calls it working 'in the shade' in a way that will never gather political clout. This is perhaps less than just to what has been achieved by many of the non-French agencies through cooperating with journalists.

Sans-frontiérisme can lead to such absurdities as MSF's abortive mission to China in 1989 to aid the victims of the Tiananmen Square massacre, as if China were not adequately staffed with doctors. Such swashbuckling quixotries are understandably disliked and a little despised by many who work with British and many other NGOs. Sending young people to Africa for a short period without proper instruction in its culture is not always successful, and MSF volunteers have sometimes been criticized for living in colonial-style compounds rather than attempting to share the lives of the local people.[26] Yet within the context of French society – traditionally less generous to private charity than Britain – *sans-frontiérisme* has accomplished a great deal at the level of symbolism in galvanizing the medical profession and enthus- ing the public. The injection of myth and theatre has been quite deliberate. It is probably helping to effect a permanent change in international law, and has also helped the French to be more conscious of poor public health and deprivation within the 'Hexagon' of the Republic. It has helped to ginger up some of the older agencies, as the London Technical Group did in Britain (in much more down-to-earth style) in the early 1970s.[27]

The movement now needs urgently (as its leaders know)[28] to adapt to changing times and invest more heavily in education and training, relying less on a technical approach to medicine and giving more attention to sanitation, prevention and public health. When the movement began, Britain and America were still sending untrained volunteers to the Third World, a practice soon discontinued; and it was then an important innovation to send trained doctors to the Third World as a kind of rite of passage before they settled down to a conventional middle-class career. Now, however, it is recognized that training in Western hospitals is by itself inadequate for effective operation in Third World countries, and there is much other knowledge that overseas field officers need. Dependence on the recently qualified and on a reserve army of medical volunteers reads well in the annual accounts, but it presents problems for a modern agency primarily concerned with strengthening a community's own response to emergencies. Already, about a third of MSF's activities are devoted to technical assistance, with priority given to the transfer of knowledge.[29]

The movement has also generated a number of smaller agencies of great seriousness and value. For instance, Dr Jean-Baptiste Richardier and two other doctors, having gained extensive experience with MSF, founded Handicap International in 1982, an agency based in Lyons (with branches in Belgium and Denmark) which specializes in the care of victims of war, but also of polio, leprosy, tuberculosis or sheer poverty. It has 115 kinesitherapists, technicians, doctors and administrators on missions in 26 countries. Handicap International pulls no punches and is now conducting a vigorous campaign against the sale and massive use of anti-personnel mines, under the slogan 'The Coward's War'.

Typical of the problems which MSF faces was the

Armenian earthquake, discussed in our last chapter. Xavier Emmanuelli went with the MSF kidney dialysis team to treat victims of 'crush syndrome'. In the event, only fifteen victims of this syndrome were treated and saved.[30] According to the economics of disaster relief, most professionals would say that the mission was not justified; in the jargon of the agencies, it is not 'appropriate' (let alone 'replicable'). Fifteen probable deaths, however tragic, do not compare with the terrible damage which a major earthquake does to the local economy and its capital base; and the priority for relief aid should be to help this to become independent again. However, before we dismiss such a mission, we should reflect, with Dr Emmanuelli, that 'if one had asked the fifteen patients who were saved whether their lives were worth such a great effort, their replies would surprise no one'. Medicine has always incorporated a strong individualistic strain which runs against the grain of epidemiology and other collective approaches to health and disease. Emmanuelli concludes his combative book with the challenging observation that there can be no mass humanitarian action, for 'God only knows how to count up to ONE'.[31] (Here Emmanuelli, Catholic by conviction, echoes the Christian philosophy that animated the ancient crusading orders of chivalry, of which the Hospitaller Order of Malta survives, and which must be inimical to any statistical or veterinarian approach to medical relief.)

Kouchner's and Emmanuelli's books both seem to radiate a stereotypical French *gasconnade* or boastfulness, the qualities of brilliant cavalry which can sometimes disconcert foot soldiers. The *panache* shown by Mitterrand and Kouchner in their dangerous visit to Sarajevo in June 1992 is of the same order. Some zippy maxims imparted to new MSF recruits are far from the high seriousness of Oxfam or Christian Aid:

> *Action does not like democracy.*
> *Everything is allowed except what is forbidden.*
> *Only describe a situation in terms of the solutions that you bring to it.*[32]

A leading Paris journalist, Christine Ockrent, has written

that analysts of the humanitarian scene in France should 'treat as they deserve the sickening polemics for Parisian initiates';[33] but polemics, even while they boost fashions and individual egos, can also bring out analytical issues. For instance, Kouchner distinguishes between those humanitarians who are 'owners of the miseries of the world', wanting to 'continue to live off afflictions' (presumably the current directorate of MSF?) and those who intend to eradicate those afflictions. The former have grown self-important as they turn the charity machine. The latter have a 'political apprehension of humanitarian activity' and 'hope for a respite in the assassinations of man by man'.[34]

Behind the flourishes is much solid and careful work, such as that which has earned international standing for the Groupe Européen d'Expertise en Epidémiologie Pratique (Epicentre), a 'satellite' of MSF staffed by paid specialists. It must also be set down to the credit of the 'French doctor' organizations that they are managed in an impressively open way, so that even the weaknesses and contradictions are exposed and subjected to unrestricted critical debate. Most important of all, as a previous UN High Commissioner for Refugees has written, 'The initiatives of Bernard Kouchner and his friends have opened lasting breaches in the anti-humanitarian *realpolitik* of governments'.[35]

THE INTERNATIONAL COMMITTEE OF THE RED CROSS

The ICRC has recently been spurred by events in general, but more particularly by the high profile of Médecins sans Frontières, to become much more media-conscious. However, it is worth looking back in history to see how it once led the way in publicizing humanitarian action; indeed, how the movement's emblem has become to some extent a victim of its own success in becoming so widely disseminated that it is vulnerable to abuse.

Only a part of the ICRC's work is in fact directly concerned with material relief – whereas its role in, for instance, protecting and assisting prisoners and other victims of war and internal strife, including 'political' detainees, in family tracing and in negotiating ceasefires or truces, is unique. But the ICRC is too important an institution to ignore in any study of international relief aid, which it effectively founded in modern times.

Whereas any biography of Florence Nightingale has to come to terms with her imperious personal influence – her canonization as the epitome of dedication and foresight – the founder of the Red Cross, Henry Dunant, is more reminiscent of the Good Samaritan in that his seminal work was the result of accident. A Geneva businessman, he just happened as a young man in 1859 to be trying to negotiate the renewal of a concession in Algeria with the French Emperor, Napoleon III, who was leading the allied French and Sardinian armies to liberate Italy from Austrian rule. Dunant caught up with the army in northern Italy on a hot June evening after the battle of Solferino, where lay tens of thousands of dying and wounded soldiers without medical attention, water or other help. Dunant mobilized help from local people, and – at least according to the oft-repeated legend – he persuaded them to give it equally to the wounded Austrians as well as to the French and Italian soldiers.

Dunant returned to Geneva and in 1862 published *A Memory of Solferino*, a horrific description of the plight of the wounded together with practical proposals for an organization of volunteers and a legal framework to facilitate impartial relief of the wounded. This book was widely circulated and had great influence. As many humanitarians have done since, he next enlisted the support of a famous military figure. General Guillaume-Henri Dufour had in 1847 crushed the seven secessionist *Sonderbund* cantons in Switzerland's civil war; now he was made President of the International Committee for Relief to the Wounded – later to become the ICRC. Henry Dunant then devoted his life to lobbying; and in 1863–4 international meetings were held in Geneva which led first to the founding of the Red Cross, and second to the first Geneva Convention, a treaty ratified remarkably quickly by all the powers. Following a number of revisions to this and the addition of other conventions, the four existing Geneva Conventions were agreed in 1949. The ICRC draws its legal authority from these and two additional protocols adopted in 1977.

Dunant himself became so engaged in his Red Cross work that he neglected his own business affairs and went bankrupt at the age of 39, which in respectable Genevois circles of that day meant becoming a non-person. As an old man he was discovered by an enterprising journalist in an old people's poor-house in a Swiss mountain village. However, during the last fifteen years of his life until his death in 1910, he received many honours including the Nobel Prize.

It is clear that Dunant and his associates used the appropriate medium of their day, a widely circulated printed book, to great effect. The choice of the red cross emblem was itself a master-stroke of publicity. It seems that, before 1864[36], different countries used a variety of different coloured flags to mark their ambulances and hospitals, and these were neither widely recognized nor backed by law. Field hospitals therefore tended, for safety, to be far behind the lines, which resulted in long, distressing and dangerous journeys for the wounded. A symbol was chosen which would be recognized at a distance, universally accepted and backed by law. It would be an emblem of respect and protection for the wounded and those caring for them. The red cross on a white background is now said to have been chosen simply as a compliment to Switzerland, being a reversal of its national flag – without religious connotations. The emblem and treaty were meant to be universal in their appeal, and the religious connotations were probably unintentional.

The Swiss flag is a white cross on a red ground because a white cross was once added as a sign of Christian devotion to the arms of the canton of Schwyz, till then a plain red shield. Schwyz was one of the founding cantons of Switzerland in 1291. The white Swiss cross was used as a symbol to rally the confederate cause against the Austrians in the fourteenth century. Moreover, the cross carries in the European sub-conscious all the connotations of the saga of the Crusades, and a red cross was in fact the badge of the Templars.[37] The official ICRC literature avers with emphasis, citing even the support of the Vatican, that the symbol is as neutral in religion as the organization;[38] but unfortunately it is not possible for even the most influential organization to regulate the connotations of such a powerful emblem as the Crusaders' cross.

As early as 1876, the Ottoman Empire complained that the Red Cross gave offence to Muslim soldiers, and said that it would use the Red Crescent as the protective sign for its own ambulances. Since 1906 Iran was permitted to use the Red Lion and Sun, until in 1980 the Iranian government and hence the national society adopted the red crescent. Israel uses the Red Shield of David for its armed forces medical services and its own national society, though states have never admitted this in the Geneva Conventions, which is the source of some friction. More than 25 Muslim countries now use the Red Crescent. The movement is now known as the 'International Red Cross and Red Crescent Movement', which creates problems in some countries where communities of several faiths co-exist – whether Christian, Muslim or other – and an insoluble problem in a country where neither Cross nor Crescent is acceptable. The presence of the two emblems side by side in many contexts probably gives their religious connotations a salience which they would not have otherwise in the late twentieth century, for the cross itself in one form or other has been adopted by nation-states for all manner of military and civil purposes. The protective power of the red cross would be that much stronger if it could be accepted as the sole emblem, devoid of any religious connotation, but this seems a most unlikely prospect at present.

Another serious problem arises from the extraordinarily successful 'penetration' of the red cross emblem. This is that it is misused so widely to mark first-aid posts or medical equipment and supplies that its significance as the hallmark of the medical services of the armed forces, and the International Committee of the Red Cross, is diluted. Use of the emblem for commercial or publicity purposes is, in fact, forbidden by law but this is not widely enforced in most countries. National Red Cross and Red Crescent Societies are allowed to use the emblem to identify premises, vehicles, equipment or personnel, but it must be small. The European Community requires a white cross on a green ground, rather than a red cross on a white ground, to be used to identify first-aid kits and the like.

Some pharmacists' shops in the UK have chosen to use the sign of a green cross on a white background.

It is a serious breach of law to transport armed troops by ambulance, or to fly a red cross flag over a munitions dump, but in parts of the world where the writ of international law is weak, the emblem is often abused. For instance, in Liberia in 1991 the emblem was commonly displayed in shop windows and on vehicle windscreens. The ICRC delegation and the National Red Cross Society have cooperated with the government to try to curb this practice.[39]

During the civil war in former Yugoslavia in 1991–2, the emblem was frequently abused to shield the transport of arms. From August 1991, the ICRC appealed regularly on television and radio, and in the newspapers, for respect to be shown for humanitarian values and the Red Cross emblem – amid hysterical, frantic and vengeful propaganda broadcast by the television stations on both sides.[40] By the middle of May 1992, the ICRC was the only foreign agency left in Sarajevo, capital of Bosnia-Herzegovina. On 19 May, an ICRC delegate, Frédéric Maurice, died as a result of an apparently deliberate attack on the Red Cross convoy bringing medical supplies to the beleaguered city; a local Red Cross worker was wounded.[41] The ICRC was forced to leave, so Sarajevo was left without any international humanitarian presence. Some Red Cross personnel present said that they had never witnessed such brutal atrocities, and a number of agonized articles in the Swiss press argued that the world was seeing a regression to the state of affairs before Dunant and Solferino.

Deliberate abuse of the emblem, and ignorance of its meaning in some parts of the world, are matters of grave concern to the Red Cross directorate. The issue should be of wider concern, too: for any erosion of respect for the red cross emblem, which has been the subject of steady 'promotion' since 1864, will surely weaken efforts to establish much newer badges such as those of the UN, the EC and voluntary agencies such as MSF and Save the Children. None of these symbols, however, carry the Red Cross's message of protection as well as neutrality, which derives from international humanitarian law.[42]

The International Red Cross and Red Crescent Movement

has a structure which is little understood except by those who work with it in some way. The ICRC has no management control over the National Societies, which have been set up in almost every country in the world. The International Conference has approved fundamental principles which apply to all components of the movement; the ICRC has statutory responsibilities to see they are maintained and disseminated. The ICRC recognizes new societies according to the conditions set out in the movement's statutes. The National Societies themselves vary greatly in their strength and in their range of activities across a wide medico-social field. The National Societies are all independent from each other: there is even a Swiss Red Cross, quite separate from the ICRC, though sometimes confused with it by the non-Swiss press. The National Societies are members of the International Federation (formerly League) of Red Cross and Red Crescent Societies, which has a secretariat office in Geneva entirely separate from the ICRC and concentrates for the most part on coordinating National Society assistance to the victims of 'natural' disasters, developing National Societies, and caring for refugees in non-conflict zones. The Federation, the National Societies and the ICRC meet together every two years, and meet with representatives of the States party to the Geneva Conventions at the International Conference of the Red Cross and Red Crescent, usually every four years. A number of representatives of NGOs and others may attend in an observer capacity.

As one might expect from such a complicated structure, there is a considerable amount of micro-political tension within the movement. At present, the leadership of the Federation secretariat is hoping to become a more operational body, but is meeting resistance from many of the larger National Societies, who wish the secretariat to be the coordinator and to preserve their own freedom of action – particularly in order to be able to show their own domestic donors where and how their money is being spent.

The movement is also subject to pressures of a macro-political kind. For instance, in 1986 the International Conference, held in Geneva, voted to suspend the South African governmental delegation from taking part in that conference, despite the wishes of the ICRC and over 50 National Societies (who declined to take part in the vote on the issue, in order to preserve their own political neutrality).[43] Even taking account of the abhorrence in which the South African State was generally held at that time, this political issue was a dangerous precedent for the movement, since one of its 'fundamental principles' is to endeavour '*to relieve the suffering of individuals, being guided solely by their needs*'. Further- more, '*the Movement may not take sides in hostilities or engage at any time in controversies of a political, racial, religious or ideological nature.*'

A similar macro-political blow hit the movement in 1991. In November, its 26th International Conference, in Budapest, was abandoned because the Israeli and the US governments would not accept that observer status be given to 'Palestine' – possibly in reprisal for the PLO's attitude during the Gulf war. The delegation was to have been led by Yasser Arafat in person, despite a special visit to him in Tunis by the ICRC's President and the Chairman of the Standing Commission, who was also head of the Jordanian Red Crescent, to try to reach agreement. The ICRC was ready to risk a vote, but the Federation and some of the National Societies on the Standing Commission responsible for the conference were not, and the conference was cancelled at the last moment. In particular, some European and especially Scandinavian societies were worried about the effect of any scandal on their home constituencies. The result was that the huge effort put into planning the conference – intended to cover humanitarian law, the protection of civilians in war zones, and new laser weapons, among other things – was to a great extent wasted.[44]

The ICRC has also had to face serious criticism in recent years. There seems little doubt that it used to be a somewhat self-satisfied organization until it was forced, by pressures from MSF and others, to change and adapt to media interest. One of the most reliable chroniclers of the Biafran war has recorded that the ICRC's 150 staff sent to Fernando Po were 'many of them entirely unsuitable for the job'.[45] Its image was also temporarily damaged by the revelation in 1988 that, although the Committee in Geneva had information about the Nazis' genocide of Jews in 1942, they decided they were not

legally authorized to take action in internal matters. The
ICRC's defence is that first, at the time they had as yet no
powers under the Geneva Conventions to assist civilian
populations; and second, that if they had protested about
treatment of the Jews they would probably not have been
allowed by the Nazi authorities to continue their work for
prisoners of war held by Germany. The historian Jean-Claude
Favez, Rector of the University of Geneva, concludes that the
Committee was under pressure from the Bern government –
and with a German regime only 6 kilometres away from their
Geneva headquarters.[46]

Even if Favez's interpretation is fair, and without seeking to
belittle in any way the horror of the Holocaust, there are few
organizations, however respected, that do not have some less
creditable episode in their history to set against their positive
achievements. The ICRC deserves credit for having eventually opened its archives to scholars. A senior official of the
ICRC expressed a personal view to me that he is more worried
about some of the outrages against human rights that have
occurred during *his* active career, and which the ICRC has not
protested about adequately – and he gave the particular
example of Tibet.

Confidentiality and discretion are at the heart of the
ICRC's protection work.[47] It may receive information from
Amnesty International about human rights abuses and seek to
alleviate them discreetly. Its reports on prison visits are
confidential. Its rare, though increasingly self-assured, de-
nunciations are confined to breaches of international humanitarian law in conditions of conflict. It seeks to *persuade* –
something which Dunant and his co-founders were evidently
good at from the beginning. But persuasion can be both public
and private, and the ICRC has usually opted for the private
mode, because guarantees of confidentiality can persuade
authorities to allow the ICRC access to victims such as
political detainees.[48]

One is tempted to see an analogy between these ICRC
characteristics and the qualities which have made the Swiss
such successful private bankers. The analogy probably has
some pertinence, but an ICRC 'delegate' (i.e., field director)
who puts his life on the line in Lebanon or Cambodia, trying

to give protection and support in desperate conditions, is as far removed as one can imagine from the upholstered banker who takes risks with cash-flow rather than blood.

A senior press official of the ICRC told me that they have a real problem today because in the past the organization adopted a disdainful response to the media. Many journalists now in key positions had been snubbed in the past and now have to be won over. Geneva newspapers cover the affairs of the ICRC generously – with a due sense of responsibility for intelligent reflection in the world's humanitarian capital, but without neglecting polite sniping between the ICRC President and Bernard Kouchner on the matter of *ingérence*. Yet the ICRC is somewhat neglected by the international press.

The ICRC is an expensive organization to run because it is located in Geneva where the cost of living is high, although its salaries are not exorbitant by Swiss standards.[49] However, it cannot be compared precisely with other NGOs, and in a sense is not an NGO at all since its authority derives from decisions made by governments. It is able (though a private Swiss institution) to enter agreements with and have formal diplomatic contacts with States, and has observer status at the UN. One journalist has described organizations like MSF as standing to the Red Cross as the freedom-fighting priests of Latin America stood to the Vatican in the 1970s: 'compromising, annoying, but complementary and indispensable'.[50] To survive amidst a more competitive environment for humanitarian agencies, the ICRC emphasizes that it does not merely provide assistance and relief, but chiefly *protection* underwritten by international humanitarian law – and this protection cannot be provided by MSF, Oxfam, Save the Children or anyone else.

One of the effects of the mediatization of aid is that all donors, not only individuals but also States, want to see how their money is being spent and take a degree of credit for it. This is true of the National Societies (who in 1990 contributed 4 per cent of the budget of 360 million Swiss francs, and an additional 50 million SF in kind and/or services), it is true of donor states (who contributed 75 per cent, including 9 per cent from Sweden and 20 per cent from Switzerland), and it is true of the European Community – which contributed 18 per cent and is increasingly keen to establish a media profile in its emergency work. The ICRC is thus keenly conscious of the need to propagate a wider knowledge of its work; as many as 65 of its 650 employees are in its Communications Department. In October 1991 its press office published a detailed and lively leaflet describing its work during the Gulf crisis of 1990–1, with articles by 20 ICRC staff,[51] admitting in the introduction that this kind of illustrated publication is 'rather unusual for us'.

The discretion of the ICRC has sometimes been criticized as leading to paralysis (Kouchner has been one of the critics). The disciplines imposed on their delegates must sometimes be hard to bear in the field, when a more obvious human response would be to denounce or to help individuals escape from oppression. Dres Balmer, a disillusioned delegate in El Salvador during the civil war, writes in a fictional account of his unease in meeting the eyes of a Swiss compatriot who is trying to help individual Salvadorians gain recognition as political refugees:

> She blanches and asks me 'What do you do then?' In spite of my rapid explanations and my manic listing of our principles and limitations, I feel I am rather shabby. I think of our delegates, administrators, secretaries, auxiliary staff, cars, offices, transmitters, apartments, all our equipment, and I have difficulty in doing anything that relates usefully to her desire to give immediate help. . . .[52]

Balmer writes as a disgruntled ex-delegate. Supporters of the ICRC point out that some of its greatest achievements must by their nature be unpublicized – in particular, negotiating the exchange of prisoners or saving civilian lives, which can benefit many tens of thousands of people on a single occasion,[53] but which would not be agreed to by local authorities without an assurance of confidentiality. When we think of the ICRC we should recall not only the discretion of private banking, but the discretion of medicine and pastoral care. One of the reasons why psychoanalysis sometimes has difficulty in proving its efficacy is that its practitioners are prevented by professional ethics from parading their successes, while patients who have been helped are usually unwilling to give testimony – and psychoanalysts are soft targets for criticism or ridicule by colleagues or patients who are disaffected.

It is clear that if there were no ICRC, something like it would have to be invented. For example, during the 1962 Cuban missile crisis, arrangements that the ICRC should inspect Soviet ships were put in place at the request of the UN Secretary-General, and would have been an indispensable backstop against nuclear war breaking out if the two superpowers had not backed off from confrontation, as they eventually did.[54] Recently, after the Gulf war ceasefire, the ICRC presided over meetings between senior officers of the Iraqi and coalition armies to negotiate the repatriation of prisoners-of-war and other matters.[55]

The most serious threat to the ICRC's unique position flows from the fact that its neutrality has been associated historically with the neutrality of Switzerland. Switzerland's own once bloody ethnic and religious internal conflicts now seem far in the past, and resolved as satisfactorily as any human conflicts are ever likely to be. Its army is indeed an important part of its national life, but it is dedicated almost entirely to defence of the land from a hypothetical invader. Switzerland has built up a unique position for itself: Geneva is the city where envoys of nations in conflict can meet in relative harmony and safety. The Swiss Confederation is host to the United Nations yet not a member of it, like a benevolent bachelor uncle who provides a lakeside holiday home for squabbling kids. But Swiss industry is now under pressure from German and Japanese competition and Switzerland may eventually agree to join the EC. It is becoming a country more like others where money inflates, stock markets crash and even the odd bank is known to fail. It has also, to its honour, tightened up its banking laws so that the country is no longer freely used as a centre for the profitable laundering of 'narcodollars' and other tainted money.

The ICRC has hitherto provided an outlet for the public spirit and adventurousness of young Swiss men and women who seek a cosmopolitan and challenging field for their efforts, sometimes at grave risk to their personal safety,[56] while retaining their affiliation to a Swiss institution. One should not forget, however, that the ICRC's hundreds of 'local employees' do a great deal to ensure the institution's continuity and institutional memory: in Israel and Lebanon, some local staff have been working for 20 years or more, whereas a delegate may move on after one or two years. In common with other European agencies, the ICRC pays them local rates though their responsibilities are sometimes similar to those of an expatriate relief delegate. Until recently, only Swiss staff could undertake 'protection' work.

In exchange for the Swiss government's annual contribution of 73 million Swiss francs to operating costs, Switzerland gains immense international prestige – and it may be that the contribution is regarded to some extent as a financial setoff against the benefits which Switzerland gets from the presence of the UN through spending by the various agencies and handsomely paid expatriate employees.[57] The ICRC President, in reply to a journalist's question, has not denied that the ICRC may bring more to Switzerland financially than the value of its contributions – for he is currently in need of an increased budget to cover a huge expansion of its commitments, and urges the government to be even more generous than it is. But he says that it is on the prestige and political image which the ICRC gives to Switzerland that the institution rests its case.[58]

The current president of the ICRC, Cornelio Sommaruga, is faced with the extraordinary challenge of steering it through the inevitable process wherein the Swiss polity becomes less rarefied, more like that of its neighbours. With Jesuitic finesse, he is attempting to detach conceptually the neutrality and independence of the ICRC from that of Switzerland. An observer new to the scene might well suggest, as the solution to his dilemma, the thorough internationalization of the ICRC, changing its image as the private domain of a Swiss governing body – for at present only Swiss citizens may be members of the governing Committee, though about half the medical staff and a fifth of head office staff are non-Swiss. Sommaruga, however, deprecates this line of argument on the grounds that a fully internationalized ICRC would risk becoming an arena for political intrigue and manipulation, like the UN. Sommaruga robustly defends the 'mononationality' of the ICRC,[59] claiming that it is possible for the members of the Committee to abstract themselves to a great extent from their own cultural and social context. He adduces a case in which the ICRC once had to negotiate about the release of hostages from some hijacked airliners, one of which belonged to Swissair; this was never raised as an obstacle by any of the parties involved in the affair. Another example he takes from the recent Gulf conflict, when Iraq might have doubted the impartiality of the ICRC since Switzerland had adopted sanctions against the country, but it 'rediscovered in the field the Committee's independence'.[60]

Speaking as the *de facto* reserve banker of humanitarianism, Sommaruga alludes to the 'capital of confidence of which the ICRC is the depositary'. He goes on: 'Even given the hypothesis of a Switzerland no longer neutral, the ICRC can remain Swiss and neutral and it can act effectively thanks to its moral authority as the servant of those who suffer.' It refrains from acting in situations where it can only do so under the military protection of parties to the conflict, or even under the protection of observers such as those appointed by the EC.[61] 'If a State's neutrality is passive, or at least reactive, humanitarian neutrality is disposed towards action.'

During the Second World War, some ICRC convoys carried the Swiss flag beside the red cross flag. But when the ICRC embarked in 1941 on a major operation for the relief of German-occupied Greece, the Allies did not rate the neutrality of Switzerland high enough to lift a blockade and allow provisions to pass through to Greece. Sweden's neutrality was invoked as being more creditworthy than Switzerland's.[62]

These subtleties have evidently not been communicated to a senior executive of one National Society of the Red Cross to whom I spoke, who saw the ICRC's position of independence and neutrality more simply, as being closely tied to that of the Swiss nation and likely to be eroded if and when Switzerland joins the EC. For one thing, all EC citizens should under Community rules be eligible for employment.

The future of the ICRC is of the greatest importance. M. Sommaruga is a former secretary of state for foreign economic affairs in the Swiss government. Not everyone believes him when he declares that the Swiss government and the ICRC are, though cordial, totally independent of each other.[63] The membership of the Committee, which perpetuates itself by cooptation, was in the old days 'the preserve of good Genevan families' and doubts were expressed about their expertise as a group in the context of such great and specialized responsibilities.[64] Now membership is extended to personalities drawn from Switzerland as a whole, and there is a growing tendency to appoint professionals. Sommaruga himself now acts as an executive chairman of an executive board which includes members of the management as well as the governing Committee. By all accounts, the president is a personality of the greatest energy, dedication and administrative ability, yet from the perspective of the British voluntary sector, governed by English charity law, it is surprising to see no clear separation of responsibilities between the governing body and the executive. Though Sommaruga is on record as wishing to resist the encroachment of bureaucracy on humanitarian agencies, he operates an organizational structure with an executive Presidency which is nearer to that of the Vatican, or large companies that combine the posts of chairman and chief executive, than it is to that of Oxfam. The size of the headquarters staff in relation to the field remains a target of criticism – though this may be misguided, since the head office staff have responsibility for many non-field responsibilities, such as the development of international humanitarian law.

Whatever the theoretical virtues of mononationality, there are also dangers of insularity or provincialism which the Red Cross movement does not quite escape. For instance, the magazine *Red Cross Red Crescent* (the popular magazine of the movement as a whole, distributed in three languages to 160 countries) used as the front cover for its May–August 1991 issue a photograph of the glaring, reproachful face of a sickly African child – which would not, in 1991, have been published in a similar publication from one of the major British agencies. Even though this particular choice of picture could be defended, it seems that the whole anguished debate in the agencies about visual imagery (Chapter 5) has passed the ICRC by.

It is rumoured that the ICRC has some difficulty in recruiting enough employees of high calibre from Switzerland, and retaining them when they have been trained. This problem does not exist for British agencies, where low salaries are compensated by high job satisfaction and strong competition for the jobs.

For those who contend that democracy and representativeness are often inimical to effective action (as the MSF slogan quoted above would have it), M. Sommaruga may be the strong man that the ICRC needs to guide it into the next century which Kouchner declares will be the 'century of the humanitarian'.[65] He is clearly concerned about the fate of the United Nations ideal. The UN was originally conceived as an international civil service independent of national governments; but it has been politicized ever since its staffing policies were first manipulated by the Americans, then by the Soviets and the Third World bloc.

The National Societies of the Red Cross and Crescent (despite being auxiliaries to the humanitarian services of their governments) ought to maintain their autonomy in order to be able to act in accordance with their fundamental principles. This is not always true in practice. One observer has estimated that only a small proportion of National Societies are genuinely independent of their governments, and the movement's independence suffered particularly in eastern Europe during the Communist period.

It is not only in 'second-tier' nations that their independence is called into question. The French Red Cross lost a great deal of prestige in January 1991 as a result of the *affaire Habache*, when a hard-line Palestinian terrorist leader from Tunis was admitted to Paris for medical treatment, under Red Cross auspices. The president of the French Red Cross, Georgina Dufoix, who was forced to resign, was also a close political supporter of President Mitterrand and one of his governmental advisers. The incident may be seen as lending support to the ICRC's concept of mononationality.

Yet we now inhabit a world where national borders are blurred in so many ways, and where in most other fields of action insularity is a recipe for decline. Switzerland is a small country, likely to be at an increasing disadvantage in bilateral relations with larger countries until it is completely integrated with the EC. The ICRC is sometimes sucked unwillingly into disagreements between the Swiss government and others.[66] The mononationality principle, which was endorsed by the International Conference, involves risks which it will require political genius to avert. Ultimately, the future of the ICRC's *suissitude* will depend on whether the majority of Third World governments are prepared to accept it.

'The unsung heroes of the Red Cross tend to avoid publicity since it can compromise their ability to negotiate the delivery of aid to victims.'[67] As a nation, Switzerland is deeply distrustful of would-be heroic posturing, and has produced few examples of what is conventionally regarded as individual 'greatness'. Whatever human failings the ICRC may be accused of, it must stand as an exemplary institution and reminds us that among the 'great' individuals that Switzerland *has* produced was perhaps the greatest engineer in the history of bridge-building – Robert Maillart, whose well-known bridges are 'immaterially spun in space'.[68] Red Cross delegates spin bridges between human beings, never losing touch with the idea of the individual (which is why family tracing is so central to its work). In this respect, ICRC differs from an organization like WHO or CARE International which concentrate on general programmes. Dr Rémi Russbach, the ICRC's chief medical officer, told me:

> Some values are universal. When I was visiting some prisoners of war in the Middle East, the group was very politicized, continuing the fight on a political level. They thought that by improving their conditions we were helping their enemy to improve his reputation, so they refused to fill in family messages for ICRC. I entered the prison, took my stethoscope and spoke to an old man about his health, and whenever I was alone or in a dark place some prisoner gave me a family message. The group was politically against us, but each prisoner was very happy to give news to his family. So in *private* there are universal values. The ICRC is based on this value, and it's very exceptional not to find this value with an individual. Only one or two times in my life I was not

able to find human feeling in someone, he was so completely politicized.

Which other agency would you work for if you couldn't work for ICRC?

The ICRC corresponds most closely to my philosophy of human beings rather than programmes. As for children, I am a paediatrician but I don't accept the separation of children from adults, though this is done by other agencies for purposes of fund-raising. . . . In the ICRC, we are big but still individual-oriented.

Under Sommaruga, the ICRC has not only become more vocal in denunciation, but has also encouraged public debate about the grave dilemmas that it faces. Is it right to arrange for the evacuation of Bosnian Muslims from Serbian prison camps, when this is actually contributing to the Serbian goal of 'ethnic cleansing'? Is it right to pay armed soldiers to protect food and personnel in Somalia, as the ICRC like other agencies has been obliged to do in order to save thousands of lives? In its largely unnoticed but actually momentous adaptation to the media regime, the ICRC leadership has shown determination and intelligence, and it has stuck unswervingly to its principles. Internally its major problems relate to organizational structure. Externally, it must address its relationship to its host State and the wider comity of nations.

WORLD VISION

World Vision, with a turnover of US $259 million in 1991, is among the largest and most globally integrated aid organizations, and it has been particularly prominent in its use of the media and modern marketing techniques, including the telethon. It is also easily the most controversial of the larger agencies. I shall outline its history[69] and its present position, with special reference to World Vision of Britain, showing how the controversy surrounding World Vision points up problems in the NGO scene as a whole. To avoid any misunderstanding, I should make explicit that I am personally unsympathetic towards evangelistic protestantism, but seek to describe the situation as objectively as possible.

World Vision was founded in 1950 during the Korean War by Dr Bob Pierce, who had been travelling in Asia for Youth for Christ. He is said to have written in the flyleaf of his Bible, 'Let my heart be broken with the things that break the heart of God'. While in Korea he preached, visited schools and orphanages, and made documentary films to motivate Christians for mission. WV's early work included help for war orphans and refugees, a children's hospital and evangelism in Korea. During the 1960s its work spread to Taiwan and Vietnam, and it responded to an earthquake in Iran and a volcanic eruption in Indonesia. In the late 1960s Pierce was replaced by W. Stanley Mooneyham, a former press secretary to Billy Graham and organizer of the first Graham-inspired world evangelism congress. Between 1970 and 1990, WV grew rapidly: from 20 countries served to 96, from 357 projects to 6,057, from annual expenditure of US$7 million to US$224 million. WV was active during the Vietnamese 'Boat People' crisis with Operation Seasweep, also in and around Cambodia[70] and in most of the highly publicized disasters of this period, both natural and man-made. Its budget was greatly augmented in the mid-1980s by public response to famine in Africa. From showing films on Korean refugees in church basements, WV had turned in the early 1970s to fund-raising in the home, through television.

In 1978 a 'Declaration of Internationalization' was signed by key executives which established World Vision International (WVI) as a separate entity, with the result that now the presence of Americans on the international board and in senior WVI leadership is no more than about 25 per cent. Some 52 per cent of WVI's revenue (for 1990) still comes from the USA, but it is also one of the major agencies in Canada, Australia and New Zealand. WVI runs a liaison office in Geneva and has working relationships with major UN agencies. The British offshoot was founded in 1982 and is constituted as an autonomous independent trust under English charity law, but with close affiliation to WVI. WV of Britain's revenue for 1991 was £11.4 million – a sharp increase on the year before when income had been depressed on account of a hostile television programme broadcast by Channel Four. This resulted in a shortfall in donations, and was the subject of a successful action for libel by WV.

Officials of WV urge that the agency should be evaluated on the basis of what it actually does today. But it has to be noted that WV's impressive financial and operational growth has been dogged by unrelenting criticism – both from secular liberals and from Christian agencies, especially all who are opposed to Christian evangelism in the Third World in the context of dependence on relief work. These charges will be summarized before we seek to assess their weight.

One line of criticism has been allegations of association with the right wing. WV officials have conceded that the agency's early history was rooted in cold-war attitudes when 'part of being a missionary was to be anti-Communist'.[71] Billy Graham and his associates at that time were stridently patriotic. Persistent but unsubstantiated rumours used to mention too close an association with US foreign policy or even a possible involvement with the CIA. A supporting allegation is that WV is too unthinking a promoter of capitalist values.

A second criticism has focused on the agency's avowed commitment to evangelical Christianity. The mainstream Christian church agencies – Britain's CAFOD and Christian Aid and their worldwide counterparts – draw a sharp demarcation between missionary work and humanitarian aid, though everyone admits that in earlier less enlightened days it was common practice for missionaries of every denomination to gain converts among people in adversity by means of material aid. 'WV's long-range goal', stated an official handbook to policy in 1980, 'is that every childcare project, every relief program, and every other ministry of World Vision should draw people to Christ our Savior.'[72] Some critics have gone further and accused WV of espousing fundamentalism. Its official Statement of Faith asserts a belief in the Bible as 'the inspired, the only infallible authoritative Word of God', in 'regeneration by the Holy Spirit' as 'absolutely essential' for the 'salvation of lost and sinful man', and that those who are not 'saved' will be 'lost unto the resurrection of damnation'.[73]

Third, the agency has been accused of excessively emotional fund-raising campaigns. Answering this point, the same 1980 handbook defends them vigorously:

> WV's programs and informational pieces are often emotional, and there's a very good reason for that. The needs with which WV works *are* very emotional. It is difficult for most of us to realize the extreme physical and spiritual needs of people thousands of miles away. But WV field workers have been with these people, and have seen their desperate needs. When they report what they see, it would be unethical for us *not* to relay the severity of the situation to concerned friends. Emotional involvement is a part of decision making and WV shows emotion not to unfairly arouse false feelings but to present reality and invoke caring, proper decisions.[74]

Fourth, it has been argued that WV is operated too much as a business. For instance, WVI uses a centralized banking system with the Crédit Suisse in Singapore to coordinate its international transactions by telegraphic transfer. In general it makes clear that pumping money into the organization is a top priority.

Fifth, WV is sometimes accused of fragmenting Third World communities by creating new patronage and leadership structures. In certain donor countries too, such as New Zealand and Ireland, there has been conflict with the traditional churches over the churches' traditional Christmas and Lenten appeals in which WV's participation has been felt as intrusive.

Sixth, WV has allegedly acted in ways which promote dependence – by giving handouts, for example, or in emphasizing short-term relief more than long-term development.

Seventh, it is claimed that WV is ethically unscrupulous in trying to be 'all things to all men'. For instance, its '24 Hour Famine' campaigns aimed principally at young people, in which donors abstain from solid food for 24 hours, raise some £2 million a time in the UK; the promotional literature makes no mention of WV's evangelical aims and is entirely secular in content. Its dual aspect, humanitarian and religious, enables it to present whichever face it chooses as the more advantageous. Similarly, WV of Britain can present itself either as a home-grown national institution when responding to local insularities, or as the most sophisticated of global networks.

Let us deal one by one with these objections in the context of the actual current policies and practices of WV and, particularly, its British arm. First, though probably WV did have connections in the early days with the American 'evangelical' Right, it would appear that these have been severed. WV United States dissociates itself from conservative groups such as Focus on the Family. WVI and WV of Britain consistently support Palestinian rights, to give one example. Again, the Australian President of WVI has recently published his view that 'a fair reading of history will show the roots of the Gulf War go back far beyond Iraq's occupation of Kuwait; that the occupation and the war might have been averted by patient, sensitive diplomacy'[75] – which amounts to an indictment of President Bush. As regards capitalism, WVI is firmly committed to the promotion of community development through small enterprises, revolving loans, and so on, but this policy – whatever its problems of adaptation to local conditions – can hardly be excoriated at a time when state socialism is losing credibility everywhere in the world.

The second charge exposes a real theological division between WV and many of its liberal Christian critics. WV has no connection with the peripheral sects such as the Jehovah's Witnesses. Evangelistic Christianity in many parts of the USA is not peripheral, as in Europe, but mainstream. The executive director of WV of Britain, Charles Clayton, maintains that WV adheres to what he calls 'historical Christianity' and that there is nothing in the Statement of Faith which contradicts the traditional teaching of the Anglican or Catholic churches.

Yet in practical terms probably the majority of practising Anglicans and Catholics in Britain today do not believe in the automatic damnation of those who do not embrace Christ. Teaching about sin and hell is widely discouraged as likely to have undesirable psychological consequences. Moreover, the

influence of relativistic thinking and anthropological knowledge has caused the more sophisticated churchpeople concerned with the Third World to damp down Christianity's
claims to exclusiveness, recalling that 'There are many
dwelling-places in my Father's house' (*John*, 14.2), and that in
global terms Christianity is still a minority religion despite its
huge missionary success over the centuries. Christian Aid and
CAFOD confine their objectives, on the whole, to relieving
suffering and promoting material development. Christian Aid
does enclose printed prayers with its appeal circulars for
supporters to use privately, and it takes its Christian
commitment seriously – for instance, in publishing a book of
prayers in solidarity with poor people. CAFOD, likewise,
produces each year a number of liturgical materials at the
time of Family Fast Day for inclusion in religious services, as
well as theological reflections for Advent and Lent.

Proselytism, in the sense of offering aid with religious
strings, is explicitly forbidden by WVI official policies.[76]
Bearing witness to the Gospel seems to be more permissible
but is 'strictly regulated', according to a WV of Britain
spokesman. In practice, the churches with which WV
cooperates in many countries, especially in Africa, are often
the same as those with which Christian Aid and CAFOD
work. If evangelistic Christianity in industrial countries is a
reaction against secularization – it is perhaps fairly characterized as a simplified form of belief which avoids some of the
challenges of multi-cultural societies – then it may find a
ready welcome in countries which have not yet experienced
modernization, or those which are recovering from the
collapse of Communism as a religion-surrogate. Though WV
protests that it has no wish to usurp the role of churches, its
loyalty to a model of Christianity which is in some ways 'neo-
colonial' is likely to draw continuing criticism both from
secular agencies and from the more self-critical church
agencies.

Yet in another sense WVI is the opposite of colonial in that
it takes the lead in indigenization and the phasing out of
'expats'. For instance, World Vision of Malawi employs 125
people of whom all are Malawian except for one Ghanaian.
(Incidentally, WV of Britain's overseas director is a Malawian,

Jeff Thindwa, who has earned approval even from those who dislike WV's ideology.)

Charles Clayton, who happens to be a former theology student as well as an engineer, contends that Christians from the West ought to offer an 'all-round' version of development, including a spiritual component, rather than deliberately limiting their aims to material relief and uplift – as the mainstream Christian agencies now do, in order to avoid repeating the blunders that Christianity committed in the past in the course of its attempt to establish itself as the leading world religion. WV's presence thus highlights a dilemma for Christians today, Clayton argues: should they be exporting materialism?

WV's support for a Palestinian homeland has recently brought it into conflict with the Israeli state, which has accused it of anti-semitism. The only evidence, it would seem, inheres in a proselytizing attitude to the Jews which some traditional Christians inherited but which modern liberal Christianity, certainly, has striven to repudiate.[77]

The third charge, of over-emotional fund-raising material, must be considered in historical context. Accepted norms in the area of visual imagery have changed considerably over the last 15 years, as is shown in Chapter 5. Most of the other agencies have also, from time to time, used highly emotional imagery; and in the USA the general tone of all advertising is more brash and crude than in Britain.[78] All the recent literature published by both WVI and WV of Britain seems to fall squarely within current accepted guidelines for agencies, except for one poster I saw in the Northampton office, showing an emaciated African child with an empty bowl. This, it turned out, had been produced by an outside advertising agency rather than in-house, and had provoked sharp debate within the office. One could defend the *occasional* use of such a poster: for with only 'positive imagery' showing happy faces and people hard at work bettering their lot, there is a danger of the facts of starvation being forgotten.

The fourth charge, of commercialization, can be levelled at many other agencies. WV has pushed the multinational corporate model to an extreme with its unashamed emphasis on marketing, and with its cultivation of relative autonomy for national WVs while exploiting the advantages of a global banking network and corporate identity. Whereas in a typical African country there may be several SCF or Oxfam offices from different donor countries, there is one World Vision office only, with funding from many different countries channelled through the bank in Singapore – which, in principle at least, ought to allow for more effective planning and coordination. Each national office is subjected to a field audit by international auditors.

Fund-raising, administration and publicity expenses in the UK office of WV appear to be considerably higher than those of the major DEC-member relief agencies.[79] This is presumably recognized as a problem, since the international President has recently called for a 'lean' organization.[80]

As regards the fifth point, WV's present methods of operating in the field do not seem to be much different from those of agencies such as CAFOD or Christian Aid, which concentrate more on 'working with the poor' than on technical intervention. WV's current policy emphasizes the need for poor people to take the lead in development. Alan Whaites, of WV of Britain, says that 'perhaps the only area in which it can be said that we call into question traditional structures is through the involvement of women in project planning and implementation, which in some societies is contrary to traditional practices.'[81]

Relations with other Christian churches and agencies in donor countries are, however, strained. In the High Court in Dublin in October 1991, World Vision of Ireland secured an apology from the Catholic Primate of All Ireland, Cardinal Ó Fiaich, and six Archbishops, as trustees of Trócaire, the Irish development agency. Trócaire withdrew a statement which it had circulated in 1990 to the Irish bishops and to some Catholic schools, alleging a link between WV and a child abuse scandal in the Philippines.[82] Trócaire also said it accepted that WV did not countenance proselytization by its officers or partners, and acknowledged that Catholic communities and projects in the developing world benefit from some WVI projects. On 31 October 1991, Trócaire made a grant of US$158,200 for the World Vision Relief Programme in Ethiopia.[83]

The root of the problem is that WV, while holding to what they call a 'traditional' protestant view of the church, works willingly with all those who call themselves Christians. In Britain the biggest single denominational grouping among their staff is the Anglican church, and in the USA 20 per cent of the staff are Catholic. Yet WV prefers to bypass church hierarchies: only one of the 19 members of the WVI Board of Directors is ordained, and not a single member of the UK Board. By contrast, the longer established Christian agencies are directly controlled by the various churches, and hence have an inbuilt accountability which runs deeper than that of the secular trusts like Oxfam. These Christian agencies would appear sometimes to wish that World Vision would go away, and they are in general slightly more antagonistic than are the secular agencies, forgetting perhaps that WV's constitution as a religious ministry outside the established churches is comparable to that of the Salvation Army, which is not generally regarded as a threat.[84]

The sixth charge, of promoting dependence through handouts, would appear to be largely out of date. All relief and development agencies have matured enormously over the last 20 years. (On the other hand, there may be special emergency situations where a handout, for instance in cash to individuals, is the most effective way of giving help.) However, it is impossible for an outsider to form an impartial opinion of the general standard of field operations in such a large international organization.

The seventh objection, of being 'all things to all men', would seem to reflect WV's extremely practical approach to marketing. Its slogan in Britain, for instance, is 'Practical Christian Caring'. The first Christian Aid Weeks in Britain in the 1950s showed a similar marketing skill in basing their appeal on a compromise between religion and humanitarianism.[85]

To sum up, World Vision is in some ways a distorting mirror for the other agencies. On the religious side, it owes much of its success to taking advantage of the divisions in the Christian churches. This is surely the main reason why the other Christian agencies find it so hard to accept. Yet with its financial muscle it is most unlikely to disappear, especially (in

Britain) while evangelical Christianity has found an influential supporter in the current Archbishop of Canterbury, George Carey. It might be more sensible to welcome WV to the comity of NGOs in the expectation that it can be influenced.

On the business side, WV's emulation of the multinational corporation is a distorting mirror for all those charities where mission statements, organograms, trading subsidiaries, legacy marketing and baffling acronyms have taken over from the old-fashioned charity offices which were amateur by definition.

The major British agencies, like the Red Cross, look back proudly to their founding fathers and mothers. In 1923 Eglantyne Jebb, who founded SCF, drafted the 'Rights of the Child', which, with little modification, were the basis of the UN Convention on the Rights of the Child adopted by the UN in 1989. Save the Children UK has also built up a base of support running right through British life – from royalty, the aristocracy and the diplomatic service to trade unions, fundraising branches and shops all over the country. Oxfam's history resounds with the reputation of the distinguished intellectuals who have supported it. The 'faith entrepreneurship' of Bob Pierce and W. Stanley Mooneyham carries American overtones which are played down by World Vision of Britain in its quest for naturalization as an accepted British charity. It may be that as well as the doctrinal differences separating World Vision of Britain from the other British agencies, secular and Christian, there is at play a little of the nation's besetting disease of snobbery.

Whatever criticisms may be made of WV, its relief programme following the floods in central China during the summer of 1991 testifies to an organization which can operate speedily and efficiently, using the media to constructive effect and without being clogged by bureaucracy. Almost continuous rain fell over the eastern part of China from mid-May to mid-July. A World Vision Hong Kong assessment team with a Hong Kong film crew (three WV staff members and four media people) visited the most seriously affected areas from 8 to 12 July to authenticate the facts and record them with photography and video. This was followed by a seven-person team from 19 to 26 July. WV was, in fact, the first NGO to respond to this disaster, and the only one to establish a formal operational base in the field.

The Chinese Communist Party's organ the *People's Daily* announced on 2 August 1991 'the most serious flood of the century'. A Médecins du Monde doctor reported to Paris that in Jiangsu province, two million peasants had taken refuge on all the high land which stayed above a stretch of bluey-green water on which there floated pigs' carcasses, human excrement, and debris from what used to be rural life in the country's rice granary.[86] The estimated death count at that time was only some 2,500 compared to millions in 1954, which is probably why the disaster never got much coverage in the western press. However, some estimated figures from the government's damage report at that time indicated the scale of the distress:

Affected population	320 million
Evacuated population	13.9 million
Houses collapsed	2.1 million
Houses badly damaged	4.1 million
Hospitals badly damaged	more than 1,805
Grain loss	13.2 billion kilos
Total direct loss	more than US$7.69 billion (equivalent)

The Chinese authorities sent nearly 80,000 doctors and paramedics to the stricken provinces of Anhui, Jiangsu, Hubei and Henan, and some 12 million army and civilian workers to Anhui province. For the first time ever, they appealed for assistance from the international community (US$200 million).

They made it clear that they were not opposed to Western humanitarian agencies bringing assistance to the field, as well as material supplies. Médecins sans Frontières and Médecins du Monde both sent medical missions. The plight of the flood victims prompted the citizens of Hong Kong to raise huge sums for relief (already about US$75 million by 7 August). World Vision was in a strong position to respond because of its Hong Kong office, founded as long ago as 1962 when it was the fifth national office to be opened and now contributing a regular US$2 million per year to WVI's budget.

WV's needs assessment indicated that the first priority was shelter, since tens of thousands of flood victims were living in the open air in crowded and unsanitary conditions. The only shelters available were makeshift and inadequate for protection from 36–40°C heat. Medical supplies and food were also needed, but the government had already made some provision for these. In order to avoid duplication, WV decided to concentrate its efforts on reestablishing primary schools, township clinics and medical stations, along with shelter building.

By 5 August, after a three-day visit with his team, the Revd David Ngai of World Vision China (who is also a Vice-President of WVI) had signed a formal Relief Cooperation Agreement with the Civil Affairs Department of Anhui, the worst affected province, through which the Yangtse and Huaihe rivers flow. This is one of the poorest provinces in 'China proper', and some rural areas had had to be sacrificed, just when the summer harvest was coming in, to divert the floods from the cities. Among 44 million victims, 13 million had lost most or all of their belongings. WV decided, amid such vast need, to select the most devastated counties for action, and within these counties it selected communities who had lost more than 80 per cent of their assets.

The agreement paid special attention to financial accountability and efficient cooperation between local and WVI personnel. Seven WV relief officers were already working to identify villages to receive aid. Ngai applied to WVI for a budget of US$5 million, to be spent in Anhui and another province.

WV found it hard to allow for the people themselves to participate in the planning of their relief project, since the Chinese government's management system is very much a top-down model. However, mass meetings were held in each of the shelter sites to select beneficiaries. Project beneficiaries were encouraged by both the government and WV to make cash contributions to their shelters, in order to encourage responsible use. Where loans from relatives could not be arranged, bank loans from the government were provided.[87]

The reconstruction project hit some problems such as unprecedented snowfalls in November–December 1991, and a government decision to divert local labour towards autumn sowing and large-scale water conservancy projects. But WV's temporary shelters were all completed by October 1991, their permanent shelters by February 1992, and their clinics and schools between November 1991 and April 1992.[88]

The Hong Kong people's generosity to the Chinese flood victims has obvious political overtones – an attempt to reach the Chinese people, bypassing their Communist leaders who are generally detested in Hong Kong – and implications for the future. When such a massive disaster occurs in a country like China, no external aid is likely to provide more than marginal additional help. However, as we have seen from a review of the Armenian earthquake, devastating disasters of this kind, and efforts to bring relief across national frontiers, dramatize the need for peoples to help one another and to transcend ideological differences. World Vision may well have been influenced to some extent by the possibilities for missionary activity in China, looking forward to the eventual collapse of the Communist state.

For those who believe that humanitarian agencies should model themselves on the integrated, market-oriented, multinational corporation, World Vision is probably the nearest to that ideal yet achieved – but a heavy load of religious ideology comes with the package.

NULL CASES: TWO PRE-MEDIA NGOS

This chapter has been concerned with NGOs for whom relations with the media are in different ways of the greatest importance. There remain some large NGOs for whom relations with the media are, for one reason or another, undeveloped. Two examples of these are given here, to show the difference between what might be called the 'pre-media' and the 'mediatized'. Whereas Oxfam, Save the Children, Médecins sans Frontières and World Vision have always been mediatized (in different ways) since they were founded, the

ICRC is currently undergoing the transition from one state to the other.

CARE

Though the American origins of World Vision are crucial factors in its current style of operating, it would be mistaken to regard WV as representative of the United States agencies. Even bigger than World Vision International is CARE International, which has an annual budget of over US$300 million from the USA alone and is the largest non-political, non-sectarian organization operating in the developing world. CARE Britain's budget for 1990/1 was £18 million, and there are affiliated international members in nine other industrial countries.

CARE was founded in 1946 by a group of American businessmen who arranged for millions of American families to send CARE packages to European countries recovering from the Second World War. A million packages were sent to Britain. In the 1950s CARE turned its attention to helping poor communities in the developing world.

By contrast with WV, CARE has minimal administrative and fund-raising expenses (3 per cent of expenses in the USA, 2–4 per cent in the UK) but by the same token it secures nearly all its finance from government sources: all but 11 per cent in the USA and 4 per cent in the UK. It spends little if any of its budget on development education, advocacy or profile-building.

From a technical point of view CARE is highly thought of, with a commitment to working with the poorest on field-driven projects, identifying population growth as one of the world's major problems. Like many other agencies, it has been forced by recent crises to commit itself more to emergency work, whereas it sees its main preferred role as long-term development. Its weakness is that it is widely seen from outside as a kind of sub-contractor for governments. Four out of eleven of its UK Board are retired senior civil servants. Though it does have its base of private and corporate supporters, it lacks the public voice with which other agencies have learned to speak. It tends to put its point of view privately to governments rather than in public. It receives relatively little coverage from the media except in news reports of relief projects, and is probably still widely seen as an American organization.

The Order of Malta

The Order of Malta was founded in Jerusalem in the eleventh century and is the only existing Sovereign Order of Knighthood in continuous tradition. It looks back to a double role of caring for the sick and protecting pilgrims. After the fall of Acre in 1291, it was ejected from the Holy Land and founded its first state in Rhodes. In 1530 the Order was forced by the Turks to leave Rhodes and it took up residence in Malta. In 1798 Napoleon drove it from Malta and it took up residence in Rome, where it still has extraterritorial status and is recognized as a sovereign state by 53 nations, with its own passports, postage stamps and uniforms. It has 10,000 members or Knights, all Catholics, some of whom take religious vows while others merely commit themselves to supporting the Order and living Christian lives. About 50,000 volunteers support the Order and about 900,000 contribute financially. The Order's Grand Master has the rank of a cardinal. It has branches in 33 countries and gives medical or social help in 90 countries.[89]

The Order is much decentralized and considerable latitude in policy is given to national organizations. However, the total value of the Order's programmes, including the value of goods distributed as well as budgets, has been estimated at an astonishing US$500 million per year,[90] more than even CARE International or Catholic Relief Services and easily topping International Save the Children Alliance or World Vision. This said, a large proportion of the Order's charitable work has nothing to do with the developing world. The accounts are not consolidated and there is no figure available for public as opposed to private funding. For instance, its major medical programmes in Romania and other Eastern European countries are privately funded, but its relief work for the Kurds in Iraq in 1991 was entirely funded by the EC and the German and Austrian governments, to the tune of about $3 million.

In some fields of medical aid, such as the relief of leprosy, the Order of Malta is a world leader, and it has an extensive network of care for aged and terminally ill people. Some of its less well-known projects are breaking new ground: for instance, a programme to support traditional medicine, healing and mental health in refugee camps in Thailand, which scores high for cultural and personal sensitivity: 'the programme offers a place where refugees, in helping others, can recover a dignity which their status usually deprives them of'.[91]

In disaster relief, the Order as a whole seeks to avoid competition with other agencies. One of its more recent initiatives is to build up small but self-sufficient and well-trained action groups to move in soon after a sudden disaster.

In the past the Order has been reticent about itself, not needing to be involved with the media because of its access to private wealth through a membership which is in principle aristocratic. It is more concerned with the threat of 'False Orders' trying to milk unsuspecting people of funds. In the context of modern agencies the Order of Malta may seem to be an extraordinary anachronism, and, as one might imagine, concepts like development education have not yet reached it. Yet in some of the former Communist countries of eastern Europe, the symbolism of nobility has – as a result of the repression of religion and independent association – regained some of the lustre for ordinary people which it has lost in the democratic West, and the Order is likely to attract support and interest there.

The Order is regarded by some outsiders as a snobbish club for mutual advancement. Its house magazines contain numerous group photographs which transport one to *The Prisoner of Zenda*. Yet this must be a superficial reading of an organization which has established itself as one of the largest humanitarian organizations outside the UN system and the Red Cross and Red Crescent Movement. Observers of the humanitarian scene may ask themselves whether the Order will be able in future both to maintain its detachment from the marketplace of image and profile, and to continue to draw funds successfully from governmental bodies that are increasingly image-conscious.

NGOS SEEN FROM THE SOUTH

We have concentrated in this chapter on the cultural differences within the club of Western ('Northern' or Euro-American) NGOs – differences which are more substantial than has often been appreciated. However, when viewed from the Third World (or South) their common factors are more pronounced than the differences. Generally speaking, Third World countries are hospitable to NGOs that seek to better the lot of deprived sectors of their populations. The NGOs see themselves as corrective elements to the West's political and economic dominance, but increasingly some Third World intellectuals are indicting them as representative of that dominance. Professor Mahmood Mamdani, for instance, director of the Centre for Basic Research in Kampala, Uganda, accepts that NGOs are coming to be increasingly influential in many African countries, but argues that they are a mixed blessing because they are based on the idea of philanthropy and they lack the principle of accountability to beneficiaries, which gives practical legitimacy to much less sophisticated local operations.[92]

The demand for accountability is indeed likely to become more pressing in NGOs, and we have touched on some of the problems already in this book (see, for instance, Chapter 1, note 13). Evaluation of NGO projects is generally carried out as an internal exercise, though when funds are provided by a government it may appoint outside consultants, often from a university department. There is no doubt that evaluation is now treated by the major agencies as an important part of their management responsibilities, and there is a growing literature on the subject.[93] However, Mahmood Mamdani has a valid point that control of the evaluation process is still generally paternalistic. What is lacking is the direct voice of the beneficiaries, which even the most refined methods of social research have difficulty in conveying to readers.

Television and video can now allow the voice of beneficiaries to be heard by means of techniques of observational filming – especially through the use of sub-titles, long takes and minimal narration. Video is already frequently and effectively used to publicize the work of NGOs in the field, and television crews are accustomed to making expeditions that result in news and current affairs programmes. There is new scope, however, for the making of observational films, based on solid ethnographic research and conducted with the cooperation of local communities, that would give an impartial picture of the reception of NGOs' work at the grassroots. In the new climate of healthy self-criticism that is growing among the major NGOs, led by the august ICRC, news that the grassroots perception is not invariably favourable will not do irreparable damage. Even Professor Mamdani, who was invited to state his views at a meeting sponsored by London-based NGOs, would probably concede that despite his criticisms the NGOs represent the least damaging aspect of Western intentions towards the Third World.

5   Images and Narratives of Disaster Relief

Much of this last chapter could be regarded as a free essay in semiotics, the theory of sign systems, which has been defined inclusively by one its leading exponents as 'the study of everything that can be used in order to lie'.[1] Intentional outright lying is mercifully uncommon in the Western media's treatment of peacetime disasters: we benefit from the tradition of a free press and responsible broadcasting authorities. But in times of war, civil strife and revolution, truth is notoriously 'the first casualty'. Disinformation, twisting of the truth, lack of self-criticism, unconscious bias, self-censorship – these are common even at times of peace. And when we think of how a television bulletin sets out to 'cover' the whole wide world, with all the hackneyed imagery of swirling globes and flashing rays, it would be naïve to conceive of a *singular* truth.

Semiotics is supposed to embrace the study of visual imagery and of narrative forms, all of which may be summed up under the heading of 'representations'. Semiotics is obliged to draw on many different fields of enquiry, for no one intellectual discipline has any monopoly in explaining how signs and representations work.[2]

Hence this final chapter will of necessity be somewhat eclectic in styles of approach. It will consider how disasters and disaster relief are represented across a range of visual imagery and narrative devices. Special attention will be given to television as the medium which is coming in many ways to dominate the others, unmistakably so in the coverage of disasters and relief.

AGENCIES AND THEIR LOGOS

Well-established European institutions, from universities to banks, used to have heraldic coats of arms. The Sovereign Order of Malta still does. Nowadays, any institution that wishes to keep in the public eye has to have a logo, and the NGOs are no exception. The word 'logo' will be used here in the sense of any identifying symbol consisting of a simple picture or design and/or letters. Despite the attentions of graphic designers and advertising creators, no agency emblem has approached the success of the red cross, which is well protected by virtue of the near-universal ratification of the Geneva Conventions, and because it stands for a principle broader than the work of any single organization.[3]

The 'French doctor' organizations have adopted 'heraldic' variants of the red cross. Médecins sans Frontières is the most irreverent, using a red cross which slopes forward and is half erased by a red squiggle: it is almost saying 'Not the Red Cross'. The Red Cross is not amused – claiming that such usages actually dilute the semiotic power of their unique protective emblem and may even put their representatives at greater risk. Médecins du Monde uses a more discreet white on blue, and the limbs of the white cross are transformed into the tail, wings and head of Noah's dove bearing the olive-branch across a map of the world. The Swiss Disaster Relief Unit uses the cross of the Swiss flag (white on red) against a ground of rightward-sloping parallel upright bars whose colour changes from red to black, presumably to suggest carnage returning to normality.

The United Nations uses a map of the globe as it would be seen from a satellite over the North Pole (though many would argue it should now be the South), surmounting Olympic laurel leaves – to which the World Health Organization adds a medical caduceus. UNHCR adds to the laurels a pair of hands offering shelter to a 'lego' man; UNICEF a mother holding up her baby; UNDRO a streak of lightning. CARE and the Disasters Emergency Committee use a style of lettering inspired by the stencilled letters on emergency consignments. CAFOD, 'On the side of people in need', has an ear of corn emerging from the initial C of the acronym.

World Vision uses a Christian cross apparently impaling the globe like a sword from North to South Pole.

Oxfam has never settled on a graphic design for long, relying no doubt on its pithy and well-known acronym.[4] When it prints a map of the world, it normally uses Peters' projection, which focuses on Third World countries, placed prominently in the centre of the map. Oxfam's extraordinary success in the 1960s seems to have been linked to the recognition by the public of what became known as the 'Oxfam child' (see p. 181). One of these images of an emaciated child was even designed as late as 1968 to be hung from the family Christmas tree.

In 1992, to mark its fiftieth anniversary, Oxfam abandoned a logo it had used for several years – a stylized head with raised arm – which may have been too similar visually to Save the Children's. Instead there is a new logo, 'OXFAM: Working for a Fairer World', in which the capital O has become a globe with cross-hatchings presumably representing divisions and injustice, the X possibly expresses anger, the F slopes backwards, the A and the M stand four-square on their own feet.

Christian Aid again uses a stylized image of the globe, but viewed, unlike the UN's, from somewhere above the Equator. Spreadeagled from the North to the South Poles is a thin human figure with tapering arms and legs. This symbol was designed for a poster by Maurice Rickards, who was a consultant designer on appeals to Inter-Church Aid in the 1950s and who proposed the idea of an ecumenical Christian Aid Week in 1956. 'CHRISTIAN AID', he wrote, 'a phrase which could through repetition over the years, achieve the status, sympathy and currency of SAVE THE CHILDREN or RED CROSS.'[5] The symbol and the title 'Christian Aid' were adopted in the early 1960s. Rickards later rendered it as a three dimensional maquette and proposed that it should be erected on a plinth, about twice life-size, outside St Martin-in-the-Fields church in Trafalgar Square with a donation box. The maquette survives and can be seen in Christian Aid's offices in London. Rickards' name for his concept was 'The Victim'. 'This figure', he wrote 'is a monument to millions. It represents the concentration-camp victim, the refugee, the oppressed, the outcast and the disaster-stricken.'[6] It has always been known in-house as 'Slim Jim'.

Save the Children Fund has always, since its foundation in 1919, made use of the publicity techniques of the day. Eglantyne Jebb, its principal founder, used a former newspaper reporter to help increase funds, whose policy, in a contemporary's words, 'was to adapt to the needs of philanthropy methods which had hitherto been reserved for the publicizing of patent medicines.'[7] SCF's first badge was borrowed from a well-known plaque, the *bambino* (baby boy) designed by Andrea della Robbia in 1419 to decorate the Foundling Hospital in Florence. The baby is wrapped in swaddling clothes and his arms are outstretched, the hands at hip level, with the motto added '*Salvete Parvulos!*' (save the children). This lasted until the 1960s – except that when the Fund started the Karamandian Hospital in Patras, the first paediatric hospital in Greece, the baby on this plaque wears a modern nappy instead of the swaddling clothes which Greek nurses had been making great efforts to teach their people to abandon.[8]

In the late 1960s the bambino ceased to be used and SCF experimented with various designs. In the early 1970s a new logo was introduced, representing a stylized, ungendered child still with its arms outstretched but now above the shoulders. Its in-house nickname is 'Charlie Brown' after the cartoon character. Save the Children is now of all the NGOs the one which has most potential to emulate some of the worldwide influence of the Red Cross. Unlike Oxfam's loose extended family (see note 4, p.248), the International Save the Children Alliance has a constitution, broad policies in common, and a representative in Geneva. Its simple, striking logo is no doubt of some help. The SCF logo is used to some extent in emergency conditions in the field, for instance on vehicles supplying relief aid, and it carries with it a considerable reputation. On occasion, probably, it has the effect of restraining local or other people from behaving badly since it implies the presence of what Médecins sans Frontières call *témoignage* (witnessing). The International Save the Children Alliance is now expanding its role and recruiting agencies from European countries to the consortium: they do not all have to use the name 'Save the Children', but unity will be maintained by their shared use of 'Charlie Brown'.

The qualities which the original della Robbia *bambino* represented – total dependence on paternal funding and maternal swaddling – are exactly those which a progressive agency concerned with the rights of children today strives to combat. The new 'Charlie Brown' image is equivocal, for the stylized child may be seen as raising its arms not necessarily in supplication or gratitude, but possibly in sheer *joie de vivre*. Charlie Brown, like the Red Cross, is literally a 'stereotype', for the metaphor derives from printing. Modern agencies' educational efforts concentrate to a great extent on challenging stereotypes; but the merchandizing of a brand image depends precisely on maximizing their diffusion, with the help of bold and self-standing graphics which impart a mystique and encourage brand loyalty.

DISASTER IMAGERY BEFORE THE 1980s

Anti-racists sometimes claim that charity appeals representing starving Africans embody a particularly racist, colonialist motivation. Band Aid was at one time criticized by *Black Voice* as 'the racist event of the decade'.[9] Charities are said by such critics to reflect a 'colonial desire to save the unfortunate in distant lands'.[10]

It is true that virtually all appeals for charity until the 1980s tended to picture helpless, passive victims and heroic saviours. Virtually all imagery of disasters in 'distant lands' was (by present-day standards) patronizing to the victims. Later in this chapter, I shall explore, with special reference to contemporary television reporting, how accounts of suffering and relief continue to fall almost inevitably, even today, into this pre-set narrative structure.

But we should be sensitive to historical epochs when looking at the efforts of relief agencies in the past. For evidence of a British appeal untainted by either colonialism or what we now call 'racism', we may examine a typical eight-page leaflet published by Save the Children in about 1922, priced at threepence, appealing for funds for relief of the Russian famine. Save the Children sent out its own teams of Russian speakers to administer relief (as agents of fourteen different nations) throughout the province of Saratov, which is about two thirds the size of England and Wales and had a population of about 3 million.

The leaflet is sub-titled 'Our Errand of Mercy into the Regions of Death'. The text emphasizes that the Fund assists both Russian children and the children of Russian refugees. 'It has never made the politics or the creed of the parents of the children an excuse for leaving the children to die.' The photographs, which also appeared in a film at the time, show 'abandoned children who had laid down to die in a deserted house', 'corpses waiting for the Death Cart' and 'corpses in a common grave'. Another photograph shows Dr Fridtjof Nansen the explorer, now High Commissioner for Russian Relief, and 'launched upon the most heroic adventure of an adventurous life', inspecting the careful precautions taken to guard trainloads of food so that it is not stolen. Under the heading 'From Death to Life', a row of children is seen eating from metal bowls in front of wall-to-wall della Robbia *bambini*. Since 'the local bread is made of oak leaves, chopped straw, weeds, clay, etc.', it is 'no wonder Save the Children Fund bread seems to the children of Saratov as delicious as cake to the children of happier lands', and it only costs three halfpence per head per day to feed them. Donors of £100 or more 'may have a Kitchen called after them.'

Since the 1920s, generations of photo-journalists like Alfred Eisenstaedt, W. Eugene Smith, Robert Capa and Werner Bischof have established a genre of searing, compassionate realism in their portrayal of war and disaster. Some have been markedly predatory and sensational, like 'Weegee' (Arthur Fellig); others have been markedly aestheticizing, like the currently fashionable Sebastião Salgado.[11] Photo-journalists were mainly responsible for disseminating such images until television took over much of their role. The humanitarian agencies have always depended indirectly for their support on this kind of journalism, and have often made use of it directly in their appeals.

The victory of television over photo-journalism was gradual but the closure of the leading picture magazine, *Life*, in 1972 may be taken as a watershed date. However, the victory is only partial, for news photography is still able to provide a lasting emotional intensity and images that abide in the collective memory. It seems certain that the horrors of the Vietnam war will be remembered most vividly by means of such classic photographs as that of a Buddhist monk burning himself to death, the street execution of a Vietcong prisoner, and children fleeing a napalm strike, and it may well be that in due course the Falklands, the Gulf war and Bosnia will be remembered by similar images.[12]

1960s photography produced the 'Oxfam child' and the horror images of Biafra. In 1973 came Jonathan Dimbleby's television programme on Ethiopia, *The Unknown Famine*, which eleven years later came to be regarded by experts as 'very nearly unwatchable and more gruesome than anything shown in 1984'.[13] The incidence of disasters, fund-raising pressures and the growing influence of advertising experts produced by 1981 perhaps the most blatant of images, the helpless hand of a dying African child clasped by a fat and healthy adult white hand. Other agencies, too, used this image, particularly Oxfam around 1970, but Save the Children's poster of November 1981, 'Sentenced to Death: Save the Innocent Children' (plate 4), is perhaps the most extreme and insensitive, and can justly be described as racist. It was posters like this which brought discontent within the agencies to a head and precipitated a period of intense questioning and criticism of visual images which is still with us. A poster like the Red Cross's '125 Years' (plate 5), published in 1989, shows an unusual condescension – for its date – to the subjects of the photograph, no doubt because the debate about visual imagery and so-called 'disaster pornography' has taken a long time to get through to the Red Cross's corridors in Geneva. The red crosses on white feeding-bowls are part of a blatantly composed tableau.

THE AWKWARD AGE OF VISUAL IMAGERY

'Visual images of colonized peoples' was the subject of an influential Social History Workshop in Oxford in 1984, and the 1980s saw a current of interest in this subject across the whole range of art history, photographic history, anthropology and education, as well as the specialized field of charity appeals. Oxfam was the leading agency to effect a fundamental change in the coverage of disasters and to criticize the role of the media. For instance, in 1985 their Youth and Education Department published a four-page broadsheet, 'The News behind the news: reporting on disasters'. The front page reproduces front pages from the British tabloid press screaming 'Ethiopian famine: *Mirror* to the rescue' (in the person of the then mighty businessman, Robert Maxwell) and 'Race to save the babies!' (from the *Sunday People*), and the rest of the broadsheet is devoted to criticizing the assumptions behind the headlines. Oxfam, then as now, was a leader among British agencies in seeking to examine the underlying causes of poverty rather than merely providing palliative aid. Part of the leaflet's back page includes a photograph (often reproduced since) by Wendy Wallace of news photographers lining up to photograph a single starving child.

At about this time, Oxfam, Christian Aid and War on Want all set up working groups to develop guidelines on visual communications. Oxfam and the European Economic Community sponsored a report on 'Images of Africa'[14] which showed clearly, by means of research with young people in Britain, that negative images of Africa were reinforcing stereotypes of a doomed and helpless continent which dated back to the colonial era and gave no weight to the point of view of Africans themselves. When children in a school were shown a photograph of a *smiling* woman and her child in Burkina Faso,[15] the majority of responses were that 'if they looked contented "we must have helped them."' The researchers concluded that

> 'The public's perceptions, though they were influenced by other factors like family, friends and school, were ultimately formed by the media. . . . The visual images were dominant, and the images were remembered when even significant facts and figures had been forgotten. . . . While the Ethiopian famine brought the continent to the British public's attention, it also added its own particular

distortions to those which already existed. Given that an interest had been generated, might it have been possible to develop this further, to enable people to take a deeper look at the economic, social and political background to the continent? The evidence of this research is that it might. Time does not seem to be proving that it has. It is for the NGOs and the media to ask themselves why.[16]

The 'Oxfam child' of the 1960s would be outlawed by current Oxfam recommendations on images:[17]

An image has a lot of power. It conveys information and excites emotions. It provokes response, and it can leave a lasting impression.

But the power of images can be damaging if they are handled insensitively. They can generalise, over-simplify and distort. They can reinforce stereotypes. They can deny people their dignity.

Oxfam, like other aid agencies, has had to struggle with a legacy of its own creation. Poster campaigns in the 1960s depicting vulnerable, starving, pot-bellied children were successful in raising funds. But the association of these images with what was then a new term, the 'Third World', has characterised public perceptions of poverty and need in vast regions of the Southern hemisphere ever since. . . .

Images:

1. Should respect people's dignity as individuals.
2. Challenge our prejudices rather than reinforce them.
3. Should convey that Oxfam works *with* people who are actively striving to improve their lives. Disaster situations particularly challenge the capacity of Oxfam to select appropriate images which convey and reflect need but do not portray people merely as recipients of aid.

Meanwhile, a number of writers took to asking awkward questions about the aggressive character of photography and film when there is an asymmetry of power between those who make images and those who are 'subjects'.[18] The agencies were accused of 'exploiting' Third World children through publishing such 'squalid images',[19] or of generating a 'brand image' of African impotence and misery.[20] A schizoid incongruity emerged from 'images of starving Tigrean mothers and children . . . in the pages of the *New York Times* usually jumbled together with glamorous advertisements for sable jackets and the latest symbols of middle class consumer sovereignty.' Concern was dispelled rather than mobilized, because of an ambiguity or inadequacy inherent in the photographic image itself.[21] Writers like Alex de Waal[22] argued that journalists and agencies who look for pathetic pictures in famine-threatened areas can make it advantageous for people to present themselves as helpless victims.

In April 1989 the General Assembly of European NGOs adopted its Code of Conduct on Images and Messages Relating to the Third World. This is designed to counter fatalistic images of the Third World by providing

> more realistic and more complete information, thereby increasing awareness of the intrinsic value of all civilizations, of the limitations of our own society and of the need for a more universal development which respects justice, peace and the environment. It is the duty of NGOs to provide the public with truthful and objective information which respects not only the human dignity of the people in question but the intelligence of the public at large.

The Practical Guidelines are quoted here in full:

1. Avoid *catastrophic or idyllic images* which appeal to charity and lead to a clear conscience rather than a consideration of the root problems;

2. All people must be presented as human beings and sufficient information provided as to their social, cultural and economic environment so that their *cultural identity* and *dignity* are preserved. Culture

should be presented as an integral part of development in the South;

3. *Accounts given by the people concerned* should be presented rather than the interpretations of a third party;

4. People's ability to *take responsibility for themselves* must be highlighted;

5. A message should be formulated in such a way that *generalisations* are avoided in the minds of the public;

6. The internal and external *obstacles* to development should be clearly shown;

7. *Interdependence* and *joint responsibility* in underdevelopment should be emphasised;

8. The *causes of poverty* (political, structural or natural) should be apparent in a message in order to enable the public to become aware of the history and real situation in the Third World, and the structural foundations of these countries before colonisation. It is the situation today, coupled with a knowledge of the past, which should be the starting point for examining ways in which extreme poverty and oppression can be eliminated. Power struggles and vested interests should be exposed and oppression and injustice denounced;

9. Messages should avoid all forms of *discrimination* (racial, sexual, cultural, religious, socio-economic);

10. The image of our Third World partners as dependent, poor and powerless is most often applied to *women* who are invariably portrayed as dependent victims, or worse still, simply do not figure in the picture. An improvement in the images used in educational material on the Third World evidently requires a positive change in the images projected of Southern women;

11. *Southern partners* should be consulted in the formulation of all messages;

12. If an NGO calls on the services of other partners (institutions, organisations or private companies) for a fund raising activity, it should ensure that the recommendations of this Code are respected by all parties. Reference should be made to the Code in the *sponsoring* contract(s) between the NGO and its partner(s).

A number of technical problems are of course raised by the guidelines. For instance, the third guideline seems to favour direct filmed interviews with members of indigenous groups, but fails to recognize that such material can be just as manipulative as old-style narration – by means of choice of interviewee, cueing of questions, cutting and editing, etc. As regards the fifth guideline, it is impossible to convey *any* message with a guarantee that it will not lead to generalizations being formed in the 'minds of the public'. Furthermore, the guidelines apply only to development education, which is but a part of an NGO's work. The agencies do not find the guidelines easy to work with, but they are a landmark in the history of development education.

In September 1991 Save the Children UK published 'Focus on Images', which is the most carefully thought-out set of guidelines published by any agency to date.[23] These apply to everyone involved in promoting SCF, including fund-raisers, volunteers, illustrators and commissioned freelances. The leaflet gives visual examples of 'dos' and 'don'ts'. No more pictures of dominant relief workers dispensing aid to passive villagers; disabled persons should if possible be photographed doing something rather than sitting in a wheelchair; cropping and captioning should be sensitive to the dignity of individuals and communities; coverage must be both accurate and balanced, and so forth. SCF's guidelines are not advisory but mandatory, carrying the full authority of the Council and directors, yet the intention is to encourage creativity rather than muzzle it. Clearly a great deal has changed in ten years.

A kind of progress has been made in attending to and studying the impact of visual imagery. However, television news editors do not adhere to the same guidelines and are still ready from time to time to screen horrifying footage that shows starving and dying people – subject, in Britain and many other countries, to the broadcasting organizations' own guidelines. Arguably the agencies, which benefit indirectly from television news coverage, are maintaining a slightly sanctimonious position since they still depend for their support, to a great extent, on the public's exposure to such images through the news media. Save the Children – and the broadcasters – would respond that horrifying imagery may have its rightful place when it is absolutely necessary to inform and is genuinely representative of a community's predicament. Some of the major British agencies are now discussing the possibility of imposing their own image guidelines on television crews who make use of their facilities such as feeding centres to film a news report.

In reaction to negative imagery of Africa, the Hunger Project, a New York-based organization dedicated to eradicating world hunger by the year 2000, makes a policy of only showing up-beat images and conveying encouraging messages about how Africans are bettering their own lot. Unfortunately, despite some prestigious supporters, the Hunger Project presents itself with a Madison Avenue razzmatazz that does not adapt successfully to non-American audiences. By comparison, Comic Relief at its best is able to allude sensitively to the sharp facts of suffering while also showing that they are not the whole truth about any African society, and demonstrating how communities can help themselves.[24]

Avoidance of negative imagery, while timely and on balance desirable, can lead to blandness. Annual reports and other literature published by British agencies are now becoming sensitive, tasteful, considerate – but rather similar to one another and not exactly challenging or conducive to a strong response. 'Positive imagery' of beaming children and citizens of colonies has long been used by State propagandists, if for very different political purposes from those of the NGOs today, and it typically carries a latent message of reassurance. In properly recognizing the validity of the reforms carried out by the agencies in their visual imagery policies, one should not fall into the error of feeling superior to the Oxfam publicists of the 1960s. One can almost hear the acerbic James Cameron, Oxfam supporter and one of the great journalists of his generation, retort that Britain in the materialistic 1980s became too squeamish to include the truth about African famine in the domestic rituals of Christmas. To reinforce images of dependency is indeed counter-productive; but the dogmas that prevail in the agencies today will seem equally dated in another 25 years' time.

REPRESENTATION OF THE OTHER

Since the 1980s, much thought has been given to the question of visual images of 'the other',[25] especially images of colonized or formerly colonized peoples. There is a long-standing tendency to represent such people either as exaggeratedly romantic, glamorous and 'exotic' (a word which originally meant simply 'other' or 'outside'), or alternatively as inferior in some way – either as lacking in some moral quality which 'we' assume that we possess, or as victims, or both.

It seems that these two modes of representation are in fact complementary, and that they parallel the way in which a male-dominated society tends traditionally to represent its own women. Women are invested with glamour and valued as objects of desire, yet the majority of them are called on to lead harsher or at least more demanding lives than their menfolk, and without complaining about their subordination. They are in fact less expendable than males insofar as the reproduction of society is concerned, and they are widely defined as being closer to 'nature'. Both the way in which 'we' picture colonized peoples, and the way in which we [males] picture women, betray an anxiety about our expendability and a fear of forces felt to be beyond normal control. (The argument may be applied to our perception of children as well as women.)

We may extend this analysis to the representation of any Third World peoples. Regardless of the historical reasons for the underdevelopment of most Third World countries (and whatever the true reasons may be), the West sees this poverty as threatening to its security, not least because of the perceived link between poverty and mass migration. Photography and the ensuing technologies of film and television – though in principle they can be, and sometimes are, adapted for all sorts of liberating purposes – are in practice often used to reinforce stereotypes which have a controlling function in our society.

Romantic images of Africans and Asians, especially, appear all the time in the media – especially, nowadays, to assist the promotion of tourism and even (increasingly) European high fashion. But the *dominant* imagery, especially in television news and current affairs, is of helplessness and negativity. 'For the western news media', comments a leading writer on television, John Fiske,[26] 'the Third World is a place of natural and political disasters and not much else.' A leading historian of Africa, Roland Oliver, complains in particular about the distorted picture of Africa that results:

> Until recently, there were at least the Cold War and the struggle against apartheid to provide some ongoing themes of continent-wide dimensions. Now, it seems that, except for riots in South Africa (always portrayed with the same bobbing crowd scenes), we are presented only with civil war, famine and AIDS, with the same or similar pictures used over and over again. It is not that the scenes depicted are untrue. It is that they represent such a small part of the truth. It is as if all the television time and all the column inches that can be spared for Africa had been preempted by the aid charities to serve only their compassionate purposes – and at a pretty mindless level. I have talked to the employees of the aid charities, and I find them very well aware of the problem. They know that they are causing Africa to be misrepresented, but their publicity departments know what pictures bring in the money, and that decides what is put out. The fault of the media is to take what is fed to them, without much attempt to balance it. During the last century, the issue of slavery must have played something of the same role in supplying the public image of Africa, but it was then at least confined to the sermon, the Exeter Hall meeting and the missionary magazine.[27]

In fact, Western perceptions of Third World poverty are often exaggerated. Peter Adamson recently reported[28] on a questionnaire that he regularly gives to 16–17-year-olds and their teachers in British schools. He asks what percentage of the world's children are 'visibly malnourished' and is usually told 50–75 per cent, whereas the true answer is 1–2 per cent.[29] What percentage of the world's families are living in such absolute poverty that their most basic needs are not met? Estimate: 75 per cent, correct answer, 20–25 per cent. What percentage of 6–12-year-olds start school? Estimate: 10–20 per cent, correct answer, 90 per cent. Adamson comments that these pronounced misconceptions are not confined to schoolchildren, but derive largely from the news media and the fund-raising agencies. All the misconceptions are skewed towards the negative. It is easy to see how this happens when the public has few alternative sources of information or none at all. When a true catastrophe occurs – such as famine, or the coming HIV pandemic – it is not perceived against a background of healthy normality.

DISASTER RELIEF AS A FORM OF FOLK NARRATIVE

Whereas much attention has been devoted to the visual imagery of disasters and their relief, perhaps the underlying narrative form has not yet been sufficiently understood. From now on in this chapter, special attention will be given to television: because it integrates the visual and the narrative; because it is (as will be shown) the pre-eminent means whereby knowledge of the Third World is gained by most people; and because of its extraordinary power.

A Russian scholar, Vladimir Propp, published *Morphology of the Folktale*[30] in 1928 and it was translated into English in 1958, since when it has had a great impact on folklorists, linguists, anthropologists and literary critics. Here I will analyse the narrative of disaster relief, as it is typically represented in news and agency publicity, as a series of what Propp calls 'functions'.

I suggest that even when only a part of a narrative relating to disaster is shown on television – for instance, pictures of starving babies, or an aeroplane setting off from a familiar airport bringing supplies, or an ambassador thanking the public for their generosity – viewers come to recognize it as part of the total narrative convention.

On this reading, the central character of the narrative is the travelling *hero*, who may be an expatriate fieldworker, such as an officer of Oxfam or MSF, or a foreign correspondent. There is also in some cases a *villain* – a Pol Pot in the Cambodian crisis of the late 1970s,[31] Saddam Hussein during the Gulf war. But, as Propp says, in those tales where no villainy is present, 'lack' or misfortune can serve instead, and it is noticed by a *dispatcher*. 'One can imagine that, prior to the beginning of the action, the situation has lasted for years, but the moment comes when the dispatcher or searcher suddenly realizes that something is lacking. . . .'[32]

Propp describes another essential character whom he terms the *donor*. The donor provides the hero with a *magical agent* sometimes in the form of a *magical helper* – clearly, in our case, the embodiments of Western abundance and technology in its various forms. After the hero has undergone various ordeals and solved difficult tasks, the misfortune or lack is liquidated. Hence we learn from an Oxfam *Bulletin*, admittedly twenty years old but commendably lacking in guile, of an Indian peasant sighing that the drought 'may be too big a problem for God; but perhaps OXFAM can do something.'[33]

Propp also draws attention to the *false hero* who presents unfounded claims and is eventually exposed. These are the impostors who start fake charities, or the incompetents who dissipate funds and send grotesquely wrong medicines, or the 'lords of poverty' – to borrow from the title of Graham Hancock's polemic against the UN.[34]

The final member of Propp's cast is the *princess*. This may be any person of rank and/or charisma who intervenes and rewards.[35] Save the Children (UK) has prospered particularly well since it acquired a real one in Princess Anne, its tireless and effective President.

Fairy tales, as everyone knows, have to have a happy ending. The agencies try to provide this, especially in their annual reports to donors and staff, with a favoured alternative to the image of distress: the image of gratitude.

The above analysis is not meant to be cynical. The agencies

deliver real relief to assuage real needs. The Save the Children team that risked their lives in Mogadishu in the spring of 1992 to feed at least 5,000 children, who would otherwise almost certainly have died amid a senseless civil war, are genuine heroes in anyone's estimation. But the agencies depend on representations to publicize both the need and the relief. The point of my analytical exercise is merely to stress that when one wants to tell a story, it is hard to avoid certain stylistic constraints. The listener needs a way into the story.

Surgical teams are invested with a particular glamour and are successful in saving lives. Yet far more lives are saved by the sanitation engineers who provide clean water and dig latrines.

> An ex-warrant officer next to an 'appropriate technology' row of latrines is a far cry from the 'magical white man' with electronic gadgets and a spattering of other people's blood on his starched operating clothes, particularly if seconded by a devoted and braless nurse looking on admiringly. . . . I doubt if even the French version of 'sanitation engineers without borders' would have quite the dramatic ring of 'Medecins sans Frontières'.[36]

The image of the French doctors, as we have seen in Chapter 4, is one of panache. By contrast, the image of the ICRC is one of persuasion and discretion. The result is that it has an 'image problem'. Though perhaps the most active agency during the Gulf war, they received little publicity compared to the French agencies. Paul-Henri Morard, head of ICRC's press division, is well aware of the importance of the right choice of television spokesperson for an interview and of the way spokespersons allow their image to be managed. As he charmingly said, 'Switzerland as such is very hard to "sell". A Swiss man is not something terribly sexy to sell.'

The most thoughtful of the operational agencies are restrained about playing up the heroic aspects of their work. They are concerned most of all with trying to strengthen weak points in a community's own 'immune system' so that it can muster its own resources to face an emergency. The appro-

priate therapeutic analogy is not invasive surgery or pharma-
ceutical remedies, but a homoeopathic approach which gives
priority to an organic system's power to recover from outside
disturbance.

NARRATIVE AND NEWS PROGRAMMES

Most people would readily accept that popular fiction and
drama on television, whether sitcoms or soap operas, follow
more or less pre-established formulae. They are clearly
variations on themes – mostly the perennial themes of sex,
money, kinship, status, ethnicity, generation conflict and so
on. It may be more of a surprise to see apparently factual
programmes analysed in the same way, 'as if' they were
fiction. 'I think', says Stuart Hall,

> we make an absolutely too simple and false distinction
> between narratives about the real and the narratives of
> fiction.
>   When a journalist is socialised into an institution, he
> or she is socialised into a certain way of telling stories.
> And although individual journalists may perform opera-
> tions (or what is called originality) on top of that, they
> are working within a given language or within a given
> framework, and they are making those adjustments
> which make the old and trite appear to be new. But they
> are not breaking the codes. Indeed, if they constantly
> broke the codes, people outside wouldn't understand
> them at all. . . . I think that journalists learn them very
> habitually, rather unconsciously, and they are not aware
> that the mode in which you construct a story alters the
> meaning of the story itself. They think it is just a set of
> techniques. . . . The stories are already largely written
> for them before the journalists take fingers to typewriters
> or pen to paper.[37]

It is recorded that during the Vietnam war, GIs sometimes
behaved as if they were making war movies. 'So it is not
difficult to understand', writes Phillip Knightley,

how, when seen on a small screen, in the enveloping and cosy atmosphere of the household, sometime between the afternoon soap-box drama and the late-night war movie, the television version of the war in Vietnam could appear as just another drama, in which the hero is the correspondent and everything will come out all right in the end.[38]

During the 1991 Gulf war, the plight of John Simpson, the BBC correspondent who remained in Baghdad, became an absorbing topic of interest for British viewers. Viewers are enticed into identifying with the reporter seen on the screen, or alternatively with military personnel on their own side whose good or ill fortune is tracked. As ITN's Editor in Chief has publicly admitted, 'the media talked lightly about the "light" [Allied] casualties, but could have done with a few more mentions of the thousands of Iraqi casualties'.[39]

John Fiske claims[40] that the timing of news bulletins at the beginning of an evening's viewing is designed 'to draw the male of the household into the TV audience'. He cites research findings that mothers are commonly urged to keep children quiet 'while father watches the news'. The news typically ends with a ' "softer" item that is intended to bring the female back into the audience', and this is often followed by a local news programme designed to appeal to women. For Fiske, the news is 'masculine soap opera'.[41] In fact, empirical evidence suggests that (in Britain at least) evening news programmes are watched equally by men and women.[42]

CLAWBACK

Fiske and Hartley borrow the neologism 'clawback' to describe the way television news and documentaries constantly strive to keep control of potentially deviant or disruptive events by drawing them into a preordained central focus. 'For example, nature programmes will often stress the "like us-ness" of the animals filmed, finding in their behaviour metaphoric equivalences with our own culture's way of organizing its affairs.'[43]

In a later study, Fiske writes of television news[44] that it typically works with three successive stages of clawback: first, the news reader, who appears to be conveying the authoritative, objective truth; second, the reporter, who signs off as both an individual and an institutional voice, thus acting as a bridge between the final truth and 'raw reality'; and, third, the eye-witness or spokesperson or recent film footage, which are the guarantees that what we are being told is 'fact'. Clawback, according to Fiske, allows that which has been interpreted to present itself as objective.

Fiske somewhat spoils his analysis by blaming these processes on 'the bourgeoisie'. One could speak, more precisely, of clawing back to a political centre of gravity which gradually shifts from time to time in every country (more crudely than this in countries where television is directly controlled by the government). For instance, in the late 1980s in Britain far less coverage on domestic television news was given to trade union leaders than over the previous fifteen years, on account of a shift to the Right in the centre of gravity. What is excluded from the spectrum of politically acceptable opinions? There is, for instance, a minority view of the extreme Right that British citizens have no obligations of any kind to the Third World, as there is a minority view of the extreme Left that all restrictions on immigration into Britain should be rescinded; neither of these extreme voices is heard in the political news bulletins except perhaps as an occasional news item that is itself deemed worth reporting. This conforms with a tendency for television and other mass media to be pacifying and consensual, and to reproduce without frequent questions the hierarchic distribution of power in society.[45]

This is sometimes presented as a discovery by students of the media. But it would be extremely surprising to find the converse true: a national television devoted indefatigably to shaking up its audience's social and political assumptions and giving a voice to unknown and unaccredited people. A moment's thought surely suggests that any alternative state of affairs would enable single-issue campaigning agencies and demagogues to manipulate the programming schedules and exert a possibly sinister influence on public opinion.

It should be noted here that efforts are made in Britain by the broadcasting organizations – principally Channel Four and BBC2 – to counter the 'pacifying and consensual' role of media, for instance by giving limited opportunities for minority groups to use air-time. Moreover, a trend in recent academic research rejects the assumption that the viewers are mainly passive and treats them instead as sophisticated and critical.[46]

THE TELEVISION PERSONALITY

Television techniques are highly convention-bound and unlikely to change quickly. The television personality as hearthside 'friend of the family' has great importance. There is at present a dearth of personalities who could do for the field of development and disaster relief, what Sir David Attenborough has done in Britain for wildlife and zoology, or as the late Lord Clark did for art history. This would seem to be a definite job vacancy in international broadcasting, though perhaps a difficult one to fill.

There is an increasing tendency for British newscasters to be bland, personable, reassuring figures on to whom the viewer can project emotions of affectionate confidence – Martyn Lewis of the BBC has set an unmatchable standard in that department, and Trevor McDonald of ITN is well-known for his suave air of relaxed authority. By contrast, the 'anchormen' (or -women) for major documentaries have to be distinctive or even flamboyant. It is official BBC policy that 'It is not appropriate for a regular BBC reporter, normally associated with news or programmes related to matters of public policy, to present a personal view programme on a controversial matter.'[47]

Newscasters such as Reginald Bosanquet or Alastair Burnet, who were conspicuous 'characters', seem to have few counterparts today in Britain, though one must acknowledge the passionate commitment to Ethiopia of Michael Buerk in the 1980s, and as one of the BBC's principal newsreaders he still exercises some influence over the content of news programmes through *personal* authority. In February–March

1992, Michael Buerk gave four hard-hitting radio broadcasts on Radio 4, *Africa: Deadline for the Dark Continent*, rather too apocalyptic in some people's opinion but persuasive in its reporting on Somalia as a 'nihilist nightmare'.[48] Though this series was featured on the front cover of the *Radio Times* and was followed up by television reporting, it did not yet succeed in carving out space for Somalia on the national agenda.

Jon Snow of Channel Four News, another colourful and respected figure, has also shown a clear personal commitment – to publicizing the truth about atrocities in East Timor which the world has chosen to ignore.

One agency, Unicef, has regularly used film stars like Peter Ustinov and Audrey Hepburn as 'ambassadors' to support its general fund-raising. As discussed in Chapter 2, the rock star Bob Geldof revolutionized fund-raising for famine relief in the 1980s, and Comic Relief has successfully adopted for its purposes the attractive personality of Lenny Henry, the Black comedian from the British Midlands. However, the need is for education and awareness as well as fund-raising, and this can only be done by those who have a thorough grasp of the issues as well as the required vivid television image. The intervention of another pop star, Sting, in trying to help solve the problems of the Amazonian Indians through his home-made Rainforest Foundation ran up against easily predictable problems of organization. Among agency officials, one like Sadruddin Aga Khan who combines long experience with an attractive media image can make a considerable impact.

Mother Teresa, who founded her own agency for the relief of the poor and dying, is held in immense esteem and is one of the best-known women in the world. While this is mainly due to her extraordinary charisma, it is also worth noting that she and her entourage are expert manipulators of the media – as was noticed by Bob Geldof when he met her while raising money for Band Aid ('She does a sort of "Oh dear, I'm just a frail old lady" schtick.')[49]

An elusive but essential qualification for a major television personality is credibility. Politicians, civil servants, sportsmen and entertainment stars generally lack credibility in the field of disasters and relief – though there are a few exceptions such as Bernard Kouchner (who only recently became a government minister) and Bob Geldof. International reporters have the credibility but if they get too close to promoting the humanitarian agencies' interests, they risk losing their reputation for journalistic objectivity. Academics and agency workers may have credibility, but seldom the communicative skill and charisma.

NUMBERS AND EMPATHY

Occasionally, a major disaster strikes people with whom the viewer in a Western country can personally identify without difficulty. Examples would be the Townsend Thorensen ferry disaster in 1987 off Zeebrugge in Belgium, or the PanAm air crash over Lockerbie, Scotland, in 1988. As Shawcross notes, the Western media can at times be preoccupied by the fate of a single person such as a boy who had fallen down a well in southern Italy;[50] other examples are hostages, hi-jack victims, or small children whose lives could be saved by expensive advanced surgery. 'Suffering is not increased by numbers', says the narrator of Graham Greene's *The Quiet American,* 'one body can contain all the suffering the world can feel.'[51] This is no doubt correct from a theological or philosophical point of view, but from the point of view of practical action we ought to be swayed by numbers. Disasters affecting very large numbers of victims and survivors nearly always involve populations far removed, both physically and culturally, from Western television viewers.

As we have seen above, news and documentary from foreign parts are mediated by a succession of people: eye-witnesses, reporters, commentators, celebrities, newsreaders. The ultimate guarantee that we are in the presence of a raw tragedy is the image of a suffering person, or sometimes a dead person; sometimes we are shown dead animals; or material evidence of a broken way of life, such as uninhabitable housing or scattered possessions; or we may be shown, more subtly, an image of someone whose distress has been relieved. The most brutal evidence is censored off the screen – according, it seems, to rules which become more restrictive according to the closeness of the victims to the assumed audience. 'In British culture', the BBC guidelines rightly say, 'grief is a predominantly private emotion', and intrusion or apparent intrusion on this privacy makes many viewers angry.[52]

We have come to gauge the scale of disasters according to the number of deaths. Television news is not well suited to exploring the social and economic disruption which follows disasters and which affects far more people than the immediate victims; though attempts are sometimes made during the extended current affairs programmes which achieve much smaller viewing figures. (For instance, BBC2's 10.30 p.m. Newsnight, which lasts for around 45 minutes and is intended to present selected news issues in greater depth than is possible in a half-hour bulletin, attracts only 1.2 million viewers or so, compared to the 7.2 million who watch the BBC Nine O'Clock News or 6.7 million who watch ITN's News at Ten. The comparable programme for ITN is the 50-minute Channel Four news at 7 p.m., which attracts slightly fewer viewers than Newsnight.[53])

THE CULTURE OF THE NEWS ROOM

Some of these ways of thinking about the news are unacceptable to those who work within the system. For them, the news story is like prey to be chased while it is still fresh and alive, for 'today's news wraps tomorrow's chips'. As they say in the USA, 'timing is to journalism as location is to real estate'.

Television news favours strong visual images. But what is strong today may be weak tomorrow. When the first Boat People from Vietnam sought a haven in other south-east Asian countries in the late 1970s, they were thoroughly documented by Western television despite being thousands of miles distant. Vietnamese refugees still risk their lives to piracy and other hazards of the sea, but the media have for the most part gone away. The boat people, as Shawcross says, 'outsailed their symbolism'.[54]

Television journalists are invested with fame and glamour, and have a fair degree of control of the content of their reporting, but they have relatively little power to control schedules and choice of subject-matter, and they work under constant pressure to deliver hot news, thus justifying the great expense of having sent out a crew. Effective power might seem to reside with television editors. But editors, too, are subject to pressures and expectations from directors and governing boards, to the need to get a yield from expensive investment in technology, and to competition both with other channels and with radio and the printed press.

Television news, at least in Britain, does not seem to work in the same way as a newspaper or magazine, when one strong editor can impose his or her policy over the whole organ. In British television there is an important split of responsibility between 'intake' (the commissioning editors) and 'output' (the editors of individual news programmes), and both are run by 'hands-on' people in shirtsleeves who report upwards to a hierarchy of panelled offices which they are not part of themselves. This means that major decision-making is diffused among a group of about eight people. Though the ambience is glamorously high-tech, television news is a craft based on apprenticeship rather than formal instruction. House values are absorbed by recruits 'in the mother's milk', as one editor of a major news bulletin put it to me.

The managers of television news tend to be preoccupied by time pressures and not much inclined to looking at themselves from outside. Whereas every profession tends to develop its own 'deformation', it is a mark of the more sophisticated ones in Western countries that they habitually engage in a dialogue with outside commentators and researchers. This is becoming true even of the more conservative professions, such as judges and surgeons.

British television news editors subscribe to a value system which includes a strong commitment to fairness, taste and ethical standards, and to withstanding pressures from powerful political interests which fully appreciate, and would like to co-opt, the power of television. I have seen one of the weekly memoranda about current news which is circulated within the BBC, and it was impressively thorough – dealing responsibly with difficult questions such as how to report the policies of terrorist organizations, whether to publish the name of a politician named in a sex abuse trial, and similar matters of ethics and privacy. The BBC's formal guidelines for producers and editors are thorough and conscientious, as is exemplified by the following extracts from the section on 'Accidents and Disasters':

> Bodies should not normally or needlessly be shown. Great care should be taken even when they are covered by blankets.
>
> Other difficult scenes may need to be shown only briefly: an acceptable picture can become intolerable because it is shown for too long – even by a few seconds.
>
> Show as little as possible of the news gathering process unless it is part of the story. It is often a tough, unattractive scramble. When the focus of it is a survivor or a bereaved person the sight and sounds of jostling reporters and cameramen is usually too much.[55]

However, the value system does not appear to include a commitment to institutional self-examination, constantly reviewing how by imperceptible shifts of emphasis the practice of the newsroom might from its position of immense influence become more rationally and equitably responsive to human need. Yet this is the kind of approach which many other branches of the broadcasting system adopt.

There is anecdotal evidence, which I have not been able to substantiate, that a BBC medical officer once found, in those responsible for putting together the 9 o'clock news, levels of stress higher than those of air pilots landing or taking off in the Concorde. Anyone visiting a news room will be aware of the high level of stress. Such pressures induce superb technical perfectionism and devotion to duty, but they also help to cement a fixed ideology. Television news editors and their subordinates seem to assume that the news proceeds irresistibly as a series of 'stories', almost as if beyond the power of individuals to influence it. Yet in fact it is constructed by a small group of professionals who tend, like all other professionals, to keep in mind constantly what their colleagues and competitors are thinking of their work.

No one would suggest that when a large bomb explodes in the centre of London, or when a major head of state dies, this should be anything other than the lead story. However, when one examines the secondary stories on television there is clearly a good deal of scope for opinion about what can make the grade. (The wedding of a minor Royal? Another leak of classified information from a ministry that is under political pressure? Foreign ministers getting in and out of limousines?) Without proposing any radical changes to the practice of news editors, some gradual alterations could be made to the emphasis and mix.

'Television executives', comments William Boot, 'seem wedded to the idea that sensation is essential.'[56] But this is only half the truth, for sensationalism is systematically balanced by hypnotic repetition of the reassuringly predictable: the dollar, the yen and the Deutschmark performing their endless *contredanse*; politicians yapping at one another. It would be foolish to plead for a complete disavowal of values which are arguably intrinsic to the medium of television. But there is some room for gradual adjustments. Individual editors and journalists do make efforts to compensate for the apparently irresistible momentum of the big story. An example would be the return of an ITN journalist, Terry Lloyd, to Kurdistan in late 1991, bringing back a series of reports about the latest skirmishes with the Iraqi army, at a time when public interest in the Kurds was at a low ebb. A committed reporter like the BBC's George Alagiah, who in his spare time advises Christian Aid, is able to respond to agencies' suggestions for coverage of Third World emergencies through translating them into the language of the scoop. However, the credit given a television channel for making such an effort in parts of the world defined as marginal cannot be compared with the derision they can suffer if a 'big story' is bungled.

The success of CNN in getting to places with amazing speed has given it a new salience in television news which is somewhat ominous for journalistic standards, for it is by no means matched, despite recent efforts to broaden the focus, by ability to see in proportion and contextualize. The BBC and ITN are well aware of the need to stand back from the adrenalized excitement of 'being there'. The alternative is for television to offer what one critic has called a 'reality show'.[57]

THE DOMINANCE OF TELEVISION NEWS

The value system described above is undoubtedly inherited from the highly competitive world of the printed press and news agency services. Television news editors possibly still look for leadership to newspaper editors, and newspapers still maintain their influence among the opinion-forming élite. However, there is massive evidence that television is now the leading news medium, especially with regard to knowledge of overseas affairs. To start with, about 95 per cent of households in the industrialized countries have at least one television set.

In 1989–90, the UN's Department of Public Information commissioned surveys in many of the larger countries by national or international research organizations to ascertain (among other things) the public's sources of information about the UN and its agencies. In all the countries surveyed except three the leading source was television.[58]

Annual surveys undertaken in Britain by the Independent Television Commission reveal the following clear trend towards television becoming the first mention by viewers as their source of world news (see table).[59]

	1982	1983	1984	1985	1986	1987	1988	1989	1990	1991
	%	%	%	%	%	%	%	%	%	%
TV	58	60	62	62	65	65	65	58	69	70
Radio	12	10	13	14	10	9	9	14	11	11
Newspapers	27	28	23	23	23	25	25	25	18	19
Magazines	0	0	0	0	0	0	0	0	0	0
Talking to people	1	1	1	1	1	0	1	1	2	0

The switch in dominance from newspapers to television probably took place around the early to mid-1970s. There can be little doubt now not only of the dominance of television, but of the continuing trend towards the press losing out still further. The declining trend seems to be slower with the 'quality' press as opposed to the mass-circulation press, and the press retains much of its importance as a medium in which it is possible for public opinion to be changed and new ideas introduced. A rearguard action is currently being fought by British newspapers to maintain their share of advertising, and they adduce in their support the fact that in many households the television set appears to be left on while 'viewers' are in fact talking to one another or asleep. It must also be remembered that newspapers are read by those who make the television programmes, who are influenced in their decisions by high-quality press reporting.

Bernard Kouchner has written that:

> The best causes vegetate amidst indifference, righteous causes drag on without the intervention of the cameras. Men are dying at this moment [October 1991] in Burma, Tibet, Sri Lanka, and no one cares because they are not 'known', they are not seen to die. Television has created a worldwide familiarity. Westerners receive great men and little men in their bedrooms. This habit is damaging to those who are not discovered. They are disregarded, they do not exist.
>
>   . . . Modern anger and today's morality come from the eye, from the force and perverseness of images. I know the importance of a long and courageous enquiry and the elegance of a front-page article in the journals that count in France, a country where people don't read much. I deplore . . . the rareness of written texts which, through the effort of reading them, used to provoke reflection. But one must not be led astray by addiction to the past. . . . Today, a newspaper article . . . achieves its aim only if it also triggers off activity by TV teams.

Kouchner calls for a close alliance between journalists – especially television journalists – and humanitarians. They need to be joined, he says, by politicians. Unfortunately, he goes on, 'televisual memory lasts only for a fortnight. . . . Televised indignations are short and disappear with the image'.[60]

It is an obvious fact, which has often been remarked, that a television bulletin differs crucially from the front page of a newspaper in that one cannot 'scan' it in the same way, omitting what one is not interested in. Hence a news bulletin targeted at a general audience – as opposed to one self-selected by a particular interest – has to assume a short concentration span, which necessitates brevity and makes it hard for the compilers to place events in their context. Anne Winters, the Information Officer at Unicef Geneva, has written:

> The increasing trivialization of the media because of the influence of television has been a subject of concern to communication experts for some years. The world of television and particularly of television news, is what has been called a 'peek-a-boo' world where an event pops into view for a moment and then vanishes. It is a world of fragments, discontinuities, where the worth of information lies in its novelty and entertainment value rather than in its relevance to social and political decision-making and debate. 'Give us 22 minutes and we'll give you the world.'[61]

This is a somewhat harsh assessment of television news at its best, and evidently that of a reader of the 'quality' newspapers. If one recalls that the 9 o'clock BBC news in Britain is seen by nearly 8 million people, or 16 times as many as those who read *The Guardian* (the British quality daily most committed to Third World issues), a more favourable conclusion may be drawn: that the BBC gives a huge number of viewers access to complex issues with expert commentators. The same cannot be said of all broadcasting services.

Bernard Kouchner holds that it is senseless to try to change the way the media work. Rather, one should swim with the tide and accept their dictates. But this is to fall victim to the fallacy of fetishization: that is, treating something as an autonomous force when in fact it is the mobile and evolving result of the continuous work of people. There is a tradition of 'media studies' which is to hammer the British broadcasting organizations as lackeys of the status quo, the bourgeoisie, and relations of domination. An alternative approach, exemplified by the Pakistani scholar Akbar S. Ahmed, is to denounce the media as an 'omnipresent, moody demon' – but this is again to succumb to the fallacy of fetishization.[62]

The broadcasting organizations understandably pay little or no attention, as they know that the mass of the public support the BBC and the independent television companies. A more subtle approach, aimed not at undermining the news system but at facilitating gradual improvements, may be more productive. These improvements could take the form of more time for the news in general, more contextualization, less parochialism, reducing the pressures a little on editorial staff, giving more time to indigenous voices.[63] The forms of narrative themselves need to be analysed. News editors should expose their decisions and internal debates to public scrutiny.

'THE GLOBAL VILLAGE'

It would be wrong to leave the topic of television without trying to explain its extraordinary power. It is worth recalling what was said about it by Marshall McLuhan, guru to an earlier generation.

The heady 1960s threw up no pundit more celebrated than McLuhan, the Canadian literary critic turned media theorist. Dissolving the distinction between content and style, theory and practice, he proclaimed that 'the medium is the message' – 'message' being sometimes transmuted, McLuhan being an enthusiast for word-play, to 'massage' or 'mass age'. He managed to propagate his ideas about the media *through* the media, co-opting in the process a whole generation of broadcasting and advertising professionals whom he convinced that they were of the greatest cultural importance rather than – as they had been commonly regarded – debased versions of poets and artists. Already in McLuhan's lifetime Jonathan Miller, who had as a young man been captivated and stimulated by McLuhan's work, published a devastating critique which contributed to a thorough collapse of McLuhan's reputation.[64] In particular, Miller was able, being trained in neurophysiology, to expose as pseudo-scientific some of McLuhan's claims about the sensory modalities of reading print, watching film etc. Today, McLuhan figures as background reading for university courses on the mass media, but as one textbook on television has noted, 'McLuhan suffers more than most from the bad press of fashion.'[65]

If we are to assign importance in the history of ideas to people who have changed our world, then McLuhan must rank higher. This is recognized by his most innovative disciple, Walter J. Ong, who concludes that although McLuhan was too glib for some readers, 'few people have had so stimulating an effect as Marshall McLuhan on so many diverse minds, including those who disagreed with him or believed they did.'[66]

McLuhan's most serious weakness was that he underestimated the political and economic interests underlying the media. The early *The Mechanical Bride*[67] is perhaps his most successful single book: a lively and elegant illustrated account of American advertising of the 1940s. It benefits from a clearsightedness about the motives of advertisers which became clouded in his later books. His theories boil down to an over-simple technological determinism – the doctrine that a given technical invention leads irrevocably to a chain of social and cultural consequences. He was also too apt, when threatened in debate by scholars, to fall back on the defence that he was merely putting out 'probes' at some higher level than that of methodical argument, whereas when addressing an unsophisticated audience he readily assumed the prestige of natural science.

Yet in formulations like 'the medium is the message' inhere powerful truths. This was a way of saying what literary critics and art historians had known for a long time: that it is futile to separate what X is saying (or thinks he is saying) from the way in which X says it and the material qualities of the form of communication chosen. McLuhan's formulation helped to popularize the study of the specific properties of a wide variety of communications media, from print to photography and computers. Earlier in this chapter I examined what advantage can be got for our present purpose from considering the whole 'flow' of a television channel's output – advertising, news, documentary, fiction – as a unity, independent of the intentions and stylistic conventions of each programming department. This notion is borrowed from Raymond Williams's studies of television,[68] but it derives from McLuhan.

Since television's earliest days, no doubt a number of people were farsighted enough to recognize its future importance. In a remarkable essay written as early as 1935, the psychologist Rudolph Arnheim noted that 'If we succeed in mastering the new medium it will enrich us. But it can also put our mind to sleep.'[69] McLuhan's catchphrase 'the global village' was coined in the early 1960s when all television was still black-and-white, and instant satellite transmission was still a dream. No matter that, as Miller correctly pointed out, television coverage of faraway societies can be unconsciously pigeonholed by the viewer into a zone of unreality quite apart from his or her ordinary life – thus leading to the danger that the viewer becomes confused, indifferent and even isolationist. It is nonetheless true that television gives at least the astonishing *illusion* of shrinking the world, opening out limitless windows from the domestic hearth, and the illusion that one has, in a few minutes, understood and mastered problems of often stupendous complexity.

Reduction of the time-lag to virtually zero is one way in which this is done. Viewers of major television news programmes such as BBC, ITN, Sky News or CNN are used to having instant access to the world's trouble-spots, however remote. They may or may not be reflective enough to notice the extent of editing and filtering which is concealed in these artful representations of up-to-the-minute, ostensibly raw 'reality'. The newsrooms do their best to conceal this artfulness: as John Fiske comments, 'The idea that television is a window on the world, now known as the "transparency fallacy", still survives, if anywhere, in TV newsrooms.'[70] In fact, instant transmission by satellite is expensive and currently tends to be used only for the kinds of story attributed highest priority, which then receive extensive air-time in order to justify the expenditure. Disasters only rarely fall into that category.

DOCUMENTARY INNOVATIONS

An equally important, though not yet as commonly recognized, source of seeming global immediacy is the newer documentary technique of allowing people apparently very different from the Western viewer to speak for themselves so that the underlying similarities of human experience are explored. Technically, this is a matter of long 'takes' rather than the fast, restless editing beloved of conventional television; sub-titles rather than dubbing; and reduction of spoken commentary to a minor or subtle role rather than the authoritative monologue – that style which can be traced back to the old newsreel companies.

In the field of disasters, Granada Television's recent films about the Mursi tribespeople of southern Ethiopia, as their fertile land dwindles and they are threatened by well-armed marauding neighbours, are an excellent example – though commentary is still used.[71] A more copybook example of the observational style, concerned with the chronic disaster of poverty and poor public health, is Gary Kildea's raw and shocking *Celso and Cora* (1983) about the life of a young couple and their two children in the slums of Manila.[72] The skill and sensitivity of the film-maker bring to life the sufferings and privations of Celso and Cora, but also their courage and dignity. Such techniques have considerable potential for communicating effectively to a world public some of the messages about the underlying causes of underdevelopment which the NGOs are seeking to convey. But it is important to stress that the apparent 'rawness' is in fact achieved by processing of images and sound just as sophisticated as that to be found in more conventional, commentary-bound film-making.

Another new trend, thanks to the international diffusion of video cassettes which is already under way, is for more groups of people to film themselves by means of hand-held cameras. Some naïve propagandists for filming of this kind in the 'South' contend that it enables disadvantaged people to avoid being interpreted and distorted by mediators – professional mediators such as Western anthropologists, journalists or film-makers. In fact, all that happens is that mediation passes into the hands of indigenous political leaders or other prominent figures, who may have agenda of their own and do not necessarily represent the group as a whole any more faithfully. Nonetheless, the inventive use of video or television by the Kayapo Indians of Brazil or the Inuit of Canada offers great potential for the future. It is indicative of a movement among indigenous peoples to try to take control over the way in which they are represented by the media.

One difficulty which needs to be surmounted now is that films of this kind, depicting Third World societies in various innovative ways, tend to be shunted on our screens to minority channels or else scheduled in the morning or late at night. Broadcasting companies have a set opinion of the viewing public's requirements at peak hours, and the viewers themselves are accustomed to the excitements of fast editing and cross-cutting, frequent climaxes, and the reassuring comfort of familiar faces and voices.

THE TECHNOLOGY OF ENCHANTMENT

Television coverage of disasters and their relief gives prominence to what Propp calls 'magical agencies' and 'magical helpers' – the aeroplanes which can shift supplies at dead of night, the telecommunications which exchange messages between headquarters and the field, the medical kits which appear from warehouses to restore a measure of public health. But television is itself the magical helper par excellence, and to understand it properly we need to borrow another term from the study of folk narrative, that of enchantment.

McLuhan said that we swim unwittingly in media as fish are unaware of the element they swim in. It is truer to say that the element in which we Western consumers swim is, in fact, merchandising. This is well known to professionals in advertising and public relations, and to many of the heads of the large relief agencies. The hero not only has to bring rescue to the victims of privation, but also to close the feedback loop so that donors are reactivated and succour can be sent out afresh.

The power to impose on public opinion has become especially clear in the last few years. First (as Patrice Barrat shows in his film *Famine Fatigue: or the Power of Images*)[73] the leaders of the coup in Romania that toppled the Ceausescus not only made capture of the national television transmitters their prime objective, but also screened fictitious evidence of a massacre in Timisoara that never took place (corpses were laid out from a local morgue).[74] Few at the time thought to question the evidence, such was national and international loathing of the Ceausescus.

Second, Western television during the Gulf war was successful in attuning the majority of the public, especially in Britain, towards government military goals. Even those of us who fancied ourselves as being reasonably knowledgeable about the workings of the media were caught up by a grisly national suspense-thriller which opened every morning around 6 a.m. and closed around midnight. Hardened journalists passed on repetitive military propaganda – such as the famous 'video game' illustrations of 'smart bombs' landing on their targets – without always questioning the representativeness of such evidence. Television reporters playing the role of war correspondents were filmed in combat uniform under palm trees, purveying military rhetoric and heavily censored interviews with Coalition troops. Virtually nothing was heard about Iraqi civilian casualties (with the exception of those who suffered from the bombing of the Amiriya air-raid shelter on 13 February), it being in the interests of neither Iraq nor the Coalition to draw attention to them. The press officer of a leading international agency told me that during the war, whenever the words 'civilian casualties' were mentioned by a spokesman, his words would be cut off just before, if the broadcasting organization was British or American. An editorial in *British Journalism Review* comments: 'Most British journalists who were involved with covering the Gulf war have since sworn that they will never again allow themselves to be manipulated as they were.'[75]

To put it crudely, the Romanian coup leaders were highly successful in selling their revolution by television, and the American and British military command was reasonably successful in selling a campaign whose ultimate objective was mobile (was it to support a moral principle or to protect US vital interests?) and whose adverse repercussions were devastating and at best only marginally compensated by the advantages of restoring sovereignty to an undemocratic UN member-state. The American military authorities no doubt recalled how relatively free television coverage of the long-drawn-out Vietnam war resulted in national disillusion with the war in the USA, and contributed to the eventual humiliating withdrawal.

From this point of view, the relief agencies are also immersed in merchandising their product, which is arguably a palliative for troubled Western consciences, or 'absolution' as Harold Sumption has put it [76]. We are all aware, if not all the time consciously, that the relative peace and security of the domestic hearth in a Western country are a fragile political construct. Immigration officials devote their careers largely to keeping out people who want to enter the country to share welfare benefits and employment opportunities; the homeless (in a big city like London) often remind us of their presence when we step out of doors. If the news media were to make notification of human suffering their top priority, the news programmes would not be much watched. So a selection is made of disaster stories, usually one at a time. In the case of many countries like Ethiopia or Sudan, it is the aid agencies who make it possible for journalists to get an entrée. Almost as a quid pro quo, the agency is mentioned in the programme. The system is operated responsibly, at least in Britain, but in effect the news programme provides publicity for the agency, resulting generally in a surge of both earmarked and 'general purpose' donations. Press advertisements are still of some importance in maintaining an agency's presence, but it is the news that is all-important.

Alfred Gell, an anthropologist, writes of technology as a form of magic.[77] For Gell, the notion of magic is 'a means of securing a product without the work-cost that it actually entails . . . the base-line against which the concept of work as a cost takes place'. It is a fallacy that effective technology displaces magic; on the contrary, 'magic haunts technical activity like a shadow'. 'Magic, as the ideal technology, pervades the technical domain in pre-scientific societies', but it has not disappeared from industrial society, it merely becomes more diffuse and hard to identify. The 'technology of enchantment', for Gell, exists everywhere but in pre-scientific societies it is called sorcery or casting of spells. In our society it is called advertising or public relations. 'The propagandists, image-makers and ideologues of our technological culture are its magicians, and if they do not lay claim to supernatural powers, it is only because technology itself has become so powerful.'[78]

An earlier communications technology than television, the newspaper, was poetically characterized by Proust in terms of a miracle (or 'magic', though he did not use the word) which Roman Catholic believers call the Real Presence of Christ in the communion wafer:

> Then I considered the spiritual bread that a newspaper is, still warm and moist from the recent press and from the morning fog, where it has been distributed since dawn to maids who bring it to their masters with the morning coffee – miraculous, multipliable bread which is at the same time one and ten thousand, and which stays the same for everyone even though penetrating at once, innumerable, into every house.[79]

A newspaper's monetary price to the reader is trivial because the costs are subsidized by advertising. Television itself gives the illusion of being virtually cost-free because it is most commonly paid for either through advertising or through a levy on the population at large, or both. Either way, recovery of the broadcasting costs is spread so thinly amongst the whole community of consumers and/or television licence-holders that it is virtually painless for the individual. It gives the illusion of intimate presence not to ten thousand only, but to many millions.

The price which viewers do pay is that the scheduling and promotion of television are usually highly centralized, and its practitioners have become masters of the 'technology of enchantment'. For example, on British television, for the duration of the Gulf war, Coca-Cola and some other companies withdrew their advertising on the commercial channels.[80] It is easy to see why: the image such companies seek to present is one of youthful fun and freedom from care. As it happened, morning-till-night coverage of the war ended after a few weeks, when the risk of there being thousands of Coalition casualties was removed, and the balance of television returned to normal – except that 'the world's major news organisations had spent a fortune, and many of them have had to close bureaux as a result. There will be less coverage from South Africa and Asia, for example, because of the cost of covering the Gulf War.'[81] The BBC news service, though quite independent of advertising, feels obliged to compete for viewing ratings with ITN, so that in practice there is not much difference between the two services. In a subtle way, a large American multinational company – and other companies that compete with it for consumer spending through images of youth, desire and pleasure – probably have considerable influence, albeit indirect and hidden, over the general style and content of British television news. Television planning accommodates the lowering effect on the viewer of 'bad news', which often conspires to be a large proportion of the whole on a particular day, but this must be 'clawed back' to conform with an overall balance of pain and pleasure. The sports news which ends every news bulletin is one way in which this is done, another is the ITN 'And finally . . .' device of winding up with a droll item. Another technique is the 'diary event' – one which cameras have gone out specifically to film, often involving politicians, royalty or other celebrities.

It is debatable to what extent viewers are able to resist such enchantment. On the one hand, one may note the sophistication of television advertising in Britain, where perhaps a third of all advertisements play ironic games with the viewer rather than presenting a hard sell, as most American television advertising still does. On the other hand, the Eurovision Song Contest reaches more hundreds of millions of viewers every year, not only in Western and Eastern Europe but in Australia, Japan, Hong Kong and Korea; the aesthetic standard of the songs represents the Lowest Common Denominator. In the sphere of party politics, television is now a major consideration in the presentation of policies, the selection of leaders, their personal styles of communication and the planning of party conferences and election meetings. A national politician who disobeys the rules of television presentation – for instance, by moving his or her head while speaking so that it jerks out of the frame, or by energetic gesturing – will lose ratings. Contrary to the view of some researchers, it seems that the image manipulators are several steps ahead of the viewing public and it is difficult to believe that resistance to their wiles is as widespread as we would like to believe.

In any case – to follow the McLuhan-Williams principle of examining the 'flow' of television – advertising techniques have spilt over into many other sectors of television. The spillage is obvious in the case of contested party politics or the promotion of popular songs. It is less obvious when the ideology that is being promoted is uncontested. For instance, one of the functions of news coverage of Northern Ireland is to justify to the public the bipartisan policy of maintaining a British military presence there over a long period. Bombings and murders are dutifully recorded, yet the conflict with the IRA is not described as a 'war' – which would provoke uncomfortable questions as to why it was not a top General Election issue for 1992.

Some disasters fall readily into the mould of television consumables, the obverse of its 'light entertainment'. Others are ignored. But those which are recognized may as readily be dropped. What happens to politicians or entertainers can easily happen to groups of sufferers, that is to say they are forgotten. An actor is 'type-cast' and ceases to get parts. Fashion moves on. The Kurds, the Cambodians, the Ethiopians are forgotten.

'SECONDARY ORALITY' AND THE 'TRANSITIONAL OBJECT'

The power of television is universally acknowledged but not yet fully understood. Its 'immediacy' is one aspect of this power, but perhaps not enough to explain the dominance of television in so many households and in any industrial nation's popular culture – for rapidity in itself would surely in the long run become merely tedious, and the compulsive viewing of television begins early in children's lives before they have any interest in news and current affairs.

Walter Ong's notion of 'secondary orality' may be of some help. 'Primary orality' refers to the word-of-mouth culture which historically preceded any knowledge of print or writing. 'Secondary orality' is that related to today's high technology in which a new word-of-mouth is sustained by the telephone, radio, television and other electronic devices which depend for their existence and functioning on writing and print, but do not demand high literacy skills from their consumers.[82] According to Ong, secondary orality preserves some of the characteristics of pre-literate cultures such as spontaneity as opposed to analyticity, but in a deeply modified way (thus he eludes any charge of sentimentality or anthropological distortion).[83] 'In our contemporary secondary oral culture, clichés are popularly used, but at the same time, undercut and mocked because of our relentless literacy.'[84] The appeal of secondary orality is not to a locally defined community but to the 'as-if group of the mass viewing audience'.[85]

Ong's interpretation of television offers an attractive refinement of McLuhan but still does not fully account for its extraordinary power. However, a suggestion by Roger Silverstone goes some way towards a convincing complementary explanation. Silverstone adduces the psychoanalytic concept of the 'transitional object' – the blanket, cushion or stuffed animal to which young children become emotionally attached to enable them to go to sleep. The transitional object is the first possession which is neither child nor mother and thus plays a critical role in weaning. 'It is something to which the child ascribes meaning and affect, and it is affective by virtue of the intensity and familiarity of feeling, in providing a "magical" defense against anxiety, a link with the most powerful and basic feelings of attachment to the mother – a comfort.'[86] D. W. Winnicott claims that the transitional object is mentally retained throughout life as guarantor of the intensity with which we can experience art and religion.

Silverstone argues that television can occupy the status of a transitional object in that it becomes an indispensable comfort in many children's and indeed adults' domestic lives. John O'Neill, too, has observed that small children tend to prefer to watch television from close up, as if imbibing a precious nectar.[87] This insight might help to put flesh on the bones of Gell's 'technology as magic'.

And if this is how viewers feel about it, how about those

who work in television? When one of the BBC's news editors told me of his raw recruits absorbing the Corporation's values 'with their mother's milk', he may have found just the right metaphor.

CROSSING BARRIERS

Camus in his novel *The Plague* describes, through the reflections of the devoted Dr Rieux, how difficult it is for outsiders to appreciate the tribulations of a town infected by bubonic plague and cut off by quarantine measures.

> As well as the help sent by air and road, pitying or admiring commentaries swept down on the now solitary city every evening on the radio waves and in the press. Each time the tone of epic or prize speech made the doctor impatient. He was well aware that this solicitude was not feigned. But it could express itself only in the conventional language through which men try to express what joins them to humanity. . . . Sometimes at midnight, in the great silence of the deserted town, at the moment of going to bed for too short a sleep, the doctor turned the switch of his wireless set. From the limits of the world, across thousands of kilometres, unknown fraternal voices tried clumsily to speak their solidarity, and did indeed speak it, but they showed at the same time how unable everyone is to really share a pain that they do not see. . . .[88]

But *The Plague* was published in 1947, many years before television news.

Rousseau believed that, in general, 'natural commiseration' such as is experienced between individuals could hardly exist between one society and another. But he made an exception for what he called 'a few great cosmopolitan spirits' (*grandes Ames Cosmopolites*) who 'cross the imaginary barriers that separate peoples, and who, following the example of the sovereign being which created them, embrace the whole human species in their benevolence.'[89]

Many people in our time can be regarded as 'great cosmopolitan spirits': campaigners, journalists, relief and development workers, academics, religious leaders, artists, teachers. . . . But if there is one device which can enable anyone, not just an educated and well-travelled élite, to knock down barriers in their perception of human kind, it is television. Those who deny this have often not seen what television at its best can do when aiming at large audiences without loss of standards.

Bernard Kouchner is right to call for an alliance of journalists and NGO workers that will pull politicians along in its wake to secure progress in humanitarianism. The governors and managers of television, and those who appoint them, have a particular responsibility to ensure that standards of news, current affairs, documentary, drama and fiction film are kept as high as possible. These standards have dropped sharply in some countries where they were high (including M. Kouchner's own) and are under threat in others.[90] In countries whose television services are subject neither to state control nor to *laissez-faire* commercialism, we should regard them as major cultural assets, not to be taken for granted. Yet there are increasing signs in Britain that the television documentary is in danger of being downgraded in favour of a more 'tabloid' approach to broadcasting.

As David Bellamy the conservationist has written, television has the power to let voices be heard and images be seen which result in such issues as famine in Ethiopia and the green movement to be discussed at primary school, yet 'television will be rendered impotent if the predators of advertising and sponsorship are given free rein to sharpen their claws on viewing figures and profit and feed us on an exclusive diet of trivial distraction. Control of the masses by inflicting pleasure can only lead to a collapse of civilisation as it laughs itself to death.'[91] If it is true that serious factual programmes in Britain are likely to be replaced by deliberate sensationalism, as some commentators fear, the result will be equally damaging.[92] Fortunately, there are articulate and well organized pressure groups ready to do what they can to resist the trend.

 # Conclusion:
Disasters, Relief
and the Media

SOME CURRENT ISSUES

As this book nears completion, it is reported that the Yugoslav civil war is 'the first conflict in which people have fired intentionally on journalists, especially cameramen and photographers. About 30 [by the end of June 1992] have already been killed. They are most often found with a bullet between their eyes.'[1] Many journalists have shown great courage. Sarajevo is judged by one reporter 'the worst posting any journalist here has experienced';[2] and the most appalling atrocities consequent on the 'ethnic cleansing' of Bosnia-Herzegovina have probably not been properly covered because the journalists have been scared off. Using the control of information as a weapon of war is not new, but the determination of the belligerents of ex-Yugoslavia, in particular the Serbs, to eliminate or terrorize journalists is perhaps a new twist indicating a growing awareness of the power of the media.

What should be the objectives and strategies of the humanitarian agencies, both UN and non-governmental, in such a war, if they are able to gain a foothold and introduce their staff without excessive risk? 'One man's humanitarian relief is another man's aid to the enemy.'[3] How can the ordinary citizen make sense of the narratives and images coming through to us, each one serving some vested interest: of a political faction, or of a television channel which seeks to justify its investment, or of an ace reporter with a dashing career, or of an international statesman whose main motivation is to be 'visible', or of an agency that seeks better funding?

How much was actually achieved by President Mitterrand's much publicized visit to Sarajevo by aeroplane on 28 June 1992? I hope this book will help in the consideration of such questions.

Despite the extensive media coverage of the Balkans, the European public as a whole has not fully grasped the enormity of what is happening on its borders now that the Cold War is over. The global threat of nuclear war, so near-at-hand at times like the Cuba crisis of 1962, has receded; but many peoples of the former Eastern bloc, no longer controlled by powerful States, are now paying dearly for our peace of mind. Refugee and migrant movements, the most extensive in Europe since the 1940s, leave Western labour markets and standards of living and health care uncomfortably exposed.

Nor has the West grasped the enormity of the various crises in Africa, which are said by some NGO experts to be more serious than in 1991. Africa has shown that it can take a lot of punishment, but is there a limit?

Those who have emphasized the ability, often under-estimated, of communities in difficulty to help themselves, rather than become dependent on external aid, were surely correct; but maybe their diagnosis has been overtaken by the collapse of government in countries like southern Sudan, where six million people are currently living with no services and no semblance of government. In Mogadishu, capital of Somalia, where the civil war was perhaps Africa's most savage since Biafra, Save the Children Fund (UK), during the first half of 1992, saved the lives of some 10,000 children through food aid protected by armed escorts. In July, the Red Cross was bringing a meal of rice every day to 500,000 people and was seeking funds to double this.[4] In northern Somaliland, SCF and a few other agencies are providing the only health services that are available. In Ethiopia, the government is more responsible than it has been for some 15 years, yet financially it is nearly bankrupt and the international donor community is not much interested in funding Ethiopia's rehabilitation.[5] About a third of the Ethiopian conscripts currently being demobilized are estimated to be HIV-positive. Thousands of refugees from Somalia and Ethiopia are crossing the Kenyan border each day to flee from war and famine. UNHCR appealed in the summer for $34 million to help these refugees, who may number nearly 300,000 in 1992 and are 'among the most destitute the UNHCR has had to deal with'; officials are not hopeful that they will be given enough funds.[6] In southern Africa, traditionally self-sufficient in food, the current drought, the worst this century, has parched about 2.6 million square miles and eliminated half the current year's agricultural production.[7]

These food emergencies, and projections for HIV infection in the continent, will make great demands on the humanitarian agencies and probably affect the whole tenor of their fundraising and development education. For apathy about Africa seems to be growing. There are signs that in order to shock people out of this apathy, some of the agencies' fund-raising departments may decide to revert to publishing horrific imagery in their appeals. A partial case can be made for this, but it is clear that such imagery has damaging side-effects for the public's perceptions of both Africa and black people generally. Ambivalences and tensions within the agencies (see Chapter 2) will probably become sharper. It may be that the largely successful efforts of some of the leading agencies to resolve these tensions for themselves in a holistic way will be threatened by a new realism that tries to maximize cash receipts, and the count of individual lives saved, without reference to wider social, economic and political contexts.

As this book went to press, President Bush announced his despatch of US troops to protect relief supplies to Somalia.

THE RELIEF AGENCIES IN THE 1990s

While taking the media as its main theme, this book has sought to define a field of enquiry in which the relief agencies are seen as a kind of multi-axial hinge: between haves and have-nots, North and South, the local and the global, emergencies and planning, education and operations, marketing of images and meeting genuine needs, politics and compassion.

Currently the influence of NGOs in many fields – most notably, at the time of writing, on ecological issues – is increasing and is coming to be regarded by some commentators as one of the most positive hopes for the future, in particular for the expansion of 'civil society' at a global level. Jon Tinker, the environmentalist, has written recently that 'The voices of NGOs – and the strength of NGOs is that they have many voices – have been behind most of the dramatic political changes of the last few years.' Tinker sees an important role for alternative news agencies and research and educational institutes in strengthening the information capacities of NGOs and the media in the developing world.[8] It may be added that if the NGOs use the media constructively, and through their own good example, they could advance alternative models for the eventual restructuring of the UN system.

But equally, the rise of cynicism, gross materialism and xenophobia in some of the most supposedly civilized nations is a cause for concern. These opposing tendencies coexist with the rising influence of the NGOs, and perhaps we should see the processes as mutually reactive. For instance, environmental and development NGOs that call for 'frugalism' and an 'aesthetic of scarcity' in the West should realize that insofar as this movement is successful in moderating consumption, it is likely to put a brake on economic recovery as conventionally defined. Economic recession causes anxiety and fear, which in turn lead to protectionism and xenophobia.

The values and operating standards of the humanitarian NGOs at their best are indeed exemplary, but they need to be considered as institutions with normal human failings rather than as sacred cows. They deserve, too, to be respected as foci not merely of dutiful do-gooding, but of creativity in moulding and managing resources and in propagating new and inspiring ideas.

These NGOs now face massive challenges, partly from the sheer scale of need but also from the need to adapt from the 'mononational' to the global, as public opinion gets more used to operating on a planetary scale. It is essential that they both adapt to the 'media regime' and respond to the call for clearer accountability. This book has been a preliminary exploration of some of the issues.

We should be on the lookout for fresh and innovative approaches to humanitarian action. For instance, in the autumn of 1992 a 30-year-old surgeon of Pakistani descent employed by the Manchester Royal Infirmary, Dr Zia Alvi, joined a small British agency's mission to Croatia to bring Bosnian refugees back to Britain. He was unimpressed by the agency's effectiveness, and decided after his return to seek to help on his own account. He was persuaded by fellow-medics in Zagreb that priority should be given to medical supplies, which were extremely scarce despite all the shipments from governmental and other sources. Setting himself a target of £100,000, to be managed by the Infirmary's administrators as a charity (Doctors Overseas Charity or DOC), Alvi first secured publicity in the local press and television news in the Manchester area, then circulated 500 copies of a 13-minute video nationally through a burgeoning network of personal contacts, with the result that he reached his fund-raising target three times over.

The video showed footage shot in Bosnia by a Western European camera crew (known personally to Alvi but not identified), recording the gruesome results of brutal attacks on unarmed pedestrians in markets, and of tortures and brutal-ities carried out in the name of 'ethnic cleansing'. Watching the video reminded me of how much is censored out of British television news bulletins (see Chapter 5) – indeed, it was the professional restraint of our television editors which gave Aivi the space to make an impact.

Raising funds through atrocity images is a morally hazardous exercise, which could lead to systematic confidence trickery. But in my view Dr Alvi's conviction and dedication, and the extreme frugality with which he personally delivered his large consignment of medical supplies into reliable Croatian hands, justified what he did. Such qualities, joined with such a flair for exploiting the media, keep the flame of charity alight by showing what can be done by one individual. Great careers in the humanitarian field, and even the foundation of great agencies, have had similar origins.

ENVOI

We have examined the imagery and narrative structures through which disaster and relief are represented in the media, showing how the flux and immensity of individual worlds of deprivation and restoration are ordered into packages for us to consume – whether in listening to a reporter bring us a 'big story', or in showing our brand loyalty to a favoured charity. Stories of famine or civil strife in poorer countries may be conceived as exports to the North – in some cases, like that of the Biafran war, literally their principal cash-crop – subject to unpredictable shifts of consumer fashion, to political manipulation, and to control of the channels of aid by Northern intermediaries. We consumers find our way into these stories by means of Propp's invariants: the hero and villain, the donor, the lack, the magical agency and so forth.

It is from folklore that Propp's archetypal scheme derives. In most other difficult areas of human experience, we can seek help and guidance from imaginative literature. Have the great imaginative writers of the West anything to say to us on the subject of disasters and relief?

In Western literature, harking back to the Old Testament, we may find memorable representations of disasters of many kinds. Defoe's *A Journal of the Plague Year*, published in 1722, is a vivid evocation of London during 1664–5 when the author was a small child, recalling Thucydides' description in *The Peloponnesian War* of a plague that gripped Athens in 430 BC.

In 1814, Shelley travelled through war-ravaged France and he imagined in his long poem *The Revolt of Islam* a scene of macabre desolation:

> There was no food, the corn was trampled down,
>   The flocks and herds had perished; on the shore
> The dead and putrid fish were ever thrown;
>   The deeps were foodless, and the winds no more
> Creaked with the weight of birds, but, as before
>   Those wingèd things sprang forth, were void of shade;
> The vines and orchards, Autumn's golden store,
>   Were burned; – so that the meanest food was weighed

With gold, and Avarice died before the god it made.[9]

A better-known example is a devoutly Christian poem by Gerard Manley Hopkins about a shipwreck off the Kent coast:[10]

Wiry and white-fiery and whirlwind-swivellèd snow
Spins to the widow-making unchilding unfathering
    deeps.

. . .

Hope had grown grey hairs,
Hope had mourning on,
Trenched with tears, carved with cares,
Hope was twelve hours gone. . . .

Desolation and disaster exert a powerful fascination, evoking by turns horror, compassion, guilt, *Schadenfreude*, a superstitious spell to protect our own lives from harm, and, for some people, a religious awe. But what of the efforts of those who seek to relieve disaster?

Numerous sympathetic portraits of medical doctors are to be found in imaginative literature: Dr Rieux in Camus' *The Plague* or Dr Colin the leprosy specialist in Greene's *A Burnt-out Case*, where the Catholic fathers in a medical mission are also described with understanding. (Neither of these two mid-twentieth-century colonial novels, set respectively in Algeria and what was then the Congo, gives attention to indigenous points of view.) Organized humanitarian relief of a more general nature has been less diligently depicted by imaginative writers. The eighteenth century yields sympathetic portraits of individual philanthropists in, for instance, the work of Pope and Fielding.[11] But questioning of the motives of organized philanthropy, in the manner of Dickens or Emerson, became more widespread in the nineteenth century, anticipating the anthropologist Marcel Mauss's[12] insight that charity can actually wound. (The published lives of great humanitarians tend to be dull hagiographies, except when a reputation built up by the media is pulled down by the same means, as in the case of Albert Schweitzer.)

Like sex within marriage, organized humanitarian relief is one of those topics of which there are few imaginative descriptions, because writers do not think of them as having interesting potential, and are constrained by stereotypical assumptions. Some of the responsibility must rest with Cervantes, whose extraordinary novel about Don Quixote's ludicrous career as a knight-errant is a satire on chivalric texts. When Don Quixote sees the dust raised by two flocks of sheep and concludes that they are two opposed armies, he decides that he must 'favour and assist the weaker side'.[13] Since the seventeenth century, sophisticated literature has often followed Cervantes in inverting the Proppian schema and presenting us with ironic anti-heroes.

Yet the humanitarian movement today is imbued with significant tensions that call out to be explored by the novelist or dramatist. Let the last word be with Camus's Dr Rieux, who says of bubonic plague – extended by Camus as a metonym for all and any disasters and oppressions: 'it's not a matter of heroism, it's a matter of honesty. It's an idea that may seem laughable, but the only way of fighting the plague is honesty.'[14]

Notes

INTRODUCTION

1. *The Times*, 27 June 1992. A more cautious UN estimate was 1.5 million. *Le Nouveau Quotidien*, 27 June 1992.
2. Alexander de Waal's chilling phrase was intended to encompass agency consultants, academics, bureaucrats and dignitaries as well as journalists. *Famine that Kills* (Clarendon Press, Oxford, 1989), p. 20.
3. Jérôme Koechlin in *Journal de Genève*, 31 July 1992.
4. Many observers fear that the edge which British television has over other countries will soon be lost because of moves by Conservative administrations towards deregulation and submission to pure 'market' forces. Follies such as the BBC's recent investment of millions of pounds in scenery for its *Eldorado* Spanish soap opera do not help its defenders.
5. The quarterly journal *Disasters* is a focus of serious interest, the only journal to bring together research on disasters and relief and emergency management. It was started in 1977 by the London Technical Group, which included John Seaman (the first editor, now head of policy in SCF (UK)'s overseas department), the late John Rivers, Julius Holt and Mark Bowden (now head of SCF (UK)'s African operations). Its philosophy was described in the first editorial as 'a conviction that people die in disasters chiefly because insufficient money is spent saving lives. Given this, the limited money available can be spent more or less wisely. Wisdom, in this context, can only be arrived at by the application of science.' The London Technical Group turned itself into the International Disaster Institute in 1978, with Frances D'Souza as director. In 1986 she left and the name was changed again to Relief and Development Institute. In 1991 this was closed down but three of its protagonists moved to the Overseas Development Institute, Regent's College, London, to set up a new Relief and Disaster Policy Programme. ODI is now the institutional home of the journal *Disasters*, and David Turton of Manchester University has been the editor since 1989, with Blackwells as the present publisher.

6. Peter Ackroyd, *Dickens* (Sinclair-Stevenson, London, 1990) pp. 544, 971.
7. Such work can even be 'energized by a secret recoil from family intimacy. It sends [such a person] out to deal with people who give him more status and control. Behind the love was a hidden indifference, even hatred.' John Drury, *The Burning Bush* (Fount Paperbacks, London, 1990), p. 64ff., writing of certain clergy and social workers.
8. Report by Children's Defense Fund, May 1991. Families of three earning $9,985 a year, and families of four earning $12,675, are considered under the federal poverty level.
9. Some organizations have adopted a deliberate vocation to work in obscurity to change society from the bottom up. The Little Brothers of Jesus, a Catholic order of monks founded by Père Charles de Foucauld, follow the example of Jesus's life by living with poor people. However, Christianity only made its impact on the world by means of brilliant use of the media of the day by St Paul and others.

CHAPTER 1

1. Sadruddin Aga Khan, *Improving the Disaster Management of the United Nations* (United Nations Assn. of the USA, New York, 1987), p. 4ff. A subset of the fourth type, the accidental, might be called the *iatrogenic*, on the analogy of diseases caused by medical treatment. An example of this, sadly not infrequent in attempts to 'develop' the Third World, was the Polonoroeste highway project in north-west Brazil funded in the early 1980s by the World Bank, which resulted in mass migration from other parts of Brazil to almost uncultivable land, and in the impoverishment of indigenous Indians. David Price, in his *Before the Bulldozer: the Nambiquara Indians and the World Bank* (Seven Locks Press, Arlington, VA., 1989) argues that 'the devastation is more widespread and more lasting than that caused by a hurricane or an earthquake. But instead of receiving aid for disaster relief, Brazil is expected to pay the World Bank for helping make the disaster happen' (p. 189).
2. WHO leaflet, *En Cas de Catastrophe*, p. 5.
3. Pär Stenbäck, secretary-general of the Federation of Red Cross and Red Crescent Societies, in *ibid.*, p. 6.
4. The Committee has urged that 'by the year 2000, all countries, as part of their plan to achieve sustainable development, should have in place comprehensive national assessments of risks from natural hazards, with these assessments taken into account in development plans; mitigation plans at the national or local levels, including long-term prevention and preparedness and community awareness; and ready access to global, regional, national and local warning systems.' The Committee has also

called for a world conference on natural disaster reduction in 1994 for the national committees, of which nearly 100 have been formed worldwide. The Committee estimates that, in 1990 alone, natural disasters caused economic losses of $47 billion, and that, in the last 20 years, natural disasters cost the lives of some three million people and affected at least 800 million human beings (UN *Development Forum*, November 1991).

5. Graham Hancock, *Lords of Poverty* (Mandarin, 1989). For a more measured critique of the UN's response to famine, see Chapter 4 of Peter Walker, *Famine Early Warning Systems; Victims and Destitution* (Earthscan Publications, London, 1989).

6. Sadruddin Aga Khan, *op. cit.*, pp. 21–2. 1987,

7. Richard Reeves, *International Herald Tribune*, 25 July 1991.

8. 'The International Response to Emergencies' (ISCA, Geneva), August 1991.

9. *The Independent*, 14 February 1992; *Le Nouveau Quotidien*, 26 February 1992; *Journal de Genève*, 28 February 1992.

10. SDR cooperates with other national bodies which together with it form the Rescue Chain – the Swiss Red Cross, the Federal Office for Air Protection Troop, Swiss Air-Rescue and the Swiss Disaster Dog Association – and also with international agencies, including, of course, the ICRC. The volunteers are divided into ten groups: *general management* (administrators, lawyers); *health services* (physicians, nurses, laboratory personnel); *construction* (architects, engineers, foremen, bricklayers, carpenters); *supply services* (logistic specialists, dieticians, book-keepers, storage personnel); *transportation* (mechanics, drivers, pilots, ground crew personnel); *radio communications* (radio and telegraph operators); *air-sea rescue, chemical and nuclear expertise, disaster prevention* (e.g., seismologists) and *documentation/information* (journalists and photographers). SDR also has a warehouse of necessary materials valued at over SF5 million. In order to ensure immediate action by SDR in case of emergency, SDR has signed agreements with a number of countries frequently struck by national disasters. It is increasingly giving attention to disaster prevention and mitigation.

11. Recent statistics for British government responses:

	No. of responses	Expenditure
1988	90	£22.94 million
1989	41	£19.34 million
1990	66	£21.37 million

(These figures exclude food aid and long-term aid for refugees.) Source: ODA.

12. Press release, Brussels, 6 November 1991.

13. John de Salis, 'Opinion', *The League* (Red Cross, Geneva), October

1986. In the context of long-term development rather than short-term relief, some of the techniques of commercial market research have already been adapted to help ascertain the attitudes and aspirations of client groups who, because of their lack of purchasing power, are too often regarded as silent beneficiaries. See T. Scarlett Epstein, *et al.*, *A Training Manual for Development Market Research Investigators* (BBC World Service, International Broadcasting and Audience Research, London, 1991). Cf. Alexander de Waal: 'Currently there is no dialogue, no exchange of views, between relief organizations and the people they avowedly serve, the rural poor. . . . If, however, we listen to the rural poor of Africa – not only to their voiced concerns but to an articulated understanding of the principles that underly their actions – a lively debate will follow, and a new agenda will be set.' *Famine that Kills: Darfur, Sudan, 1984–1985* (Clarendon Press, Oxford, 1989), p. 1.

14. There are some 500 million disabled people in the world. 'It is a sorry state of affairs when a very poor group of people have so low a profile in our thoughts and strategies, that they are even excluded from our clichés.' Chris Underhill, 'Disabled people in development: challenging traditional attitudes', paper published by Action on Disability and Development, 23 Lower Keyford, Frome, Somerset, UK, May 1990.

15. Nonetheless, a low ratio of administrative costs to turnover is sought by all responsible agencies. Agencies may differ in the way they account for, e.g., staff travel and regional office expenses.

16. Chen Yong, *et al.*, *The Great Tangshan Earthquake of 1976: An Anatomy of a Disaster* (Pergamon Press, Oxford, 1988).

17. See Eugenia Shanklin, 'Beautiful deadly Lake Nyos: the explosion and its aftermath', *Anthropology Today*, February 1988.

18. Patrick Poivre d'Arvor, a leading French news anchor-man, in the film by Patrice Barrat, *Famine Fatigue, or the Power of Images*, 1991.

19. Personal interview.

20. 'Africa: the Reality of Famine' (Save the Children (UK), April 1991). 'Famine Myths: Setting the record straight' (SCF (UK), May 1991).

21. The 1991 estimates seem to have derived from WFP, and SCF had misgivings about using them, mindful perhaps of Alexander de Waal's warning that 'Failing to comprehend how rural people really survive, disaster tourists often predict that in the absence of external aid, millions will starve' (*op. cit.*, p. 23). On 31 January 1992, Christian Aid issued a statement anticipating the journalists' question, 'The Past Year: Whatever Happened to the 27 Million?' Christian Aid's conclusion was that international action such as the UN Special Emergency Programme for the Horn of Africa (SEPHA), additional EC food aid, and support by NGOs did make a difference, though thousands did die quietly and unseen as a result of malnutrition and

lack of food. In the event, many fewer people died than was feared – often by staying at home and trying to eat less and less. Most of the agencies would agree that Western aid did help to save a large number of people. Also, the effectiveness of local coping strategies was, fortunately, underestimated, and in some countries such as Ethiopia transport and warehousing are much more efficient than in 1984–5. The big camps of earlier famines, filmed for the TV screens, gave a greater sense of crisis to stir the world's conscience. The wars in Angola, Eritrea and Ethiopia were over, allowing reconstruction to begin, but wars continued in Liberia, Somalia, Mozambique and Sudan. For their 1992 'Skip lunch' appeal, SCF decided to avoid using any specific estimates for people at risk in Africa as a whole.

22. Disasters Emergency Committee, Report on Activities, 1990–1.
23. 'Famine prevention and food security', SCF internal conference report, 19–22 February 1991. Alexander de Waal (*op. cit.*, Chapter 1) has distinguished 'famine' as a period of shortage and hunger, to which a society adapts albeit with difficulty and hardship, from famine as widespread starvation. De Waal's important book was sponsored by SCF.
24. *A Moveable Famine: Tackling Food Security in Africa* (SCF, March 1992).
25. *The Guardian*, 15 April 1991, report by Kevin Watkins.
26. *The Guardian*, 19 April 1991, 'Hunger that cries out beyond appeal'.
27. Internal agency memorandum, July 1991.
28. Oxfam memorandum, 26 April 1991.
29. Sadruddin Aga Khan, Report to the Secretary-General on Humanitarian Needs in Iraq, United Nations, 15 July 1991.
30. 'The economic impact of the Gulf crisis on Third World countries', memorandum to the Foreign Affairs Select Committee, jointly submitted by CAFOD and 5 other British agencies, March 1991.
31. SCF Emergency update, 7 May 1991.
32. See Rosalind Shaw, 'Living with floods in Bangladesh', *Anthropology Today*, February 1989. According to some experts, excessive deforestation of the Himalayan foothills in Nepal and Assam is a major cause of the increased severity of flooding. A barrage built by India on the Ganges close to Bangladesh's north-western border has also been blamed for increasing river flow during the wet season, as have various other possible factors.
33. WHO, *op. cit.*, p. 5.
34. Trevor Page, quoted by Peter Gill, *A Year in the Death of Africa* (Paladin, London, 1986), p. 99.
35. *British Overseas Aid 1975–1990*, Aid Report no. 7 of Christian Aid's Policy Unit (January 1992).
36. The ICRC receives approximately 270 million Swiss francs per year

from governments and only about 7 million Swiss francs from individual gifts and legacies.

37. ActionAid Harris poll survey, June 1991, cited in Oxfam Briefing no. 1, January 1992, p. 10.

38. Jean Drèze and Amartya Sen, *The Political Economy of Hunger* (Oxford; Clarendon, 1990), Vol. 1, p.6.

39. N. Ram, 1990. 'An independent press and anti-hunger strategies: the Indian experience', in Drèze and Sen, *op. cit.*

40. In *Starving in Silence: a Report on Famine and Censorship* (International Centre on Censorship, London), pp. 127–39.

41. War on Want unfortunately declined in the late 1980s amid charges of financial mismanagement. The scale of operation was reduced but the agency is now expanding gradually under new management. It is now a member of Entr'Aide Ouvrière (International Workers Aid–IWA), an organization based in Bonn whose members are NGOs from the whole of Europe. War on Want's current focus of attention is Latin America. Historically, War on Want were the leaders among NGOs in the early 1950s in arguing the need to change the attitudes and policies of the rich Northern countries.

42. A quango is a 'quasi-autonomous national government organization', of which there are many in the UK.

43. These are cash figures and ignore the fact that the Retail Price Index in the UK has risen approximately 8 times since 1966. Famine in Africa has of course been greatly exacerbated by war. One appeal for relief of famine in Ethiopia in 1984 was not an official DEC appeal but a fund opened to receive donations following a massive response to TV news. The figures include British Government contributions totalling £3 million made to two of the appeals for Africa.

44. DEC Handbook (revised October 1989).

45. For example, the BBC appeal for 'Crisis in Africa' on 10 January 1991, just before the Gulf war. Presented by Gavin Campbell, a television personality, this featured Jenny Borden, deputy director of Christian Aid. A German nurse was shown helping some famine victims. By contrast, the ITV appeal used a popular ITN newscaster, Trevor McDonald, but showed no agency personnel and gave barely any explanation of how funds raised would be spent. (Here it is worth noting the practice of television reporters in the field who sometimes deliberately do not shave, look dishevelled etc., in order to enhance the 'field' look. Agency field officials who take the trouble to shave and wash before an interview may be rejected by TV camera crews.)

46. Leader, 1 December 1989.

47. Leader, 29 November 1989.

48. *The Times*, 29 November 1989.

49. *The Independent*, 30 November 1989.
50. 2 December 1989, letter from John McCormick and Kenneth Blyth, Secretaries of the BBC and IBA respectively. The letter also denied that the broadcasting authorities had been concerned about the political character of the rebel movements in Tigré and Eritrea.
51. There had been two DEC appeals for famine in Africa in 1984, however, which together raised £15.97 million.
52. *Evening Standard*, 2 October 1991.
53. Articles by Colin Adamson, 2 October and 16 December 1991.
54. The Disasters Joint Appeal Committee is based in Dublin, has been in existence in one form or another for over 10 years, and consists of five agencies: Christian Aid, Church of Ireland Bishops Appeal, Gorta, Trócaire, Irish Missionary Union. Of these, Trócaire (which is Roman Catholic) is the biggest, and the Irish Missionary Union is not a funding agency but an umbrella-body comprising all the Catholic church and missionary groups with personnel abroad. IMU takes no share of income raised through joint appeals, but lends its collective voices to the appeal. The second-largest agency in Ireland, Concern, is not a member of the Committee, by its own decision.

   The Committee is inactive except during the weeks of a joint appeal. Such appeals take place on average about once every 18 months. Appeals are launched by unanimous agreement of the members, and, during the three weeks of the appeal, individual appeals for the particular disaster area are suspended by the member agencies. There are standing arrangements with radio and TV stations, so that appeals can be advertised immediately. There are also arrangements with the banks. Income from joint appeals is divided among the members of the committee, in direct proportion to the relative size of the agency. In 1991, the structure and status of the Committee were being examined. It may be that the committee will link in with CONGOOD, the confederation of development NGOs. (Information from the Rev. F. Maher, CSSp.)

CHAPTER 2

1. Elizabeth Stamp, Oxfam, personal interview.
2. *Individual Giving and Volunteering in Britain* (Charities Aid Foundation, 1992), reported in *The Guardian*, 18 June 1992.
3. Nicholas Hinton, SCF, personal interview.
4. Henrie Lidchi read a paper, based on doctoral research on SCF's marketing practices, at an Open University seminar on NGOs, 12 November 1991.

5. Peter Adamson, speech to Unicef National Committees, Geneva, 29 January 1991. Italics in original.

6. Richard Behar, 'SCF's little secret', *Forbes Magazine*, 21 April 1986.

7. Peter Adamson, *op. cit.*

8. *The Guardian*, 25 February 1982.

9. Peter Thompson-Smith of Colman RSCG advertising agency, quoted by Steve Platt, 'The hidden holocaust', *New Statesman and Society*, 23–30 December 1988.

10. Guy Stringer, quoted in Maggie Black's history of Oxfam, *A Cause for our Times: Oxfam, the First 50 Years* (Oxfam and Oxford University Press, Oxford, 1992), which is strong on the tension within Oxfam between political campaigning and traditional charity.

11. The multi-culturalists welcomed the richness of a polyethnic society such as Britain is increasingly becoming, and they laid stress on appreciation of diversity – in the arts, food, even religion. Their opponents from various camps criticized them for naïvely giving less attention than they should to racialism and to economic inequality, and for advancing policies which could strengthen the boundaries of cultural and racial ghettoes rather than assist to weaken them.

    The anti-racists condemned racial discrimination and prejudice in Britain as an evil, but often went on to insist that they were somehow the exclusive failing of white capitalist imperialists. Some anthropologists were unhappy with the anti-racists for pinning so much blame on 'race' that social problems such as drugs and crime risked becoming excessively associated with the ethnic minorities; also for giving renewed currency to the scientifically disreputable concept of race (though 'race' was for anti-racists the subjective perception of ethnic difference, regardless of the biological facts), and for ignoring that there can be intense political conflict *within* 'racially' similar peoples such as the Irish or the Belgians. The anti-racists seemed to be in the ascendant until the *Satanic Verses* affair in 1988, which clearly showed that cultural differences, and specifically religious intolerance, were as much of a threat to social harmony as racialism was to social justice.

    For consideration of these issues by anthropologists of different views, see John Corlett, 'Anthropology in British education', *RAIN (Royal Anthropological Institute News)* No. 59, December 1983; Gareth Parry, 'Anti-racist anthropology', *RAIN*, February 1984; Jean La Fontaine, 'Countering racial prejudice: a better starting-point', *Anthropology Today*, Vol. 2, No. 6, December 1986.

12. Cf. Frances D'Souza, 'Charities and politics', *Royal Anthropological Institute News*, No. 34, October 1979. Maggie Black (*op. cit.*) gives an informative account of Oxfam's tribulations with the Charity Commissioners in recent years.

13. Both these agencies have demonstrated how Adjustment Plans, which African countries have been encouraged to adopt, often leave the poorest of people suffering from cuts in subsidies. For instance, in Zimbabwe maize prices have now increased substantially, leaving the poorest unable to afford what food there is available during the drought (Oxfam news release, 1 June 1992).

14. 'Africa: meeting the challenge', Oxfam Briefing, No. 1, January 1992, p. 4.

15. Personal communication, 13 March 1992.

16. For an extremely biased but intermittently provocative attack on Third-Worldism, see Pascal Bruckner, *Le Sanglot de l'Homme Blanc* (*The White Man's Sob*) (Seuil, Paris, 1983).

17. *The Human World*, Vol. 12, August 1973, pp. 60 ff. There is a response by Leslie Kirkley, director of Oxfam, in Vol. 14, February 1974, with riposte by Robinson. Robinson criticizes Oxfam for its subsidies to the *New Internationalist*.

18. Second revised edition, Oxfam Education Department, 1989. The first edition was published in 1985.

19. 1991.

20. SCF information sheet No. 2, *Family Planning Policy in Developing Countries*, July 1988. A later edition (October 1992) stresses SCF's commitment to reducing child mortality, improving the economic capacity of communities, and improving the health, nutrition, education and status of women, as well as supporting family planning programmes.

21. Christian Aid, revised interim policy statement, 'Population', 14 February 1992.

22. Vicky Johnson, 'No safety in numbers', *Common Cause: The Magazine of ActionAid*, Autumn 1991.

23. IBT, a charity itself, has a subsidiary commercial company which is allowed to make programmes of a rather more overtly political complexion than is allowed for charities.

24. *Prospects for Africa* (Hodder & Stoughton, London, 1988) and *Prospects for Africa's Children* (Hodder & Stoughton, London, 1990).

25. See Alex de Waal, 'Misgoverned continent: war, starvation and the hidden economies of Africa', *Times Literary Supplement*, 13 September 1991, p. 5.

26. Charles R. Beitz, 'Democracy in developing societies', in ed. Raymond Gastil, *Freedom in the World: Political Rights and Civil Liberties* (Freedom House, New York, 1982), pp. 145–66.

27. S. A. Hewlett, *The Cruel Dilemmas of Development* (Basic Books, New York, 1980). See also Larry Sirowy and Alex Inkeles, 'The effects of

democracy on economic growth and inequality: a review', *Studies in Comparative International Development*, Vol. 25, No. 1, pp. 126–57.

28. Elsa Dawson, 'Indigenous NGOs, scaling up and partnership', SCF (London) *Overseas Research News*, No. 2, May 1992. See also eds Michael Edwards and David Hulme, *Making a Difference: NGOs and Development in a Changing World* (Earthscan Publications, London, 1992).

29. I. B. Tauris, London, 1991. See also Peter Loizos, 'Disenchanted developers', *Anthropology Today*, October 1991.

30. Examples of these charismatic leaders in British NGOs were Colonel Hugh Mackay, former Overseas Director of SCF, and Rip Hodson, former Chief Executive of ActionAid. Both agencies, as they have grown, have opted for more structured management systems. An example of a small agency at an earlier stage in its development is Survival International, the British-based charity to support the rights of indigenous peoples, whose director-general Stephen Corry built it up from tiny beginnings through skilful use of the media, but has also led it into a perhaps unnecessarily acrimonious dispute with the Boston-based sister agency Cultural Survival. (See letters column, *New Statesman and Society*, during the autumn of 1992, and editorial in *Anthropology Today*, December 1992.)

31. In fact, press reports in 1992 record that some large bands of Sudanese children, orphaned by the civil war, now spend their lives trekking in search of food and safety, sometimes across national frontiers.

32. WHO leaflet, *En Cas de Catastrophe*.

33. Simon Harrison, 'Ritual as intellectual property', *Man*, Vol. 27, No. 2, June 1992. Harrison writes that 'ritual is to action, as rhetoric is to discourse, as luxuries are to goods'. One might add, in equally simplified style: as fund-raising is to operations.

34. Statistics from Charities Aid Foundation report, reported in *The Guardian*, 18 June 1992. These figures should be looked at critically since they are based on a sample of only 1,020 people. According to this report, the proportion of donations as a percentage of gross income fell as follows: 1988–9: 0.75 per cent; 1989–90: 0.76 per cent; 1990–1: 0.60 per cent.

35. A telethon is a marathon TV event for charity (but also, in the US, to support political and other causes). The Jerry Lewis Telethon in aid of muscular dystrophy has been an annual event in the USA on Labour Day, the first Monday in September, for many years. The first telethon in Britain was staged by Thames Television, in the London area only, in 1981; it raised £1.25 million. for a variety of charitable causes. The ITV Telethon is now annual and runs an office all the year round; it supports thousands of local charities. Telethons now take place in

numerous countries. The USSR organized one after the Chernobyl disaster. Music and sport are in practice the only suitable elements for an international telethon, as they can translate across the whole world. Attempts are under way to organize a pan-European telethon, but language barriers are a problem. (Source: Joe Simpson, ITV Telethon.)

36. *News out of Africa: Biafra to Band Aid* (Hilary Shipman, London, 1986). This book contains useful, detailed interview material with editors, journalists and others, which I have not attempted to repeat in the present book but which is complementary.

37. Chris Cramer, then BBC TV's Foreign News Editor, quoted in *ibid.*, p. 124.

38. See Peter Gill, *A Year in the Death of Africa* (Paladin, London, 1986).

39. 'With love from Band Aid', final report, 1991. See also Geldof's autobiography *Is That It?* (Sidgwick & Jackson, London, 1986).

40. In the UK the main emphasis is on disability, homelessness and the elderly.

41. Guy Stringer, personal communication.

42. *Le Malheur des Autres* (Odile Jacob, Paris, 1991) p. 118.

43. Routledge, 1990 [1924], Chapter 4. See also Introduction by Mary Douglas.

44. Anita Roddick, *Body and Soul* (Vermilion, London, 1991).

CHAPTER 3

1. *The Scotsman*, 2 July 1968, quoted by Suzanne Cronje, *The World and Nigeria: The Diplomatic History of the Biafran War 1967–1970* (Sidgwick & Jackson, London, 1972), p. 135. Maggie Black's *A Cause for our Time: Oxfam, the First 50 Years* (Oxfam and Oxford University Press, Oxford, 1992), pp. 118 ff. gives a fairly detailed account of Oxfam's operations during the Biafran war.

2. John de St Jorre, *The Nigerian Civil War* (Hodder & Stoughton, London, 1975), p. 209.

3. *Ibid.*, p. 248.

4. For example, Thierry Hentsch, *Face au Blocus: La Croix-Rouge Internationale dans le Nigéria en Guerre (1967–1970)* (Institut Universitaire de Hautes Etudes Internationales, Geneva, 1973), p. 12.

Great Britain's administrative policy only accentuated the disparity of the territories which it governed. The method of *indirect* rule, though applied with useful effect in the North and West, never succeeded in working in the fragmented and comparatively anarchic societies of the Eastern province. This style of government conserved existing traditional structures while irremediably altering the source and nature of the indigenous chiefs' power, and so fixed each region's socio-political institutions in a particularism henceforth without an object, and consolidated the barriers which already separated the diverse ethnic groups of the country. (My translation from the French.)

5. A. H. M. Kirk-Greene, personal comment.
6. For example, this statement in July 1968 by the director of Caritas Suisse in Lucerne: 'The Ibos are distinguished by their intelligence, their energy and their ability while the Muslim Hausas give no proof of the same talent. Envy is also a source of conflict and assassination in Africa' (quoted by Hentsch, *op. cit.*, p. 92n.) The same organization also accused Nigeria of spreading the plague in Biafra.
7. John J. Stremlau, *The International Politics of the Nigerian Civil War 1967–70* (Princeton University Press, Princeton, 1977), p. 238.
8. The USA provided major finance for relief aid, especially through the ICRC. According to Joseph E. Thompson, *American Policy and African Famine: the Nigeria–Biafra War 1966–70* (Greenwood, New York, 1990), p. 166, recently declassified State Department records show that US public and private sources provided $112 million worth of relief aid during and after the conflict, out of a worldwide total of $251 million; but it is not clear how these figures were arrived at. Thompson concludes that though some humanitarian acts are politically motivated, 'the humanitarian response to the Biafran famine . . . demonstrates that America and the Americans can be moved to action through the generation of a moral issue.'
9. Stremlau, *op. cit.* p. 113.
10. de St Jorre, *op. cit.* p. 287.
11. Stremlau, *op. cit.* p. 120.
12. The Order of Malta had tried through its German association to send a medical mission to the Nigerian combat zones since October 1968, but was refused visas. *La vie de l'Ordre en France et dans le Monde*, newsletter, January 1970, p. 16.
13. Cronje, *op. cit.* p. 134.
14. Stremlau, *op. cit.* p. 239. This historian gives a figure of $250 million as his estimate of the relief funds spent to keep Biafra functioning during its last 15 months (see note 8 above).
15. Stremlau, *ibid.*, p. 248.
16. Hentsch, *op. cit.*, p. 212.
17. de St. Jorre, *op. cit.*, p. 305.
18. For example: 'On their return [from a naval battle] the Athenians put up a trophy at the place from which they had turned on the enemy and won the victory. . . . The Peloponnesians also put up a trophy for the

victory they had won when they disabled the ships in shore.' (Penguin
Classics, Harmondsworth, 1954), Book 2, Chapter 9, p. 155.

19. Ibid., p. 306.
20. Don McCullin, *Unreasonable Behaviour: an Autobiography* (Jonathan Cape,
London, 1990), p. 120.
21. Thompson, *op. cit.*, p. 63.
22. A. H. M. Kirk-Greene, *Crisis and Conflict in Nigeria* (Oxford University
Press, Oxford, 1971), Vol. 2, page v.
23. McCullin, *op. cit.*, p. 116.
24. Paul Harrison and Robin Palmer, *News Out of Africa: Biafra to Band Aid*
(Hilary Shipman, London, 1986), p. 6.
25. *Ibid.*, Chapters 2 and 3.
26. Cagnoni's photographs are extensively used to illustrate de St Jorre,
op. cit.
27. McCullin, *op. cit.*, p. 82. Here he refers to a famine in Bihar that he
covered.
28. Auberon Waugh, *Will This Do?* (Century, London, 1991), p. 195.
29. de St Jorre, *op. cit.*, p. 250.
30. *Ibid.*, p. 358.
31. *Daily Express*, 2 July 1969, cited in Hentsch, *op. cit.*, p. 192n. It is worth
remembering that economic blockade, including starvation of the
enemy, was regarded as a legitimate strategy by the Allied Commands
during both World Wars. Maggie Black notes (*op. cit.*, p. 129) the irony
that it was the intransigent policy of Churchill's war cabinet, with its
effects on non-combatants in Greece, which first engendered the Oxfam
movement.
32. de St Jorre, *op. cit.*, pp. 405, 407.
33. McCullin, *op. cit.*, p. 125.
34. de St Jorre, *op. cit.*, p. 175.
35. Michael Aaranson.
36. Dres Balmer, *L'Heure du Cuivre*. (Editions d'en bas, Lausanne, 1984),
pp. 30–1. The subject of this book (a French translation of the German
original) is the civil war in El Salvador, *c.* 1980. The book was banned
in Switzerland but sold in France.
37. From an interview with Bernard Kouchner, *Le Monde*, 30 April 1991.
38. This issue is discussed briefly in the section on the ICRC in Chapter 4.
39. William Shawcross, *The Quality of Mercy: Cambodia, Holocaust and Modern
Conscience.* (André Deutsch, London, 1984), p. 386.
40. Antonios Pomonis, 'The Spitak (Armenia, USS) earthquake: residen-
tial building typology and seismic behaviour', *Disasters*, Vol. 14, No. 2
(1990), p. 89 ff.
41. Quoted in Pierre Verluise, *La Fracture: le Séisme du 7 Décembre 1988*

Stock, Paris, 1989). This book grossly overemphasizes the relative importance of foreign as opposed to local relief.

42. For instance, Yuri Rost, *Armenian Tragedy: an Eye-witness Account of Human Conflict and Natural Disaster in Armenia and Azerbaijan* (Weidenfeld and Nicolson, London, 1990).

43. *The Times*, 10 December 1988, p. 7.

44. Rost, *op. cit.*, p. 94.

45. *The Times*, 10 December 1988.

46. The Armenian republic has a population of about 3.5 million, 90 per cent Armenian, some 1.2 per cent of the former USSR's population, mainly Christian, acutely aware of its physical isolation in the Muslim world. The republic is landlocked, with no land below 1,000 metres, and was dependent on Russian aid and markets. Armenians are relatively urbanized with a strong merchant and middle class. Muslim Azerbaijan has a population of about 5.5 million, knows that its oil wealth is drying up and looks to Iran and Turkey for its future. Nagorno-Karabakh (population 164,000) is the historic marchland between the Muslims of the plains and the Christians of the mountains. Its position was mirrored by that of Nakhichevan, an autonomous Azerbaijani enclave situated between Iran, Turkey and Armenia. For an account of the territorial dispute, see Ronald Suny, *New Left Review*, No. 184 (November–December 1990). The third republic of the Transcaucasus is Georgia, which is of Christian tradition.

   In August 1991, Azerbaijan declared its independence from the USSR and in September it annulled Karabakh's autonomous status. In September 1991 Armenia declared its independence. Violent troubles have continued since then until the time of writing (December 1992).

47. *Le Monde*, 13 December 1988.

48. *Le Monde*, 15 December 1988.

49. Rost, *op. cit.*, p. 165.

50. Personal communication, 17 July 1992. See also Rost, *op. cit.*, pp. 182–3.

51. Rost, *op. cit.*, p. 192.

52. *Le Monde*, 15 December 1988.

53. Michael Behr, formerly of British Red Cross, who played a leading role in the international Red Cross relief effort, personal communication.

54. MDM, '*Rapport narratif et financier de l'action du 9 décembre . . .*'

55. Rost, *op. cit.*, pp. 123, 133.

56. MDM, *Rapport narratif et financier de l'action du 23 décembre . . .*

57. MDM, *Rapport narratif et financier de l'action du 30 décember . . .*

58. MDM, *Rapport narratif et financier de l'action du 20 janvier 1989.*

59. *MSF Info*, No. 9 (February–March 1991), p. 14. Aide Médicale Internationale (AMI), a third French agency which is much less media-oriented, sent two doctors to evaluate needs at the end of December,

when most of the publicity had died down. AMI worked closely with two *ad hoc* organizations, S.O.S. Arménie and the Blue Cross, which was set up by the Armenian community in France, to send medical supplies, wooden bungalows, tents etc. by boat and train. AMI gave specialist help to a hospital in Kirokavan which was coping with an abnormally high incidence of cardiac illness; and also sent medical equipment to meet a need for specialist assistance in dermatology, due to the number of chemical factories in the area and the backwardness of Soviet medicine in this field. A senior representative of AMI visited Kirokovan at the end of 1989 and verified that this project had worked according to plan and could be handed over to local personnel (Pascale Sotias, AMI).

60. Xavier Emmanuelli, *Les Prédateurs de l'Action Humanitaire* (Albin Michel, Paris, 1991), pp. 166 ff. Emmanuelli includes some vivid paragraphs on devastation in Leninakan, the emergence of natural leaders in an emergency, the phenomenon of scapegoating after a disaster, and the incongruities of television with its 'gentle cynicism which is the courtesy of the profession' in a town that has become a cemetery.

61. *Injury, the British Journal of Accident Surgery*, Vol. 21, No. 3 (1990), article in special issue on the medical response to major disasters.

62. J. E. Tattershall *et al.*, *ibid.*

63. John Seaman, *ibid.* This point is especially apposite to countries where the national budget for normal health care is virtually nil. We shall revert to this question in the next chapter, with reference to the ideology of the 'French doctors' movement.

64. Pomonis, *op. cit.*, p. 11.

65. See note 46.

66. Rolando Armijo, Institut de physique du globe de Paris, quoted in *Le Monde*, 11–12 December 1988, by Yvonne Rebeyrol.

67. A. Pomonis, *op. cit.*, p. 92, states, on the other hand, that the level of seismicity in Armenia is not the highest in the world and the recurrence intervals are very long. Information from this century only is likely to have understated the actual long-term hazard, so that neither the local authorities nor the public had in mind the possibility of such a serious earthquake.

CHAPTER 4

1. Roger C. Riddell and Mark A. Robinson, *Working with the Poor* (Overseas Development Institute, London, 1992); Peter Loizos, 'Disenchanting developers', *Anthropology Today* (Vol. 7, No. 5, October 1991). See also Bernard Kouchner, *Charité Business* (Le Pré aux Clercs, Paris, 1986).

2. Frédéric Maurice, personal communication.

3. Xavier Emmanuelli, *Les Prédateurs de l'Action Humanitaire* (Albin Michel, Paris, 1991), p. 196.

4. Kouchner, *Charité Business*, pp. 210 ff. We will largely follow his accounts in this book and *Le Malheur des Autres*, though they are perhaps rather subjective.

5. *Le Malheur des Autres* (Odile Jacob, Paris, 1991), p. 113.

6. 'MSF 20 ans', *Libération*, 20 December 1991, p. 24.

7. *Ibid.*, p. 114.

8. Emmanuelli, *op. cit.*, p. 197–8. The same author also writes that MSF has a kind of indissoluble marriage to the media.

9. *Ibid.*, p. 207.

10. *Reconnaissance d'utilité publique, grande cause nationale.* See MSF, *Dossier Info* April 1991.

11. Kouchner, *Le Malheur*, pp. 74–5.

12. Emmanuelli, *op. cit.*, p. 132.

13. *Les Nouvelles: Médecins du Monde*, No. 23 (September 1991), p. 21.

14. In any case, there are wide variations between agencies in which expenses, such as travel from headquarters to field sites, are included under 'field' as opposed to administrative headings, so that all apportionments of this kind should be read with a degree of scepticism.

15. *Ibid.*, p. 33.

16. Opening of 20th general assembly of MSF, 1 June 1991, by X. Emmanuelli, Président d'Honneur.

17. Kouchner, *Le Malheur*, pp. 257ff. Kouchner seeks to distinguish the 'right of [democratic] intervention' against dictators from the 'right of humanitarian assistance'. Cf. 'MSF 20 ans', *Libération*, 20 December 1991, p. 25. MSF President, Rony Brauman replies, in this exchange, that humanitarian aid in time of war or other crisis can only come from NGOs, rather than governments, if it is not to be tainted by political partiality. Claude Malhuret, ex-MSF President, argues that humanitarian assistance is often supplied by governments with much publicity in order to relieve themselves of the responsibility to intervene politically (e.g., to protect the Kurds in 1991).

18. 'MSF 20 ans', *Libération*, 20 December 1991, p. 26.

19. Kouchner, *Le Malheur*, pp. 193ff.

20. *Ibid.*, p. 296. It seems that Kouchner has in mind the 'Third-Worldists' who used to be prominent in the French intellectual scene, not contemporary anthropologists, who for the most part do not adopt the postures that Kouchner condemns.

21. John de Salis, personal comment.

22. Edouard Mir, *Libération*, 20 December 1991, p. 30.

23. Opening of 20th general assembly of MSF, 1 June 1991.

24. Kouchner, *Le Malheur*, p. 324.
25. Rony Brauman, President, report to MSF's 20th general assembly, 1–2 June 1991, p. 8.
26. For an impartial observer's account of one MSF team's operations in the field, see Tim Allen, 'Closed minds, open systems: affliction and healers in West Nile, Uganda', in ed. D. Brokensha, *Oromo Studies and other Essays in Honour of Paul Baxter* (Syracuse, New York, 1992). Allen was undertaking ethnographic fieldwork in this area in 1987–8, with an emphasis on small-scale agriculture in a context of crisis, but he became increasingly interested in health issues. The French MSF team based in Moyo consisted of about ten people (two doctors, two logistical officers, a laboratory technician, three nurses, a pharmacist, a midwife), all on 6-month to one-year contracts and all young, altruistic, on low salaries and hard-working. The operation aimed principally to provide emergency medical facilities for returnees in the wake of the guerrilla war. Allen records that the efforts of MSF expatriates undoubtedly saved lives and cured debilitating diseases such as sleeping sickness, but they nonetheless tended to feel frustrated, partly owing to ignorance about the social aspects of affliction and healing among the local people; hence they retreated into life in the compound, where half of the main living room had been turned into a copy of a Mediterranean bar. According to Allen, MSF management did not seem to learn from the opinions of departing personnel. Also, although the duration of crisis conditions resulted in MSF's staying much longer than planned, they remained attached to the principle that they were a 'relief' rather than a development agency, thus managing to ignore critiques of top-down, interventionist medicine. 'My basic plea . . . is for those involved in medical aid to be more reflexive about what they are doing, and concentrate as hard on trying to understand what is going on around them as they do on administering cures.'
27. See Introduction, note 5.
28. Brauman *op. cit.*, p. 3. 'After these optimistic facts, let's come to the weaknesses and problems: the inadequacy of general training is certainly the first among these. That is indisputably the weak point of MSF.' This is aggravated, he said, by the continuous renewal of the membership and by the scale, depth and complexity of the problems faced. He concedes that the coherence of MSF's field operations is not matched by theoretical strength. A week-long seminar in summer 1991 in Paris on the socio-political context of MSF missions attracted a disappointingly small audience.
29. *Ibid.*, p. 5.
30. Emmanuelli, *op. cit.*, pp. 166ff.

31. Emmanuelli, *op. cit.*, p. 250, quoting Frossard, a French general. See the section on numbers and empathy in Chapter 5, below.

32. quoted by Emmanuelli, *op. cit.*

33. Christine Ockrent, 'Medias et action humanitaire', in ed. M. Bettati and B. Kouchner, *Le Devoir d'Ingerence* (Editions Denoel, Paris, 1987), p. 128.

34. Kouchner, *Le Malheur*, p. 118.

35. Jean-Pierre Hocké, *Le Nouveau Quotidien*, 24 January 1992.

36. 'What is in a symbol?', ICRC leaflet, January 1991; Jean S. Pictet *et al.*, *Commentary* on the Geneva Convention (ICRC, Geneva, 1952), Chapter VII, 'The distinctive emblem'. The primary purpose of the emblem is to designate establishments, units, personnel, etc. entitled to protection (Geneva Convention I, Articles 38–44). The 'protective' use of the emblem ought strictly to be distinguished from its 'indicative' use. The Red Cross does not 'own' the emblem. References to the Red Cross as a 'logo', for instance in the American Red Cross Identity Program's *Communicating Pride in Who We Are and What We Do* (1988), are technically incorrect.

37. The *Commentary* on the Geneva Convention states (p. 298) that is not certain that there was a conscious intention in 1863 or 1864 to reverse the colours of the Swiss flag. The first written allusion to the analogy was in 1870. The 1906 Diplomatic Conference, which revised the Convention, added a clause stating that the emblem was adopted as a compliment to Switzerland and was formed by reversing the Federal colours. The term 'Red Cross', to denote the work of voluntary relief to wounded combatants, was first adopted by the Netherlands Society in 1867, and widely used by 1885. For the origins of the Federal cross, see under 'Croix fédérale' and 'Schwyz' in *Dictionnaire Historique et Biographique de la Suisse* (Neuchâtel, 1924), Vols 2 and 6. I am indebted to John de Salis for this point. In a speech given in London in 1872, Henry Dunant recognized that the choice of emblem was the same as 'the chief standard of the Crusaders', *A Proposal for introducing Uniformity into the Condition of Prisoners of War* (National Association for the Promotion of Social Science, London, 1872).

38. 'At the 1949 Conference the Head of the Delegation of the Holy See himself recalled that "the red cross had been selected as a tribute to Switzerland and it had always been made clear, particularly in 1906, that the red cross symbol in question was devoid of all religious significance". In the face of such testimony, need we insist further?' *Commentary*, pp. 304–5.

39. *ICRC Bulletin*, July 1991, p. 4.

40. *Le Nouveau Quotidien*, 9 May 1992. Report by Sabine Esther.

41. See numerous reports in the Geneva and Lausanne press. A letter in *The Times*, 22 May 1992, by the author, argued that the attack on the convoy

and on the Red Cross emblem deserved the strongest possible condemnation from world leaders. The same point was made in a number of press articles, e.g. Jean-Pierre Hocké, *Le Nouveau Quotidien*, 29 May 1992: 'Any authority that violates the sign of the Red Cross and Crescent should be reminded that it will instantly be put in the dock: it is not possible to conceive of a continental Solferino. It is to this immediate initiative that the sacrifice of Frédéric Maurice impels us.' A number of other ICRC delegates have been killed recently.

42. A further problem may arise for the red cross emblem if, as is discussed below, the current directorate of the ICRC is successful in conceptually detaching the neutrality of the ICRC from that of Switzerland. The two flags could be confused in the heat of a crisis.

   Recently, President Sommaruga has published an article declaring that the ICRC is willing to consider the possibility of replacing the Red Cross and Red Crescent by a new emblem without religious connotation, if one can be devised that is satisfactory in all respects: 'the solution of a third sign'. 'Unité et pluralité des emblèmes', *Revue Internationale de la Croix Rouge* (July–August 1992). He rejects both the option of returning to the red cross alone, and that of using the red cross and red crescent juxtaposed.

43. *Swiss Review* (March 1987), p. 17, shortened version of leader from *Neue Zürcher Zeitung*, 1–2 November 1986; *Sunday Telegraph*, 2 November 1986.

44. *Le Nouveau Quotidien*, 28 November 1991, *Journal de Genève*, 7 December 1991 ('CICR: des bleus à l'âme', Antoine Bosshard).

45. John de St Jorre, *The Nigerian Civil War* (Hodder & Stoughton, London, 1975), p. 239.

46. Jean-Claude Favez, *Une Mission Impossible? Le CICR, les Déportations et les Camps de Concentrations Nazis* (Ed. Payot, Lausanne, 1988). Cf. also *L'Hebdo*, 8 September 1988, pp. 10–13, with defence of the ICRC's record by the director general in 1988, Jacques Moreillon.

47. They are not, however, explicitly included in the movement's seven Fundamental Principles, which are: Humanity, Impartiality, Neutrality, Independence, Voluntary service, Unity and Universality. ICRC states that 'over a century of experience has convinced ICRC that its humanitarian mission is best accomplished through persuasion devoid of all publicity. If the observations of ICRC delegates were to be made public, prisons and borders would probably be closed to them. . . . In cases of serious violations of international humanitarian law the ICRC may be compelled to depart from its usual discretion by appealing to the community of States, which have undertaken to respect and to ensure respect for the legal rules to which they are party.' *The International Committee of the Red Cross: What It Is, What It Does* (ICRC Publications, 1990). For a short but authoritative account of the

movement as a whole see Sylvia R. Limerick, 'The International Red Cross and Red Crescent movement', *Journal of the Royal College of Physicians of London*, Vol. 25, No. 3 (July 1991).

48. There are some current signs of more frequent public statements. For instance, on 14 May 1992, the ICRC's President complained to Israel's ambassador in Geneva about treatment of prisoners in the occupied territories (*24 Heures*, 22 May 1992). The Israeli government reacted with anger to the ICRC's decision to single it out for criticism and to express its opinion through the media. Some Swiss commentators, while praising the ICRC for speaking out more vocally in recent years, particularly on the Somalian emergency in 1992, have cautioned against the temptation to engage in 'rhetorical oneupmanship' (Jacques Pilet, *Le Nouveau Quotidien*, 14 August 1992). However, the ICRC's forthright condemnation of 'ethnic cleansing' by Serbians in 1992 has won general respect.

49. The director of the International Museum of the Red Cross, which is small and has recently been hard-pressed financially, was paid an annual salary of 250,000 Swiss francs in 1992, or about £95,000 – criticized locally as excessive, but roughly on a par with salaries of senior ICRC directors. The museum is, however, not part of the ICRC. *Journal de Genève*, 19 June 1992, *Le Nouveau Quotidien*, 6 June 1992.

50. Hubert de Senarclens, 'Le marathonien du CICR', *Bilan* (December 1991).

51. *Golfe 1990–1991, de la Crise au Conflit: l'action Humanitaire du CICR* (ICRC Publications, Geneva, 1991).

52. *L'Heure du Cuivre* (Editions d'en bas, Distique, 1984).

53. John de Salis, former chief delegate in Thailand, Lebanon and Iraq, personal communication.

54. Cornelio Sommaruga, 'La neutralité et l'indépendance du CICR, conditions essentielles de son action', speech to Friends of Wilton Park annual meeting, Basel, 13 September 1991.

55. Cornelio Sommaruga, 'Solidarité en action: le CICR intermédiaire humanitaire neutre', lecture to Faculty of Economic and Social Sciences, University of Geneva, 1991.

56. 'At the time of the capture of two ICRC delegates in Lebanon, one had already admired how many young Swiss people – in a country recently categorized in a comparative study as at the top of the scale for national quietude – feel called literally to leave their homes and leave themselves to become paying passengers in other people's miseries.' Obituary of Frédéric Maurice by A. M., *Gazette de Lausanne*, 20 May 1992.

57. According to a report in *Tribune de Genève*, 5 March 1992, based on government statistics, Switzerland spent 990 million Swiss francs on development projects in the Third World, but the total benefit

attributable to purchase of Swiss goods, plus goods and services purchased in Switzerland by developing countries which borrow from the World Bank, was estimated at 1,310 million Swiss francs. The British and many other governments also insist that much of the overseas aid which they fund is spent on the purchase of domestically produced goods and services.

58. *Le Nouveau Quotidien*, 1 May 1992, 'La Suisse devrait faire plus'. The ICRC's deficit for 1991 was 10 million Swiss francs. A deficit of 100 million Swiss francs was forecast for 1992 on a budget of 800 million Swiss francs (Reuter report, 8 October 1992).

59. Sommaruga, Basel speech, 1991. See also his lecture to the Musée International de la Croix-Rouge et du Croissant-Rouge, 21 January 1992, 'La neutralité suisse et la neutralité du CICR sont-elles indissociables? Une indépendance à sauvegarder'. In this lecture, he attempts to derive logically the neutrality of the ICRC from that of the stretcher-bearer in a battle. However, there is an important distinction between neutrality in the sense of 'immunity (in principle) from attack' and 'impartiality *vis-à-vis* belligerents'.

60. Sabine Estier, 'Le Comité sera-t-il encore suisse en l'an 2000?', *Le Nouveau Quotidien*, 24 January 1992.

61. For example, in the siege of Vukovar, Croatia, in October 1991, when MSF volunteers displayed great bravery in evacuating wounded people, but the ICRC declined to participate in a politico-military 'deal'. Sommaruga, Geneva lecture, 1991. But in Somalia in 1992, all overseas agencies including the ICRC have hired local soldiers to guard personnel and supplies.

62. Sommaruga, *ibid.*

63. Sommaruga, *ibid.*

64. Hubert de Senarclens, 'Le marathonien du CICR', *Bilan* (December 1991). A list of the membership committee published in the *Revue de la Croix Rouge*, No. 791 (September–October 1991) shows that it is specially strong in banking, law, medicine and diplomacy. However, one member, Jacques Forster, is Professor of Development Studies at the University of Geneva. He has been a member of the International Committee since 1989 and in March 1992 was elected to the seven-member Executive Board (ICRC press release, 19 March 1992).

65. 'MSF 20 ans', *Libération*, 20 December 1991, p. 26.

66. For instance, following the murder in France of the former Iranian prime minister, Chapour Bakhtiar, in early 1992, Switzerland was drawn into a Franco-Iranian dispute and some ICRC delegates were expelled from Iran. *Le Nouveau Quotidien*, 2 April 1992.

67. Obituary of Frédéric Maurice by Anna Orsini, *The Independent*, 19 June 1992.

68. Sigfried Giedion, *Space, Time and Architecture* (Harvard University Press, Cambridge, Mass., 1954), third edition, p. 463. Maillart lived from 1872–1940.

69. This is indebted partly to WV's own literature and information received from WV officials, especially Alan Whaites, and partly to David Stoll's *Is Latin America Turning Protestant?* (University of California Press, Berkeley. 1990).

70. WV built a children's hospital in Phnom Penh just before the Khmer Rouge's victory in 1975. It was used as a prison, then as a barracks, then wrecked. 'In January 1980 World Vision's messianic leader, Stan Mooneyham, had returned to Phnom Penh to make an impassioned plea to Foreign Minister Hun Sen for permission to rebuild the hospital. "Don't look at my face," he cried, "you will only see an American, an enemy. Look instead at my blood." And with that Mooneyham drew his penknife across his wrist and began to bleed. Hun Sen gave permission.' (*The Quality of Mercy*, p. 254.)

71. Quoted by Steve Askin, 'Hostility, conflict engulf World Vision', *National Catholic Reporter*, 23 April 1982.

72. *What's World Vision's Answer to That?* (WVI, Monrovia, California, June 1980), p. 45.

73. Statement of Faith appended to WV of Britain's Articles of Association. World Vision may be regarded as 'fundamentalist' in the strict historical sense of belonging to the US Protestant movement which from the second decade of the twentieth century attempted to assert the 'Fundamentals' of Christianity. It is probably not, or is no longer, fundamentalist in the sense of extremely conservative evangelism.

74. *What's World Vision's Answer*, p. 17.

75. 'When will we ever learn?', in *Together: A Journal of World Vision International* (April–June 1991).

76. WV's stated policy is to demonstrate respect for any other faith with which they have contact. People of non-Christian faiths are sometimes employed: in field countries there is a significant number of Muslim staff.

77. There is a strong tendency within extreme evangelicalism towards unquestioning support of Israel, possibly for doctrinal reasons connected with the Second Coming. By contrast, WV views the Palestinian issue as one of poverty and oppression.

78. As evidence of this, it is reported that when the Italian clothes firm Benetton used a photograph of a young American man dying of AIDS beside his weeping family as part of a US$80 million commercial publicity campaign, no American magazine had scruples about publishing the advertisement. In Britain, most magazines refused to publish it on the grounds that it was indecently exploiting private

distress to sell pullovers and scarves. AFP report, *Le Nouveau Quotidien*, 15 February 1992. See Chapter 5 n. 11.

79. Between 22 and 27 per cent over recent years, as opposed to SCF's 14 per cent, CAFOD's 6 per cent, Christian Aid's 11 per cent, Oxfam's 17 per cent. As stated above, WV of Britain was hit hard by the consequences of the Channel Four documentary, which resulted in a shortfall in income for 1990 when their fund-raising expenses had already been committed.

80. World Vision International, Annual Report, 1990, p. 4.

81. Personal communication, 26 February 1992.

82. The child abuse incident was a single case involving access by paedophiles as donors to WV's child sponsorship scheme. Trócaire accepted that WV acted 'with all appropriate promptitude and responsibility'.

83. Minutes of General Meeting No. 289 of the Christian Relief and Development Association, Ethiopia, 4 November 1991.

84. Many other Christian organizations, mainly lay-led, have engaged in missionary and caring work. A number of these, like the Leprosy Mission, are inter-denominational.

85. 'Inter-Church Aid: Projected National Appeal. Notes and Recommendations by Maurice Rickards', 7 September 1956.

86. Report in *Le Monde*, 3 August 1991. Other information on this disaster from World Vision sources.

87. According to WV 'Anhui Relief Operation Accomplishment Report', February 1992. The report notes that sometimes officials did not distribute according to urgency of need, but WV did their best with the help of the Provincial Relief Office to correct this problem. WV's final contribution for relief work totalled $4.7 million. This covered 19,000 shelters for 70,000 beneficiaries, 40 shelters for 480,000 beneficiaries, and 15 schools for 7,000 pupils. Blankets, jackets, food and medicine were also provided.

88. By contrast, Save the Children decided to undertake only limited flood relief work in China as it was logistically too difficult. It was awarded part of the funds raised in Hong Kong by the *South China Morning Post*, but for rehabilitation work in Anhui and Hunan provinces: helping with the reconstruction of schools, and providing training for children who were in danger of coming to live on the streets. SCF already had good working contacts with the Anhui Provincial Education Commission and the Foundation for Underdeveloped Regions in China.

89. Alfred von Boeselager, 'Nine centuries of Hospitaller works', *Rivista Internazionale of the Sovereign Military Order of Malta* (Rome, December 1991), p. 17.

90. Alfred von Boeselager, Hospitaller to the Order (i.e., director of humanitarian aid), personal communication.

91. J. P. Hiegel and C. Landrac, 'Une communauté thérapeutique originale dans les camps de réfugiés en Thaïlande', *Bulletin des Oeuvres Hospitalières Françaises de l'Ordre de Malte*, No. 52 (1989).

92. In a conference 'Television and the global agenda: the next ten years' organized by Channel Four and IBT, London, 23 November 1992. Mamdani went further and contended that television footage of atrocities and starvation in Africa is part of a process of softening up public opinion in the West to make armed intervention more acceptable.

93. E.g. eds David Marsden and Peter Oakley, *Evaluating Social Development Guidelines, No. 5* (Oxfam, Oxford, 1990).

CHAPTER 5

1. Umberto Eco, quoted by Terence Moore, *Times Literary Supplement*, 19 June 1992, p. 23.

2. Semiotics also contributes its own technical terminology, but I have avoided this here because there is a risk of merely stating the obvious in impressive terms.

3. From a legal point of view, as explained in the last chapter, the red cross is primarily an emblem to identify ambulances etc. in war-time, and only secondarily the badge of the movement.

    Another extremely successful marketing campaign, though one restricted to the British Empire, was that undertaken after the First World War by the Earl Haig Fund on behalf of wounded war veterans and families of casualties. The red poppy, blooming over the battlefields of northern Europe and simulated in millions of buttonholes, became a powerful emblem of sacrifice seeking to reassure a bereaved nation that massive bloodshed had its justification. Donations are still raised each year in the autumn in Britain for the beneficiaries of the Fund, whose scope includes the Second World War and subsequent smaller wars in which there were British casualties.

4. The Oxford Committee for Famine Relief was founded in 1942 and registered in 1948. OXFAM was originally its telegraphic address. Oxfam's name has been adopted by numerous organizations in other countries, which subscribe to the same general idea but have no personal connection with Oxford and no legal bond with Oxfam UK. The Oxfam international network was described to me by a spokesman at Oxfam House in Oxford as being like a 'family that meets every few years', that is to say not a close family. Some of the Oxfams are not

constrained by English-style charity law and stray into what Oxfam UK would regard as (at least in the UK context) inappropriate political activity. For a useful account of Oxfam's work up to *c.* 1982, see Ben Whitaker, *A Bridge of People: A Personal View of Oxfam's First Forty Years* (Heinemann, London, 1983); but this has been superseded by Maggie Black's *A Cause for our Times* (Oxford University Press, Oxford, 1992).

5. Memorandum from Maurice Rickards to Inter-Church Aid, 7 September 1956. Rickards is a writer, photographer and graphic designer who worked with Hugh Samson. Inter-Church Aid and Refugee Service, part of the British Council of Churches, became a client of Hugh Samson and Co. in 1956.

6. Proposal by Maurice Rickards FSIA, FIIP, 1 July 1978. The sculpture has been endowed with capable-looking hands which are missing in the logo. Mr Rickards told me that the drawing was meant to stress that the victim was battered, bewildered, in a bad way, but might in the long term become a victor.

7. Kathleen Freeman, *If Any Man Build: the History of Save the Children Fund* (Hodder & Stoughton, London, 1965), p. 30.

8. *Ibid.*, p. 68.

9. Bob Geldof, *Is That It?* (Sidgwick & Jackson, London, 1986), p. 291.

10. A. Simpson, 'Charity Starts At Home', *Ten*, Vol. 8, No. 19 (1985), quoted in Elizabeth Pitt, 'The Developing Image: an examination of the use of visual imagery by development agencies and the way in which we construct images of others', dissertation, SOAS, University of London, 1990.

11. 'This beautification of tragedy results in pictures that ultimately reinforce our passivity towards the experience they reveal. To aestheticize tragedy is the fastest way to anesthetize the feelings of those who are witnessing it. Beauty is a call to admiration, not action.' Ingrid Sischy on Salgado's photography in *New Yorker*, 9 September 1991. For a more positive view of Salgado, noting that he does not photograph passive victims but gives weight to their dignity and defiance (at the same time as he turns them into sacred images), see David Levi Strauss, 'Epiphany of the Other', *Artforum*, February 1991. A recent but highly significant phenomenon is the Benetton 'Life Today' advertising campaign, some of whose images were banned on grounds of taste by magazine publishers in Britain and some other countries. The most notorious image represented a young man dying of AIDS surrounded by his family; but other 'advertisements' have included a flooded street with a South Asian couple waist-deep in water trying to take some possessions to safety, and a ship teeming with refugees some of whom are trying to reach the land by swimming. The photographs are documentary in style; the caption reads in every case simply 'UNITED

COLORS OF BENETTON'. Benetton is an international fashion garment company which originated in Italy. In a brilliantly provocative article on the Benetton campaign, McKenzie Wark argues that we should avoid the knee-jerk reaction of condemning Benetton. According to him, there is no difference between Benetton's exploitation of human suffering and that of television channels and documentary photographers, except that it is middle-class intellectuals who set the rules of what is acceptable and what is not. According to Wark, such an advertisement promotes the brand image among visually educated people by its 'provocation to the mind' in questioning these rules, and the opportunity to protest against Benetton's good taste fuels the corporate publicity machine. Whereas Marcel Duchamp took everyday life into museums, Benetton take aesthetic issues into ordinary life. 'Still life today: the Benetton campaign', *photofile*, No. 36 (1992), pp. 33–6. I agree with Wark that 'Silence = Death for both social issue campaigns and corporate advertising. The purpose is different but the communicational mechanisms are exactly the same.' It follows that campaigns of this kind are likely to become more frequent in the more sophisticated industrial countries. I have refrained from giving prominence to these images in this book because that would be to play into Benetton's hands, as indeed Wark does in his article. (See Chapter 4 n. 78.)

12. 'A Buddhist monk burns himself to death to protest the Diem government in South Vietnam', Associated Press, unknown photographer, 1963; 'Street execution of a Vietcong prisoner', Eddie Adams, 1968; 'Children fleeing an American napalm strike', Huynh Cong Ut, 1972. See Richard Lacayo and George Russell, *Eyewitness: 150 Years of Photojournalism* (Time/Oxmoor House, New York, 1990). The equivalent in the 1991 Gulf war was the *Observer*'s photograph of the charred corpse of an Iraqi soldier in a burnt-out tank, by Kenneth Jarecke syndicated through Colorific. Black-and-white photography has a declining market but many serious documentary photographers are still loyal to it. The *Independent Magazine*'s picture editor, Colin Jacobson, writes ('War cry', 7 November 1992, p. 12) of the iconic power of the still image as 'the photographer's revenge on television. Television provides the primary record and the living theatre, but it is the photograph which has the power to make us stop, look and wonder. If it doesn't touch you, it has failed.' He argues that the most truly horrifying war photographs are those which concern human reactions. The ethical and political implications of war photography were covered in a BBC2 television programme by Charles Glass, *Stains of War*, screened on 6 November 1992.

13. Harrison and Palmer, *News out of Africa* (Hilary Shipman, London, 1986), p. 57.

14. Nikki van der Gaag and Cathy Nash, *Images of Africa: the UK Report* (Oxfam, Oxford, 1987).
15. This finding, cited by van der Gaag and Nash (p. 17), is by Ross Grant, with different groups of young people.
16. *Ibid.*, pp. 18–19.
17. 'Oxfam and images', internal report of Images Working Group, April 1991.
18. E.g. Peter Stalker, 'Can I take your picture?: the strange world of photography', *New Internationalist*, July 1988.
19. Paddy Coulter, 'Pretty as a picture', *New Internationalist*, April 1989.
20. Bruno Carton and Violaine de Villers, 'L'Afrique dans les représentations des médias', *La Revue Nouvelle*, 7–8 (Brussels, March 1988).
21. Michael Watts, 'Heart of darkness: reflections on famine and starvation in Africa', in R. E. Downs, *et al.*, *The Political Economy of African Famine* (Gordon and Breach, London, 1991). Watts cites John Berger and Roland Barthes as intellectual influences on this line of thinking. A particularly gross example is the cover of the *New York Times Magazine* for 6 December 1992, which depicts an evidently dying Somali child in front of a wheelbarrow of the kind used regularly by Somalis to carry dead bodies for burial. This cover announces a six-page photo essay by James Nachtwey, who took his photographs in Baidoa. Though the layout editor has evidently tried to frame off these extremely stark images by means of a black border around each print, the front cover extends into a folding colour spread of four pages. The text is headed 'The gold shivers' and claims that 'shivers of excitement', 'warmth and reward' and 'deeply felt euphoria' are elicited by the acquisition of gold jewellery from Saks Fifth Avenue.
22. Alex de Waal, *Famine that Kills* (Oxford University Press, Oxford, 1989).
23. An earlier version, 'Impact of Images Guidelines', was published in 1988.
24. *Homeward Bound (1989 Ethiopia–Children: Survivors of Famine)*, a 5-minute film with Lenny Henry, is a good example of Comic Relief at its best. Lenny is seen talking at Bati, a shelter run jointly by Save the Children and the Ethiopian government, with children who have survived the last famine but are separated from relatives. Brief flashbacks to the Korem feeding station remind the viewer of what they have been through. The children are reticent and withdrawn about the past, fearful about the future. We are told that though 100 children were left at the shelter by the time the film was made, a year later all the children had found homes and the shelter was closed. This short film is incorporated in an 83-minute cassette with comprehensive notes as *Teacher Relief* (1991).

25. Among the writers who have influenced this style of thinking are Edward Said, John Berger and Michel Foucault.

26. John Fiske, *Television Culture* (Routledge, London, 1987), p. 285.

27. 'The condition of Africa', *Times Literary Supplement*, 20 September 1991.

28. Peter Adamson, speech to Unicef National Committees, Geneva, 29 January 1991.

29. It is possible to select statistics which bear out these children's and teachers' gloomy view. A recent UN report estimates that 40 low-income, food-deficit countries (29 in sub-Saharan Africa) failed towards the end of the 1980s to provide enough food for their inhabitants to meet average nutritional requirements. The total population of these countries is 1,565 million people. As many as 78 per cent of the child population of Asia are said in this report to be malnourished, though there have been improvements in China and to a lesser extent in India. (*The Global State of Hunger and Malnutrition*, 1992 Report of the UN World Food Council, cited in *Development Forum*, July–August 1992, p. 6.)

30. V. Propp, *Morphology of the Folktale*, translated L. Scott (University of Texas Press, Austin, 1968). Cf. Sonia M. Livingstone, *Making Sense of Television: the Psychology of Audience Interpretation* (Pergamon, Oxford, 1990) and Fiske, *Television Culture*, on narrativity. P. Bell has used the Propp schema to analyse drug stories in print and television news, concluding that the media 'posit heroes and helpers acting on behalf of the administrative arm of society in just the right proportion to allay any excessive threat that the villainy of racketeers and the weakness of victims might arouse.' 'Drugs as news: defining the social', in eds M. Gurevitch and M. Levy, *Mass Communication Review Yearbook* (Sage, Beverly Hills, 1985), Vol. 5, pp. 303–20, cited by Fiske, *Television Culture*.

31. Exoticism is also an ingredient. Cf. the unnamed Oxfam official's reply to Shawcross who asked why Cambodia had become such a *cause célèbre* in 1979: 'It had everything – temples, starving brown babies and an Asian Hitler figure – it was like sex on a tiger skin.' (W. Shawcross, *The Quality of Mercy* (André Deutsch, London, 1984), p. 423.

32. Propp, *op. cit.*, p. 76

33. Quoted by Jean Drèze, 'Famine prevention in Africa', in Jean Drèze and Amartya Sen, *The Political Economy of Hunger* (Clarendon Press, Oxford, 1990), Vol. 2, p. 128.

34. A recent example is the resignation of the President of the USA's largest charity, the United Way, after a financial scandal. *The Independent*, 28 February 1992.

35. Shawcross describes the macabre visit by Rosalynn Carter, wife of the then US President, to a refugee camp in Thailand in autumn 1979, when an aide drags a priest away from a dying child to give the press their photo opportunity. Shawcross, *op. cit.*, pp. 188–90.

36. John de Salis, personal communication.
37. Stuart Hall, 'The narrative construction of reality', interview with John O'Hara, *Southern Review*, Vol. 17, No. 1 (Adelaide, 1984), pp. 3–17. The context of Hall's remarks is the British media's coverage of the Falklands war. For a summary of attempts to apply concepts from narrative theory to news, see Dennis K. Davis and John P. Robinson, 'Newsflow and democratic society in an age of democratic media', in *Public Communication and Behavior*, Vol. 2 (Academic Press, 1989). One such concept is that of the learnt 'scripts' which enable us all to react quickly to new situations and structure our own actions so that desired outcomes are reached.
38. Phillip Knightley, *The First Casualty: the War Correspondent as Hero, Propagandist, and Myth Maker from the Crimea to Vietnam* (André Deutsch, London, 1975).
39. Stewart Purvis, 'The media and the Gulf War', *RSA Journal*, Vol. 139 No. 5423, (November 1991), p. 740.
40. Fiske, *Television Culture*, p. 281.
41. *Ibid.*, p. 308.
42. BBC Broadcasting Research statistics (unpublished) tell us, in fact, that during a sample period in January–March 1991, 53 per cent of the Nine O'clock News audience, Mondays to Fridays, were female adults and only 41 per cent male adults (6 per cent children), against a proportion of the UK population which is 43 per cent female adults and 40 per cent male adults (17 per cent children).
43. John Fiske and John Hartley, *Reading Television* (Routledge, London, 1978), p. 87.
44. Fiske, *Television Culture*, pp. 288–9.
45. For a useful summary, see Ralph Negrine, *Politics and the Mass Media in Britain* (Routledge, London, 1989), Chapter 7, 'News and the production of news'. A number of American scholars such as G. Tuchman and H. Gans have argued that 'so-called objective news criteria contain an inherent bias toward the status quo.' Journalists' 'moderatism' assumes that, when reform is necessary, it will be led by the more enlightened members of the ruling élite. 'It is difficult for TV journalists to avoid coverage of dramatic, visually attractive pseudoevents staged for their cameras by élites with large budgets for promotional expenses', Davis and Robinson, *op. cit.*, pp. 64 ff.
46. See Roger Silverstone, 'Television, rhetoric, and the return of the unconscious in secondary oral culture', in Bruce E. Gronbeck *et al.*, *Media, Consciousness, and Culture: Explorations of Walter Ong's Thought* (Sage, Beverly Hills, 1991), p. 155.
47. *BBC Guidelines for Factual Programmes* (BBC, London, n. d.), guideline 52.

48. See cover story by Michael Buerk, 'Why isn't Africa news any more?', *Radio Times*, 22–28 February 1992. In this analysis, I have said little about radio, but here is an example of how this medium is used to complement television coverage – or in this case, to anticipate it. The first of Buerk's radio talks was quickly followed by items on the news, where he was still a leading newscaster. This situation was unusual because at around this time Buerk announced that he intended to retire from the constricting role of newscaster to become an active reporter again; and the radio gave him an opportunity to express strong views freely without compromising the BBC rule that a newscaster should not present a personal view programme on a controversial matter. The BBC's television news coverage in March of the civil war in Mogadishu was outstanding. They were given assistance by SCF (UK), who were running a feeding-station for 5,000 children with their stores and field team under guard by privately hired soldiers (for the first time in the Fund's history).

   Such is the power of television that radio has been somewhat neglected as a medium by broadcasters, media analysts and NGOs. It may be due for a revival. From the reporter's point of view, radio is much less disruptive in a disaster area than television; from the listener's, it does not require our undivided attention as do television and the press. The value of the BBC World Service has been widely recognized in recent years, receiving tributes from both Gorbachev and Terry Waite as a source of reliable information in coercive conditions.

49. Geldof, *op. cit.*

50. In Shawcross, *op. cit.*, p. 13.

51. Part Four, Chapter 2.3. Cf. Emmanuelli, Chapter 4 above, note 31.

52. *BBC Guidelines for Factual Programmes*, guideline 58.3.

   American television is somewhat less restrained in what may be shown. For instance, video footage of a freak flood in southern California in 1991, showing a man being swept away by the river to his death, was repeated every few minutes for a day on the US news channels. A BBC news editor told me that he only showed a few seconds. Specific decisions are left for individual editors to make within the guidelines.

53. Audience figures provided by BBC, June 1992.

54. Shawcross, *op. cit.*, p. 406.

55. *BBC Guidelines for Factual Programmes*, guideline 1.3. The last quotation illustrates neatly how the 'constructed' character of television news is systematically obscured by the editing process. Agency field officers sometimes complain about the insensitive behaviour of cameramen in, for instance, feeding centres, but it does not follow that such behaviour is necessarily typical.

56. William Boot, 'Ethiopia: feasting on famine', *Columbia Journalism Review*, March/April 1985.
57. Paul Virilio, quoted by Frédéric Burnand, *Le Nouveau Quotidien*, 27 June 1992, in an article on television coverage of the Yugoslav war.

    A promising new development is the BBC's expansion of its renowned World Service radio news into a 24-hour television news and information service, World Service Television (WSTV), to provide competition with CNN. A quasi-commercial hybrid, the service can already be seen in 6 million homes in Asia. It remains to be seen whether it will be sufficiently capitalized to compete with CNN, which already has 2,000 staff and 110 million viewing households. ('The new vision of a World Service', *The Independent*, 4 November 1992).
58. The percentages who gave this answer were as follows:

Argentina	42%	Jordan	74%
Australia	67%	Mexico	60%
Belgium	77%	Netherlands	83%
Canada	78%	Norway	90%
Denmark	89%	Poland	82%
France	71%	Portugal	69%
Germany (W.)	81%	Spain	71%
Greece	76%	Sweden	89%
Hungary	89%	UK	80%
Ireland	69%	USA	83%
Italy	73%	USSR	77%

    The three countries that did not conform were Kenya and Nigeria, where the leading source was radio (this would presumably apply to other developing countries), and South Africa (blacks), where it was newspapers (83 per cent of South Africa's whites used television as the leading source). Statistics published by UN.
59. The survey is based on all television viewers. Don't knows are excluded. The results are quite different with regard to local area news, i.e. (for 1990): TV 21 per cent, Radio 10 per cent, Newspapers 51 per cent, Magazines 1 per cent, Talking to people 12 per cent. But even here, the percentage for television has risen from 12 per cent in 1982, and the percentage for newspapers has dropped correspondingly from 58 per cent. Some researchers consider the basis of these statistics to be doubtful.
60. Bernard Kouchner, *Le Malheur des Autres* (Editions Odile Jacob, Paris, 1991), pp. 194–8. Such a quest for television publicity can often seem like opportunism. For instance, after the killing of the ICRC delegate near Sarajevo in May 1992, according to a press report M. Kouchner used the opportunity of a television appearance on Antenne 2 to criticize the ICRC for pulling out of Sarajevo, announcing that the French government would be sending an aid aeroplane - a clear case of

invoking what I have called 'magical' agency. *Le Nouveau Quotidien*, 29 May 1992.

61. Anne Winter, presentation at Unicef Information Workshop, Nairobi, 19 June 1991. It has been shown empirically that the function of television news in 'setting agenda' is greater for those issues on which viewers have no alternative sources of information. See M. McCombs and S. Gilbert, 'News influence on our pictures of the world', in eds. J. Bryant and D. Zillman, *Perspectives on Media Effects* (Erlbaum, Hillsdale, NJ, 1986). Cited by Livingstone, *op. cit.*

A substantial body of research indicates that in relation to the huge volume of information transmitted on television, little is absorbed. J. M. Wober has written a number of reports for the Independent Television Commission (London) analysing responses by over 2,500 members of a Television Opinion Panel who regularly answer questionnaires. In one of these, 'Knowledge in Britain of the [October 1989] California earthquake', he finds that only 30 per cent of the sample answered correctly that the Oakland Bay bridge was out of action, 'though pictures of the collapse of that structure had perhaps been the most frequent images of the whole disaster'. IBA (now ITC) Research Paper, February 1990.

Two US scholars, Dennis K. Davis and John P. Robinson, *op. cit.*, have challenged the widespread view that TV news is in fact the main source of information. They note the 'poor performance of television as an information medium', for 'cheap and easy access to attractive new forms of information via television does not appear to have produced sharp increases in public knowledge about the social and political environment.' It is possible that the importance of television as opposed to newspapers has indeed been somewhat overestimated with regard to domestic news and the politics of the industrial world. However, the scanty coverage of Third World issues by the mass-circulation press would seem to leave little doubt about the importance of television in that context. J. M. Wober notes that 'agenda cutting' – the non-appearance of large-scale events in Western news – is a complementary process to the more familiar 'agenda setting', *The Use and Abuse of Television: a Social Psychology of the Changing Screen* (Erlbaum, Hillsdale, NJ, 1988).

62. Akbar S. Ahmed, *Postmodernism and Islam: Predicament and Promise* (Routledge, London, 1992), Chapter 6: 'The evil demon: the media as master'. Ahmed's text does, however, throw light on how the Western media are distrusted and feared, and hence often anathematized, in the Islamic world.

63. All national media give disproportionate attention, for historical or geopolitical reasons, to some parts of the world rather than others. For

instance, the British television news barely covers Indonesia at all, though it is the fifth most populous nation in the world. In 1989–90, British news devoted only 2 per cent of air time to Central and South America, including the Caribbean. The comparative figures for the same period were: Europe 46 per cent, North America 11 per cent, Other 'North' (including Australia, New Zealand) 2 per cent, Africa 11 per cent, Asia 28 per cent, Other 'South' 1 per cent. Jane Hardstaff, *Getting the Full Picture* (International Broadcasting Trust, London, 1990).

Even in Indonesia, however, a major disaster resulting in a very large death count would be covered by British media. A recent survey of American press and television coverage of natural disasters between 1960 and 1984 showed that both the number of deaths and geographical location affected the amount of coverage. The authors found that news about US disasters got more emphasis than others, but there were no consistent biases in favour of other parts of the world. Eleanor Singer *et al.*, Nos 1–2 *Journalism Quarterly*; Vol. 68, (Spring/Summer, 1991).

64. Jonathan Miller, *McLuhan* (Fontana, London, 1991).
65. Fiske and Hartley, *op. cit.*
66. Walter Ong, *Orality and Literacy: the Technologizing of the Word* (Methuen, London, 1982), p. 29
67. Marshall McLuhan, *The Mechanical Bride: Folklore of Industrial Man* (Routledge, London, 1968). First published New York, 1951.
68. Raymond Williams, *Television: Technology and Cultural Form* (Fontana, London, 1974).
69. Randolph Arnheim, 'A foretaste of television', reprinted in ed. Richard P. Adler, *Understanding Television: Essays on Television as a Social and Cultural Force* (Praeger, New York, 1981).
70. Fiske, *Television Culture.*
71. Especially *The Mursi – the Land is Bad*, 1991. The Mursi films are produced and directed by Leslie Woodhead, with David Turton as anthropological adviser.
72. *Celso and Cora* is distributed by the Australian Film Commission.
73. Film by Patrice Barrat, La Sept/Pont Jour, Paris, 1991, screened on Channel Four Television, 27 May 1991.
74. See Kouchner, *op. cit.*, pp. 200 ff., for a first-hand account. 'The mistake of Timisoara was salutary for the press.'
75. *British Journalism Review*, Vol. 2 No. 4 (Summer 1991).
76. Personal interview, July 1991.
77. Alfred Gell, 'The technology of enchantment and the enchantment of technology' in eds Jeremy Coote and Anthony Shelton, *Anthropology, Art, and Aesthetics* (Oxford University Press, Oxford, 1992).
78. Alfred Gell, 'Technology and magic', *Anthropology Today*, (Vol 4 No. 2 April 1988).

79. Marcel Proust, *La Fugitive. A la Recherche du Temps Perdu III* (Gallimard, Paris, 1954 [1925]), p. 568.
80. Cf. Nicholas Hiley, 'Who won the Gulf reporting battle? The remarkable failure of the media to manipulate the public', *Times Literary Supplement*, 22 March 1991, p. 22. Hiley argues that the news media were biased by a desire for the conflict to be 'short and glorious' (because of its adverse effect on their advertising revenues and the increased costs of satisfying the public's demand for news), but considers that the British public views all the commercially sponsored news media with 'eternal cynicism'.
81. Stewart Purvis, *op. cit.*, p. 740.
82. Walter J. Ong, *op. cit.*, p. 11.
83. Bruce E. Gronbeck, 'The rhetorical studies tradition and Walter J. Ong: oral-literacy theories of mediation, culture, and consciousness', in Bruce E. Gronbeck *et al.*, *op. cit.*, p. 17.
84. Thomas J. Farrell, 'An overview of Walter J. Ong's work', in Gronbeck *et al.*, *op. cit.*, p. 33.
85. Silverstone, *op. cit.*, p. 148.
86. *Ibid.*, p. 57.
87. Personal communication, and see John O'Neill, *Plato's Cave: Desire, Power, and the Specular Functions of the Media* (Ablex Publishing, Norwood, NJ, 1991).
88. Albert Camus, *La Peste* (Gallimard, Paris, 1971 [1947]), p. 130. Many pages in this book evoke indirectly the German occupation of France during the Second World War.
89. Jean Jacques Rousseau, *Discourse on the Origin of Inequality* (Pléiade edition, Paris, 1753), Second Part, p. 178.
90. On French, US and other television systems, see ed. James Firebrace *Losing the Picture: the Future for Television's Coverage of Global Issues* (International Broadcasting Trust, London, 1990). On the quality of US television, Michael Tracey (director of the Center for Mass Media Research at the University of Colorado) describes it as a 'horror story. . . . The problem with American television is not that everything is extraordinarily bad, like watching TV Tirana, simply that there is an awful lot which is just not very good, born of a marked absence of any real commitment to excellence. This is not because there aren't some very clever people in American television, nor that there are not some very well meaning people.' In ed. Firebrace, *op. cit.*, p. 68. There is no equivalent in American television to the high-quality British anthropological series such as Granada Television's *Disappearing World*.
91. Preface to ed. Firebrace, *op. cit.* This report was commissioned at the time when the franchises for British independent television were under official review. Andre Ehrenberg, a marketing expert, argues in a paper

in the same publication, 'Viewing preferences and the effect of competition for revenue', that the television advertising market is highly complex, and that regulation of the range and quality of programmes is in the best interests of viewers and advertisers alike.

92. Steve Clarke, 'Endangered species', *Daily Telegraph*, 11 July 1992.

CONCLUSION

1. Representative of Reporters sans Frontières, quoted by Frédéric Burnand, *Le Nouveau Quotidien*, 27 June 1992. It is worth noting that journalists benefit from no special protection in humanitarian law, despite their evident importance in restraining the conduct of belligerents and bearing witness.

2. Kevin Myers, 'Horror at the [Sarajevo] Holiday Inn', *The Guardian*, 14 July 1992.

3. *The Times* leader, 'Playing at peace', 17 July 1992.

4. *The Economist*, 'Death by looting', 18 July 1992.

5. Report by Africa department to SCF (UK) Assembly, 14 July 1992.

6. *Development Forum*, July–August 1992, p. 5.

7. *Ibid.*

8. 'Information: fuel for change', *Development Forum*, July–August 1992, p. 13.

9. *The Revolt of Islam*, 1818, canto X, stanza 18.

10. 'The Wreck of the Deutschland', 1878.

11. The Man of Ross in Pope's *Epistle to Bathurst*, Squire Allworthy in *Tom Jones*.

12. See Chapter 3, note 43.

13. Cervantes, *Don Quixote* (1605), Chapter 12.

14. *La Peste* (Gallimard, Paris, 1971 [1947]), p. 151.

Index

Names of *individuals* and *organizations*, including *newspapers* and *periodicals*, and of *peoples* and *nation-states*, have been indexed; also the names of specific *disasters*. Names of cities, towns, counties and provinces are not included.